THE CLASSICS
OF **WESTERN**
SPIRITUALITY

THE CLASSICS OF WESTERN SPIRITUALITY
A Library of the Great Spiritual Masters

Cambridge Platonist Spirituality

EDITED AND INTRODUCED BY
CHARLES TALIAFERRO AND ALISON J. TEPLY

PREFACE BY
JAROSLAV PELIKAN

PAULIST PRESS
NEW YORK • MAHWAH, NJ

Cover Art: Detail of Emmanuel College, Cambridge, founded 1584, from an engraving by David Loggan, 1690. Courtesy the Master and Fellows of Emmanuel College, Cambridge.

Cover and caseside design by A. Michael Velthaus
Book design by Lynn Else

Library of Congress Cataloging-in-Publication Data

Cambridge Platonist spirituality / edited and introduced by Charles Taliaferro and Alison J. Teply ; preface by Jaroslav Jan Pelikan.
    p. cm. — (The Classics of Western spirituality)
    Includes bibliographical references and index.
    ISBN 0-8091-0539-X (cloth : alk. paper) — ISBN 0-8091-4038-1 (pbk. : alk paper) 1. Cambridge Platonists. 2. Spirituality—Church of England. I. Taliaferro, Charles. II. Teply, Alison J. III. Series.

BX5126.C36 2004
248.4'83—dc22

2004008867

Published by Paulist Press
997 Macarthur Boulevard
Mahwah, New Jersey 07430

www.paulistpress.com

Printed and bound in the
United States of America

CONTENTS

CONTENTS

Editors of This Volume

CHARLES TALIAFERRO, Professor of Philosophy at St. Olaf College, is the author of *Consciousness and the Mind of God* (Cambridge), *Contemporary Philosophy of Religion* (Blackwell), and *Praying with C. S. Lewis* (St. Mary's Press) and has co-edited *A Companion to Philosophy of Religion* and *Philosophy of Religion: An Anthology* (both from Blackwell). He is an associate of the Society of St. John the Evangelist, an Anglican monastic order. In addition to a PhD in philosophy from Brown University, he holds a Master of Theological Studies from Harvard Divinity School and has been a visiting scholar at Oxford University, Columbia, Princeton, New York University, and General Theological Seminary in New York City. Although this work on Cambridge Platonism is a collaboration, Taliaferro dedicates his share of the work to the philosopher William Wainwright, an exemplar of the virtues of Cambridge Platonism and the one who first inspired Taliaferro to study this seventeenth-century school of spirituality and philosophy.

ALISON J. TEPLY was born in Stratford-upon-Avon, England, and earned her Bachelor of Arts (First Class) in Medieval and Modern History at Royal Holloway College, University of London. She then entered Emmanuel College—the college where Cambridge Platonism originated—at the University of Cambridge. At Emmanuel she earned a Master of Philosophy in Intellectual History and has completed her PhD in the theology and philosophy of the Cambridge Platonist Peter Sterry.

Author of the Preface

JAROSLAV PELIKAN was born on December 17, 1923. He received a Bachelor of Divinity degree from Concordia Seminary and a PhD from the University of Chicago, both in 1946. After teaching at Valparaiso University (1946–49) and Concordia Seminary (1949–53), he joined the faculty of the University of Chicago, where he worked from 1953 until 1962. He was appointed Titus Street Professor at Yale University in 1962, and Sterling Professor in 1972, serving as Dean of the Graduate School of Arts and Sciences from 1973 to 1978; he retired from Yale in 1996. His research and writings have concentrated on the history of the development of Christian doctrine from its beginnings to the present: his five-volume work, *The Christian Tradition* (1971–89), is widely regarded as the standard work in the field for this generation. In addition, he edited and translated primary texts and has published monographs from all five periods covered by that work: Ancient, Byzantine, Medieval, Reformation, and Modern. In 2003 he published, with Valerie Hotchkiss, the four volumes of *Creeds and Confessions of Faith in the Christian Tradition* in about four thousand pages. Many of his writings examine the interrelation of the Christian tradition and the history of culture, including philosophy, literature, music, the visual arts, rhetoric, political and legal theory, and the natural sciences. His scholarship has been recognized by learned societies, academies, libraries, colleges, and universities all over the world with honors, medals, and citations, including (at present count) forty-one honorary doctorates. In 1983 he received the Jefferson Award from the National Endowment for the Humanities, the highest recognition conferred by the federal government on a scholar in the humanities. In 1992–93 he delivered the Gifford Lectures at the University of Aberdeen. He was President of the American Academy of Arts and Sciences from 1994 to 1997, and of the American Academy of Political and Social Science in 2000–2001. In 2001 he inaugurated the John W. Kludge Chair for Countries and Societies of the North at the Library of Congress. He currently serves as Scholarly Director for the Institutions of Democracy Project of the Annenberg Foundation Trust at Sunnylands.

FOREWORD AND ACKNOWLEDGMENTS

We believe the time is right for Cambridge Platonist spirituality. The mid-seventeenth century priests, theologians, philosophers, and poets known as the Cambridge Platonists articulated a comprehensive, integrated, tolerant Christian spirituality. They sought to integrate many elements that appear to conflict radically: faith and reason, the life of the mind and the body, justice and mercy, duty and beauty. We believe there is an evident and present need to take seriously the integrated spiritual life of the Cambridge Platonists. Witness, for example, the call to an intelligent faith in the encyclical letter *Fides et Ratio* of Pope John Paul II, in which irrational and anti-intellectual elements are repudiated for mature Christian spirituality. The value of an integrated, wise faith is especially apparent when one appreciates that the Cambridge Platonists lived in a time, as we do, of intense political and religious conflict. The contribution of Cambridge Platonists to the history of ideas is undergoing reassessment today, as their books are republished and conferences dedicated to them are held. While this work is refreshing and rewarding, its emphasis is often purely intellectual and cultural and neglects the spirituality of Cambridge Platonism. We are grateful to Professor Bernard McGinn and the Paulist Press for the opportunity to address the spiritual life and work of this movement.

We thank Paula Schanilec and Cleo Granneman of St. Olaf College for their enormous help in preparing this collection. We also gratefully thank Rachel Traughber, Kate Monson, Gary de Krey, Gretchen Ross, Sarah Campbell, Leif Anderson, Adam Goldhammer, Kurtis Parlin, Justin Ray, Janelle Sagness, Jerrae Swanson, Benjamin Carter, and Louise Hickman. We gratefully thank Professor Bernard McGinn for his expert, critical advice on preparing and finalizing this project. We also acknowledge the excellent work of Chris Bellitto and Joan Laflamme of Paulist Press in their expert editing of the manuscript.

All the original texts are available in the Rare Books room of Cambridge University Library and are reproduced here with the permission of the Syndics of Cambridge University Library. We thank particularly the staff members in the Rare Books room for their constant courtesy and helpfulness. Other manuscripts were also consulted at the locations listed, and our thanks are also due to the staff of Emmanuel College Library, the British Library manuscript room, Warwickshire County Record Office, and Queen's University, Belfast.

Our primary goal has been to contribute to a wider readership of Cambridge Platonist literature, and to that end we have moderized the English and the punctuation in order to increase the accessibility of the prose. We have not, however, altered the language or punctuation of the poems in chapters XI and XII.

PREFACE

Jaroslav Pelikan

Like Clement of Alexandria, Origen, and the shadowy genius bearing the name of Dionysius the Areopagite, the Cambridge Platonists have been better known to historical scholarship as speculative philosophers of religion than as men of prayer, which implies a disjunction that was as alien to them as it had been to their Greek Christian forebears. The texts and documentation assembled in this volume ought to redress the balance.

Arguably, it was Platonism no less than Christianity that shaped their spirituality. Thus, even a scholar who owes as much as I do to Aristotle for my research on the history of Christian rhetoric could not imagine a volume entitled *Aristotelian Piety* that would correspond to Morgan's book, *Platonic Piety*.[1] For, as Morgan's subtitle—*Philosophy and Ritual in Fourth-Century Athens*—indicates, it is in the relation between philosophy and ritual that we should look for the foundation of the spirituality of Socrates and its exposition in the Platonic dialogues. This principle bears distinct affinities to the Latin phrase *lex orandi lex credendi*, which goes back to Prosper of Aquitaine, namely, that what is affirmed and implied by how the church prays and worships defines how the church teaches and confesses its faith. In several striking ways, both these affinities and the ineradicable "divergence between Christianity and aristocratic Platonism,"[2] as it was identified by Jean Daniélou in the title of his seminal book of sixty years ago on St. Gregory of Nyssa, *Platonisme et théologie mystique*,[3] come to expression in this remarkable collection of sources edited by Charles Taliaferro and Alison J. Teply.

First, it is implicit throughout, though often not explicit, that it is the doctrine that everyone now seems to have learned to call

1

apophatic, or, as I have identified it, "the language of negation," that is in fact "the lexicon of transcendence."[4] Not only in overtly negative terms such as *infinite* or *immortal* but in seemingly positive words like *almighty* or *holy*, what we are in a position to say about God is, in the first instance, what God is not. Near the beginning of the selection from *The Principles of the Most Ancient and Modern Philosophy* that closes this collection, Anne Conway articulates the presupposition: "The nature and essence of God...is altogether unchangeable."[5] And Henry More takes as his subject an apophatic acknowledgment of divine transcendence in this couplet about the soul and its way of knowing God:

> If it go down to utmost nought
> It shall return with that it sought.[6]

The repeated polemic against the notion that true religion is "nothing but a little book-craft, a mere paper skill," is an attack on the presumptuousness of any theology, philosophy, or spirituality that forgets its apophatic ground.[7]

Second, much more explicit throughout is the recognition, in opposition to the anti-intellectualism that seems to beset Christian spirituality, that human reason is not only an epistemological faculty but an instrument of worship. In the only passage in the Gospels where Jesus quotes the Shema of Deuteronomy 6 in its entirety, he immediately goes on to emphasize this imperative: "The first of all the commandments is, Hear O Israel; The Lord our God is one Lord: And thou shalt love the Lord thy God with all thy heart, and with all thy soul, *and with all thy mind*, and with all thy strength."[8] The spirituality in this volume is a Christian— and Platonic—celebration of "reason, as enabling and fitting man to converse with God by *honoring him and loving him*."[9] But because it is both Platonic and Christian, it celebrates reason by recognizing its limitations as well as its powers.

Third, that recognition extends also to the physical dimension of human nature. While eschewing, by and large, the disparagement of the body that sometimes comes through in Christian monastic literature, the Cambridge Platonists made a major point of the ascetic discipline and self-denial that are an essential part of

2

Christian discipleship, not only for nuns and monks but for all
believers. In *Our Conversation Is in Heaven*, Benjamin Whichcote
provides a catalogue of "six particulars" of Christian discipline,
including "a subduing and a mortifying of fleshly and inordinate
lusts and affections" and "self-denial, and renouncing of our own
wills, so far as they stand in competition with, or rise up in opposition against God's will."[10]

Fourth, such an interpretation of Christian spirituality could
result in no hope less grand than the *theosis* celebrated by the
Greek church fathers on the basis of the New Testament promise
of "com[ing] to share in the very being of God."[11] "Christ did not
come into the world to fill our heads with mere speculations,"
Ralph Cudworth warns. Rather, "the gospel is nothing else but
God descending into the world in our form, and conversing with
us in our likeness; that he might allure and draw us up to God, and
make us partakers of his Divine form (as Athanasius speaks), 'God
was therefore incarnated and made man, that he might deify us'—
that is (as St. Peter expresses it) make us partakers of the divine
nature."[12] What Origen, the Cappadocian fathers, and especially
Maximus the Confessor describe as *metousia*, "participation," is
not merely intellectual but existential, transforming the very being
of those whom Christ came to save. To quote again from
Cudworth, "True evangelical holiness, that is, Christ formed in
the hearts of believers, is the very cream and quintessence of the
gospel."[13]

Fifth, in the seventeenth and eighteenth centuries, when
some of the most forceful statements of the case for religious toleration were based on relativism about religious teaching, the
brand of spirituality set forth here enabled the Cambridge
Platonists to make their case on the basis of profound conviction
instead. Invoking what must be one of the most colorful and forceful phrases in this or any volume of the Classics of Western
Spirituality series, Henry More speaks about inhibiting "that
wolfish and ferine humor of persecuting others for their religion"
and instead cultivating a spirit that "would live quietly by them,
and would not force anyone to their own faith, nor disturb the
public exercise of religion in others."[14] Both Platonism and
Christianity of every confessional stripe had been responsible for

more than their share of this "wolfish and ferine humor," but in the world view that they combined to produce in these writers there breathes a spirit of charity and toleration that was much needed in the religious atmosphere of seventeenth-century England—and that would be welcome in our own day, when religious conviction and religious toleration are seen by many on both sides as incompatible.

INTRODUCTION
TO CAMBRIDGE PLATONISM

The movement that came to be known as Cambridge Platonism, founded by Benjamin Whichcote (1609–83), thrived in seventeenth-century England and left a profound—if subtle—impact on the shape of subsequent religious thought and life in the English-speaking world. Besides Whichcote, the principal members of the movement included Henry More (1614–87), Ralph Cudworth (1617–88), John Smith (1618–52), Peter Sterry (1613–72), and Nathaniel Culverwell (1618?–51). All of these scholars held positions at Cambridge University. John Norris (1657–1711) and Joseph Glanville (1638–80) were later adherents from Oxford University. Anthony Ashley Cooper, the third Earl of Shaftesbury (1671–1713), may be considered a yet more distant adherent, though a vital one for the publication of many Cambridge Platonist themes. Anne Conway (1630–79), More's "heroine pupil," also deserves to be counted among these luminaries, though she is sometimes not mentioned in standard rosters of this spiritual and philosophical school.

We begin this introduction with a brief overview of some of the salient features of Cambridge Platonist spirituality. Part One seeks to show the contemporary relevance of Cambridge Platonist spirituality. Parts Two and Three then carry out the task of historically locating the Cambridge Platonists, first with an overview of the broader social context in which the Cambridge Platonists flourished and then with some biographical portraits.

The historical setting of the Cambridge Platonists is vital in order to appreciate fully their overall contribution to Christian spirituality. For, while some of their core ideas are not radically new, their articulation and defense of their convictions took place at a momentous time in the history of religion and culture. They flourished amid a violent civil war, in a period of religious conflict between Roman Catholics and Protestants, and at the outset of modern science. As we hope to establish in this collection, their witness to Platonic Christianity was a brave, dramatic contribution to Western spirituality at a point when this spirituality was imperiled by war and compromised by social division.

Part One:
Cambridge Platonist Spirituality

The descriptive title *Platonic Christianity* cannot be adopted without some qualification. Not all elements in Plato's work carry over easily into Christian thought and experience. Plato's conception of the Creator of the Cosmos as a finite, imperfect reality and subordinate to the Good does not fit in well with Hebrew monotheism or the early Christian creeds. Plato's aristocratic conception of humanity is perfectly outfitted for the proud philosophical paganism of Celsus (second century), but it is less at ease with the emphasis on grace and love found in the Christianity of Clement of Alexandria (150–215) or Origen (185–254). It will be useful here to emphasize the profundity of the divergence between Christianity and aristocratic Platonism. Origen recognizes the sublimity and awesomeness of Plato's view of the Good and the difficulty of finding God, while he counters that such difficulties can be surmounted by God's abundant generosity. Origen writes:

> The Word of God is kinder to man than Plato, for it reveals him who was in the beginning with God, God the Word Made Flesh. This it does in order to make the Word universally accessible, whereas Plato says that no one who has found him can possibly speak of him in a way that all men can understand. Plato may say that it is difficult to find the Creator and Father of the universe; he may declare that it is impossible for human nature to attain to perfect knowledge of God and even that...it is impossible for anyone to attain to much more than the

> masses have of him....God will be found by those who
> do what they can to find him but acknowledge that they
> need help from him.[15]

This picture of a bounteous, self-revealing God departs from a concept of the divine that may only be accessed through refined or elite intellectual effort. Traditional Christianity also departs from Plato's teaching concerning the transmigration of souls.

While some Christian Platonists have held that the soul pre-exists the body, this is shy of Plato's more ambitious picture of pre-natal and postmortem life. More troubling is Plato's ambivalence about the body: he describes it as a prison of the soul. Regrettably, a disdain for the body did make its way through Plotinus (205–70) into some strands of Christian asceticism, but overall, Christian theologians and philosophers view the body as fundamentally good notwithstanding the scarring of sin.[16]

Despite these and other problems, Plato did inspire an array of constructive values and teachings within Christianity, which are as relevant today as they were to the Cambridge Platonists 350 years ago. We highlight four central convictions that run through the work of the Cambridge Platonists in this collection: the sovereignty of the good, the true, and the beautiful; the goodness of inquiry; participation in the Life of God; and the goodness of Creation.[17]

The Sovereignty of the Good, the True, and the Beautiful

The Cambridge Platonists adhered to the ideal integration of goodness, truth, and beauty. In their view, if something was evil but appeared to be beautiful, its "beauty" was artificial or mere appearance. Beauty, goodness, and truth were seen as inseparable. This classic Platonic dictum was held amid the growing political realism championed by Thomas Hobbes (1588–1679), in which raw political power was the key reference point. It would be unfair to boil down Hobbes's understanding of ethics and the state to a doctrine of "might makes right." Yet one may infer from Hobbes that the exercise of political power customarily shapes what people think is right. Moreover, Hobbes assumed that without a sovereign civil magistrate capable of compelling obedience, morality was null and void. His political philosophy corresponded to a theology that gave primacy to the sheer power of God; God is to be worshiped because of God's unrivaled power. The Cambridge Platonists, on the other hand, repudiated this power-based philosophy and insisted that the world should be understood first and foremost as the creation of an all-good, just, beautiful, and trustworthy Creator. Morality is anterior to the state, as values are found in the world prior to any human artifacts. The sheer ability to wield power—the power to destroy the innocent, for example—is not worthy of respect, worship, or honor. The power of God is supremely excellent because it is essentially good and beautiful. In his famous address to the House of Commons in 1647, reproduced in this volume, Ralph Cudworth repudiated a theology in which God is characterized as "impetuous self-will, running through the world" (p. 70). On the contrary, "God is beauty" (p. 81).

Cudworth, Whichcote, and the others followed Plato in giving a central place to the good, the true, and the beautiful. As Cudworth said in his 1647 address, "Virtue and holiness in creatures, as Plato well discourses in his *Euthyphro*, are not therefore Good because God loves them, and will have them accounted such; but rather, God therefore loves them because they are in themselves simply good" (p. 70). The Cambridge Platonists explained beauty and truth in a similar way: friendship and truth are not beautiful because of divine love; rather, God loves friendship and truth because they are beautiful. The Cambridge Platonists did not subordinate God to a remote standard or form of goodness, because God's very nature is goodness.

The concord of the good, the true, and the beautiful underlies much of the practical moral teaching of the Cambridge Platonists. Whichcote's discourses on the moral life, for example, which follow in this collection, exhort us to have joy, delight, pleasure, and love for the abundant goodness of God. Evil is weighty, ugly, and enslaving, while the good elevates, animates, and frees us. The godly should relish and not merely endure goodness and truth. A moral life is, in the end, a life of harmonious, well-ordered loves. Here, Whichcote follows the Augustinian tradition, finding fulfillment in an order of love *(ordo amoris)*.

The Goodness of Inquiry

A second theme in Cambridge Platonist spirituality is that reason is a God-given faculty intended to be exercised in coordination with revelation. They resisted the anti-intellectualism that was virulent among many of the sectarians of that time. A Cambridge Platonist spirituality is not one that is built solely on emotions or unguided passions. Mature Christian faith should be wise, reasonable, and wedded to intellectual development. But for all their emphasis on the mind, the Cambridge Platonists did not advance a pure intellectualism. The exercise of sheer intellect, like the exercise of sheer political power, was problematic. In the first entry of this collection, Cudworth laments a spirituality that is hyper-intellectual as "bookish" and "ink and paper" Christianity.

The Cambridge Platonists held that the pursuit of knowledge must be conducted without vice and free from moral failures. On this front they concurred with Plato's seventh letter:

> It is barely possible for knowledge to be engendered of an object naturally good, in a man naturally good; but if his nature is defective, as is that of most men, for the acquisition of knowledge and the so-called virtues, and if the qualities he has have been corrupted, then not even Lynceus could make such a man see. In short, neither quickness of learning nor a good memory can make a man see when his nature is not akin to the object, for this knowledge never takes root in an alien nature; so that no man who is not naturally inclined and akin to justice and all other forms of excellence, even though he may be quick at learning and remembering this and that and other things...will ever attain the truth that is attainable about virtue.[18]

The Cambridge Platonists similarly affirmed the vital interplay of spiritual and intellectual values. This concord of values and reason

comes to fruition in the writings of Nathaniel Culverwell, reproduced in this volume.

The Cambridge Platonist account of inquiry may be clarified
by distinguishing two kinds of seeking: intrinsic and extrinsic. In
the former, the search itself must be shaped or animated in some
way by the object sought. When seeking justice, one must be just;
when seeking the nature of love, one must do so lovingly. It will
not do to seek justice ruthlessly or to seek the nature of love in a
malicious way. By contrast, an extrinsic search does not need to be
shaped or animated by the object of the search. One need not be
thirsty in order to search for water. Viewing philosophical inquiry
into God as an intrinsic search, the Cambridge Platonists saw that
intellectual activity itself was sacred or godly. John Smith writes:
"As the eye cannot behold the sun, unless it is sunlike, and has the
form and resemblance of the sun drawn in it, so neither can the
soul of man behold God...unless it is Godlike, has God formed in
it, and is made a partaker of the divine nature" (pp. 157–58). Thus
the intellectual and affective search for God can be a transfiguring
form of worship.

Participation in the Life of God

In Plato's dialogue, the *Euthyphro*, Euthyphro describes the
exchange between God and humanity as a commercial one. For
Euthyphro, holiness "will be a mutual art of commerce."[19] This
was emphatically not the art commended by Plato, who likened
the pursuit of the good to a lover's pursuit of the beloved. The
Cambridge Platonists, however, saw the relation between God and
the soul as one of great affective proximity and growing intimacy.
Their spirituality lay in the tradition of the Gospel of John, whose
author places emphasis on our need to abide in God. Christ calls
us to a spirituality that affectively unites us with God's will. The
divine ordinances and our moral instruction are neither imper-
sonal machinery nor techniques that enable us to reach an austere
end, for our end is a shared life in God. John Smith's three discourses in this collection describe the spiritual life as a divine art,
whereby we are drawn into God. Cudworth, in the first entry in
this volume, speaks of religion as a renewed identity, whereby we

live as children of light. Later, Cudworth exhorts the "life of God in us" (p. 61) and our being "espoused into Christ" (p. 89), for Christian spirituality ultimately involves an intimate partaking in the life of God.

The Goodness of Creation

The Cambridge Platonists did not need to be reminded about the reality of violence and deceit, as we shall document below in Part Three of this Introduction. Still, they held that human nature is structured to be essentially good in its constitution (health consists in a harmony of good bodily functions) and in our action. The evil we do is often committed on grounds that we claim (if perhaps only out of self-deception) to be good. The real horror of evil is that it is performed under the guise of some good. A murderer may paint an evil, violent act as a kind of dispensation of justice ("The person had it coming") when this "justice" is really a mask for revenge. The Cambridge Platonists, like Plato and St. Augustine, saw evil as a disfigurement of something good. The good is akin to health, which is positive, as opposed to illness, which is the loss, rupture, or violation of health.

The Cambridge Platonists' insistence upon the goodness of creation opposed Plato's low esteem for the human body. For the Cambridge Platonists, the proper functioning of body and mind is a great good. More, Cudworth, and Whichcote saw the relationship of mind and body as a "vital union" in which the soul is "passionately" present and embodied. Their understanding of human embodiment, as with their understanding of nonhuman animals and nature as a whole, was governed by their faith in God's goodness. Cambridge Platonist spirituality did not denigrate the world but generously accepted Creation as a gift—a sentiment that may best be summarized by a New Testament precept that they often cited: "Whatsoever things are true, whatsoever things are honest, whatsoever things are just, whatsoever things are lovely, whatsoever things are of good report; if there be any virtue, and if there be any praise, think on these things."[20]

Integration

In all, we believe the strength of Cambridge Platonists spirituality lies in its broad coherence and integration. Each author sought to make room for both the intellectual and the mystical, God's sovereignty and human freedom, the body and the soul, God's transcendence and immanence, morality and grace, the inner life and external political obligations. A comprehensive defense of their spiritual philosophy is impossible to undertake here.[21] At the least, however, we hope to set forth a representative collection of Cambridge Platonist writings to encourage further exploration of each of these brilliant, enduring practitioners of the religious life. We believe that their constructive Christian spirituality, as well as their quest for toleration and respect in tumultuous political and religious times, has much to offer us today.

While we emphasize unifying themes among the Cambridge Platonists, there are often important distinctions among them. We turn now to their individual biographies, where many of these differences come to the fore, followed by an overview of the historical elements of their age.

Part Two:
Biographies of the Cambridge Platonists

Benjamin Whichcote (1609–83)

In 1609, Benjamin Whichcote was born into a fairly affluent family at Stoke, Shropshire, in England. He is often regarded as the father of Cambridge Platonism, perhaps because he taught most of the group, including Smith and Sterry, and probably Cudworth and Culverwell. He was most certainly the spiritual inspiration behind the movement. He entered Emmanuel College, Cambridge, in 1626, where he was taught by the strongly Calvinist Anthony Tuckney, whose teaching "stimulated him by reaction rather than assent," and who largely inspired his focus on the natural goodness of all—contrary to the prevailing Calvinist assertion of human depravity—through their God-given reason and conscience.[22]

For ten years, beginning in 1633, Whichcote was a fellow of Emmanuel College, and in 1636, he embarked on his famous, long-running lecture series at Holy Trinity Church, which would last for nearly twenty years. Undoubtedly, it was in these lectures that he developed and spread his views on the rationality of religion and toleration. He assumed the position of provost at King's College in 1645, showing his good nature by granting half his salary to the ejected Samuel Collins.[23] Despite the fact that he never shared Cromwell's dogmatical Calvinist Puritanism, Whichcote remained on good terms with his regime, becoming vice-chancellor of the University of Cambridge in 1650, and in 1655 serving as one of the divines on Cromwell's advisory committee on the readmission of the Jews into England. Throughout his life Whichcote held various clerical posts, and after his ejection from King's College at the Restoration he came back into partial favor with the new king and was granted the livings of two important London churches successively: St. Anne Blackfriar's in 1662, and the renowned Latitudinarian living, St. Lawrence Jewry, from 1668 to 1683. While at St. Lawrence Jewry, he enjoyed continued success as a preacher; his audience included many who would become the renowned divines of the next generation, such as John Tillotson (1630–94), later archbishop of Canterbury, and Edward Stillingfleet (1635–99), later bishop of Worcester. Interestingly, the English philosopher John Locke was also a member of the church between 1667 and 1675, a crucial period for Whichcote in the development of his ideas on toleration. According to Damaris (Cudworth) Masham, Locke heard Whichcote preach and approved of his sermons.[24] Benjamin Whichcote's tenure at St. Lawrence Jewry was terminated by his death. He died in 1683 on a visit to the Cambridge house of his great friend Ralph Cudworth; being widowed and childless, he left bequests in his will to the university, his old colleges, and the poor.[25]

Surprisingly, Whichcote published nothing during his lifetime; all we have are posthumously published sermons taken from his notes and those of his listeners. The 1698 edition of his sermons was compiled by the third Earl of Shaftsbury, who felt there was much to be admired in the man he called the "preacher of good-nature."[26] Whichcote wielded great influence upon his students despite the delayed publication of his work. Uniquely, amid the standard curriculum of seventeenth-century Cambridge, he required all his students—including John Smith, Peter Sterry, Ralph Cudworth, and possibly Nathaniel Culverwell—to read Plato, Cicero, and Plotinus.[27] While Whichcote had no systematic philosophy, no one who reads his sermons—which have been described as "amongst the most thoughtful in the English language"—can fail to be impressed by their great power and undoubted relevance for us in the twenty-first century.[28]

Of all the Cambridge Platonists, it was Whichcote who most strongly emphasized the rationality of religion. The "common notions" of Christianity are clear, fundamental truths because that which is "Spiritual is most Rational."[29] God has placed "two lights" in the world to guide God's people: the light of reason, "which is the Light of his Creation" seen even by those "pagan philosophers of old," and the light of scripture, "which is the After-Revelation from Him."[30] Strikingly, amid the dominant Calvinist ideas of grace of the elect, Whichcote claimed that Cicero, the pagan, was "a better divine than some who pretend to be Christians and yet seem to deny reason."[31]

As sects proliferated in the seventeenth century, Whichcote understood only too well the dangers of religion estranged from reason. In his view, divine Recta Ratio must clearly rise as an objective principle above all distinctions of reason and faith, reason and understanding, Arminianism and Calvinism, and faith and works.[32] To use Whichcote's favorite phrase, reason, as the "candle of the Lord," unites our understanding to God.[33] Recta Ratio is the reason according to which God's own actions are ordered. God is not an arbitrary tyrant but acts in accordance with eternally unchanging, objective standards. God is neither entirely mysterious nor utterly beyond human comprehension; God can be grasped through our own understanding by the light of reason within us.[34] This unifying, transcendent, yet deeply immanent Recta Ratio is both lighted by, and enlightening toward, God.[35] In this way, for Whichcote, the "deiform seed" of the soul is in itself a form of grace implanted in our very being as a "divine life" and form of grace acting within us, rather than outside us. If we truly desire Christ—and we have the free will to choose—we can receive such "stamps and impressions" of God."[36] As a result, such a divinely rational religion will provoke neither division nor irrational "enthusiasm," nor will it merely consist in empty external ritual but will involve one's whole life, both mind and heart, in moral deeds and Christlike love.

Henry More (1614–87)

Henry More was born in 1614 at Grantham, Lincolnshire, to a strictly Calvinist gentry family. His childhood was a happy one, and he later expressed gratitude that his father had "tuned [my] ears" to Spenser's poetry by entertaining the family on winter nights "with that incomparable piece of his, *The Fairy Queen*."[37] More's education began at Eton, from 1628 to 1631, where he remembered "very stoutly, and earnestly for my Years" disputing against "this Fate or Calvinistick Predestination" that "neither there, nor yet anywhere else, could I ever swallow down."[38] In 1631, More entered Christ's College, a bastion of Puritanism under the teaching of Joseph Mede (1586–1638), who was himself hostile to extreme Calvinism. There, More developed his philosophy and spirituality into something quite different from traditional Scholasticism.[39] Indeed, it has been remarked that he found Cambridge medieval but left it modern.[40] There is no doubt that in More's blend of Neoplatonism and mechanical philosophy, Cambridge was presented with something truly original.

Considering that he remained a Royalist amid tumultuous times, it is remarkable that More never left Christ's College but maintained his fellowship, which began in 1639, until long after the Restoration. He refused several promotions, including two bishoprics and the mastership of Christ's College itself, in order to pursue his own studies in the quiet setting of his college. Amid the tranquil courts he happily followed his daily routine of study, writing, and instruction. He also found time for leisure; as he wrote, "I play at bowles ordinary twice a day, and…after supper I take a walk in the fields, and at my returne play some lessons on my lute, and after fitt myself for bed."[41]

Yet one retreat to which he went with gladness was Ragley Hall in Warwickshire, the home of his "heroine pupil," Anne Conway, and her husband. More had met Anne through her brother John Finch, who was his pupil in Christ's College from 1645. Five years later the two began a correspondence and a friendship that was to last until Anne's death in 1679. Anne's husband, Edward, Viscount Conway, was also interested in philosophy and had a high opinion of the learned More. Thus it was that More frequently joined happy groups in Ragley Hall around Lord and Lady Conway and engaged in discourse on philosophical and other matters. One such series of debates in the gardens at Ragley, in the summer of 1660, inspired More's lively *Divine Dialogues* (1667).[42] More showed his gratitude for Lord Conway's patronage by dedicating his *Immortality of the Soul* (1659) to him. However, it was Lady Conway's company—"the greatest enjoyment this world ever afforded me"—that More cherished above all. He missed her greatly when he was parted from her by death, claiming, on one return to Ragley, that he felt his life was "dead and heartless" without her.[43] The two Platonists also influenced each other's work; More introduced Conway to Descartes' philosophy, and she later convinced him to study the genuine Jewish Cabbala. More also inspired her to write her own monist philosophy of substance, a reaction to his dualism.[44]

As was the case with Peter Sterry, More's Neoplatonism was apparent very early on, and he was reputedly the first to profess Plotinus—"Divine Plotinus"—at Cambridge.[45] He further articulated his Neoplatonism in his collection of Platonic poetry, *Psychodia Platonica*, published in 1642, when he rapturously declared that Platonic philosophy was "a beam shot from the Deitie, And nearest ally'd to Christianitie."[46] This collection was the "first major philosophical document" of Cambridge Platonism.[47] It clearly expresses More's love of the "enthusiasm" associated with Neoplatonism, contrary to the "careless ravings" of the contemporary radical sects; this energy he called "the triumph of the soul of man, inebriated as it were, with the delicious sense of the divine life."[48] More's great love of mysticism is also particularly evident in his Platonic poems, and we see evidence of it again in his commending the little mystical devotional book

Theologia Germanica to Anne Conway, a text he passionately claimed could "give more ease than any physick."[49]

Despite his quiet life of teaching and writing at Christ's College, it would be a great error to think that More was out of touch with contemporary science and philosophy. He was certainly not unaware of these—indeed, he placed himself right in the middle of them. His centrality within contemporary natural philosophy is demonstrated by his membership in the Royal Society on its foundation, as well as his fascinating correspondence with René Descartes from December 1648 to October 1649. More exhibited early, qualified delight at Descartes.[50] He applauded "that admirable Master of Mechanicks" and the theistic mechanistic philosophy that was, as More believed, a revival of ancient atomism.[51] More hoped that when combined with Platonism, such a natural philosophy would prove to be an "invincible Bulwark against the most cunning and most mischievous effects of atheism."[52] Yet by the 1660s his hope had turned to despair, when it became apparent to More that Platonism and Cartesianism could never be reconciled.[53] The Cambridge Platonist was forced to admit that he could never accept radical Cartesian dualism, as it seemed to divorce the notion of spirit from the world. In More's view, spirit was right at the center of the world and, like matter, was extended.[54] In contrast, Descartes believed that spirit was not extended and indeed was divorced from the physical world; thus More claimed that Descartes was a "nullibist," or someone who claims that the spiritual exists but not how or where.[55] More's other objections to Cartesianism included Descartes' voluntarism and subjective view of space and motion. In his seminal stance on the absolute nature of space, More probably influenced the distinguished scientist Isaac Newton's (1642–1727) ideas of absolute space. More's concept of force, as well as his reluctance to exclude God and spirit from natural theology, must have had some effect on Newton, whom he definitely met in 1680, and very probably taught.[56]

Hobbesian materialism was a prime target in the Cambridge Platonists' defense of the spiritual. More was no exception to this; as an enthusiastic proponent of the spirit's presence in the world, he naturally considered Hobbes to be an enemy in the fight against atheistic materialism. He attacked Hobbes—"that confident exploder of immaterial substances"—in four separate works.[57] So great was the centrality of spirit to More that he proclaimed, in deliberate adoption of the Laudian chant in defense of episcopacy, "No Bishop, no King...no spirit, no God."[58] The danger of both Hobbesian materialism and Cartesianism was that spirit was banished from the world's mechanism and thus even God's position became tenuous. Moreover, More was prepared to use tales of apparitions at length to defend his case for the spiritual, as "they seem to me an undeniable argument, that there be such things as spirits or Incorporeal Substances in the world."[59] Such an interest in the supernatural was common at the time, and More was considered in no way eccentric for his enthusiasm and adoption of such "evidence" to prove his philosophical point.

This mission to defend the existence of the spiritual within the world is also seen in More's brief correspondence with Robert Boyle, whom he may have met in London in the 1640s.[60] More claimed that Boyle's air-pump experiment proved the existence of a spiritual force in the air. This deduction, denied by Boyle himself, seemed to vindicate More's beloved theory of a spirit of nature—an idea that was similar to the Platonic "anima mundi," and to Cudworth's "spirit of nature." This, More claimed, was forced upon him by the "inevitable evidence of Reason."[61] For More, the spirit of nature is a force that operates intimately in the natural world, pervading the matter of the universe and exercising a "plastic power thereon."[62] In this medium, God's spirit is able to display a simultaneous immanence and transcendence to the world, and More could joyfully maintain that nothing exists as a mere material body; God's "vicarious power" pervades all the matter of the universe.[63]

Henry More's writing style was more mystical than Benjamin Whichcote's more "rational" prose. It seems that More's personal disposition inclined him to the mystical; his biographer, Richard Ward, reports that he was once "for Ten Days together...in one continued fit of Contemplation."[64] Among the Cambridge Platonists, his poetic mysticism seems to fit more comfortably with the flowery style of Peter Sterry and John Smith.[65] Even so, More's poetic style buttressed the Cambridge Platonists' belief in the rationality of religion. As he declared, "Take away Reason, and all

Religions are alike true, as the Light being removed, all things are of one color."[66] Reason is aligned with a supreme faculty of the soul, "divine sagacity," with which one can "feel and smell out...what is right and true."[67]

More's major works were translated into Latin between 1675 and 1679, so that his thought could reach a more international, scholarly audience.[68] In his biography of More, Richard Ward remarked, "For ten years together, after the Return of King Charles the Second, the *Mystery of Godliness* and Dr. More's other Works, ruled all the Booksellers in London."[69] Whether Ward was overenthusiastic about his subject remains unclear. Certainly More's thought remained influential after his lifetime—perhaps, as Marjorie Nicolson claims, extending even to Coleridge and American Trancendentalism.[70]

Henry More died on September 1, 1687, "in so easy a manner, and with so calm a passage, that the nurse with him was not sensible of it."[71] He was buried in the chapel of his beloved Christ's College. His powerful, beautiful arguments for the spirit still resonate today. Nor would anything have pleased the quiet philosopher more than the thought that "when he was gone out of the World, he should still converse with it by his writings."[72]

Ralph Cudworth (1617–88)

Ralph Cudworth, in whom Cambridge Platonism takes its "most elaborate and complete expression," was born in Aller, Somerset, in 1617.[73] He was the son of another Ralph Cudworth, a distinguished clergyman in his own right, once a fellow of Emmanuel College and a chaplain to King James the First.[74] His mother had been a nurse to Henry, the eldest son of King James. On the death of her husband, she married a Dr. Stoughton, who would prove to be a kind stepfather to the young Ralph.[75] Ralph Cudworth was admitted to Emmanuel College in 1632, where it is very likely that he was taught by Benjamin Whichcote.[76] By 1639 he held a fellowship, and he may have counted John Smith, and perhaps even Henry More, among his many pupils.[77]

Of all the Cambridge Platonists, Cudworth had the most distinguished university career. He held the Regius Professorship of

Hebrew from 1645 until his death in the year of the Glorious Revolution, became Master of Clare Hall in 1645, and attained the mastership of Christ's College itself in 1654.[78] In 1654, he also appeared on a subcommittee to investigate the possibility of further revising the authorized version of the Bible.[79] Significantly, he was able to retain his positions through the Commonwealth and even after the Restoration—not so much by his detachment from politics as by his powerful friends.[80]

Cudworth married in 1654 and had several children.[81] His daughter Damaris, later Lady Masham (1658–1708), became a great friend of the philosopher John Locke, and he died in her house in Oates, Essex, in 1704.[82] Damaris bore her father's love for the study of philosophy, and she became a significant thinker in her own right; her *Discourse concerning the Love of God* was published in 1696.[83]

Cudworth has been aptly described as the "leading systematic thinker" of the Cambridge Platonists, and he was certainly the most philosophically important of the group. His lifelong ambition to write a discourse on natural ethics is detailed in the Worthington correspondence of 1664–65, which was the only time in his life when, through misunderstanding, he nearly fell out with his good friend Henry More.[84] More, along with Benjamin Whichcote, was one of his closest friends. In the end, the only work Cudworth published in his lifetime (aside from his sermons) was the mammoth undertaking entitled *The True Intellectual System of the Universe*, which he completed in 1672 but was prevented from publishing until 1678 due to opposition from various quarters of the court.[85] *The True Intellectual System of the Universe* was only the first of a projected four volumes to be published by Cudworth; the remaining manuscripts on free will are in the British Library.[86] The original folio edition of the *True Intellectual System* was a colossal nine hundred pages in length. Despite its size, it was translated into Latin and widely read in Europe and America and was reprinted in the nineteenth century.[87] The sources Cudworth used in *True Intellectual System* were of such wide variety that to call Cudworth a Platonist seems almost constraining.[88] The more general term *humanist* in this context may more aptly describe his vast range of knowledge.[89] However, it is important to remember that Cudworth's thought is founded on the Platonic world view, consisting of a dual emphasis on the goodness of postlapsarian human nature and the benign God of love and toleration. Cudworth's *True Intellectual System* attacks materialism and determinism in all its guises and contains a characteristically strong defense of a Platonic understanding of goodness. The work profoundly influenced Isaac Newton; indeed, Newton copied a large number of its passages verbatim.[90]

A number of themes reappear throughout Cudworth's writings. Not unlike More, he defends the "Attic Moses" idea of a historic correspondence between Athens and Jerusalem. Cudworth maintained his belief in a *prisca theologia*; in his view, Plato's Trinity was "in all probability...at first derived from a Divine or Mosaic Cabbala."[91] As an eirenicist and a scholar of Judaism, Cudworth, along with Whichcote and Sterry, served on Cromwell's 1656 committee to investigate the readmission of the Jews into England.[92] Cudworth shared the millenarian aspiration of converting the Jews to Christianity.[93] He also had an intellectual interest in meeting Rabbi Menasseh ben Israel, who came from Amsterdam to address the committee as a representative of the Jews.[94] The two finally met in England, when Menasseh ben Israel sold Cudworth an anti-Christian manuscript for ten pounds, the contents of which reputedly made Cudworth furious.[95]

The *prisca theologia* idea was linked with the Cambridge Platonists' tolerant eirenicism and stress on the fundamental rationality and simplicity of Christianity.[96] One of Cudworth's recurrent themes is the importance of a Christianity that is accessible to all; his particular Christian Platonism evokes Origen's God of bounteous generosity, in contrast with the more elite, aristocratic, pagan Platonism. A "shallow understanding" of divine mysteries does not bar one from heaven, since all that is needed is an "honest and good heart...ready to comply with Christ's commandments."[97] Cudworth urged his fellow Christians to promote the gospel of peace, and the "Dove-like Gospel with a Dove-like Spirit."[98] Such emphasis on love and toleration is particularly evident in Cudworth's sermon before the House of Commons on March 31, 1647, our first entry, where he addressed an audience bitterly divided along religious lines. In the sermon Cudworth espouses deiformity—the attempt to become more like God—remarking that "this Divine Life begun and kindled in any heart, wheresoever it be, is something of God in flesh."[99]

Cudworth courted atomistic mechanism as the true natural philosophy that would ultimately lead one to belief in God.[100] He supported Descartes' attempt to revive atomistic philosophy and so distinguish mind from matter.[101] Cudworth held that atomistic mechanism directly clashed with the ancient atheistic materialism that, in his opinion, Hobbes had taken from the Epicureans for his own natural philosophy; Cudworth's *True Intellectual System* was the first full-length attack on Hobbes.[102] Hobbes's argument for the self-sufficiency of matter and materialistic mechanism, as well as his attack on the spiritual—which included a devastating rejection of Christian revelation—posed a grave threat to theism in general and Christianity in particular. Cudworth, who has been described as Hobbes' "most intellectually formidable opponent," clearly perceived this threat and in 1688 personally signed the well-known expulsion order of the Hobbist Daniel Scargill, a fellow of Corpus Christi, which indicted Scargill's "Impious and Atheistical Tenets."[103] Cudworth devoted much energy to attacking Hobbes' philosophy, particularly in *True Intellectual System* (as well as in the undated manuscripts on free will), for he firmly believed in a human faculty above mere sense that could perceive and judge other senses. Mind is needed to comprehend fully the material, and knowledge and the intellect reside in a higher part of the soul than the "lower, passive, and sympathetical part, whereby the soul is vitally united to the body."[104] Cudworth aimed particularly at Hobbist materialistic determinism and refuted it with his theory of self-determination.

Cudworth's central notion of self-determination identifies a "contingent liberty" within all human actions.[105] The human soul is like a ship: though the captain is essentially passive to its movement, he still retains the power to determine its direction.[106] Yet for Cudworth, true free will is not the same as true freedom, since the perfectly free being would never have the capacity to choose evil as well as good. Rather, there exists within a person the faculty of self-determination and true freedom, with an inbuilt faculty inclining them to good.[107] Thus the true and perfect liberty of will occurs when "by right use of the faculty of freewill, together with the assistances of Divine grace," one is "habitually fixed in moral good" and only turns to evil when the faculty is abused. Evil is a privation, and only arises through our failure to use free will correctly. Once attaining true free will, one is in such a state of mind that, similarly to Neoplatonism's focus on the attainment of Truth through a participation in the Divine, one can then "freely, readily, and easily" comply with the "law of the Divine life."[108]

Cudworth disliked the way in which, for Descartes, Nature could exist without the need for any final causes and "without the guidance of any mind or wisdom."[109] Once there is no purpose or mental causality in the operations of Nature, then "reason and understanding" are also banished from ourselves and we only look on the things of Nature "with no other eyes than brutes do."[110] In order to bring a spiritual, purposeful element back to the material realm, similar to More's "spirit of nature," Cudworth advocated a kind of "plastic nature."[111] Plastic is an "inferior and subordinate instrument," executing that part of God's providence that consists in the "regular and orderly motion of matter."[112] Materialism is avoided while not detracting from God's omnipotence and the danger of occasionalism.[113] Nature is thereby able to be "incorporated and embodied in matter, which doth not act upon it from without mechanically, but from within vitally and magically."[114] Without this plastic faculty, it would so happen in nature that either "everything comes to mind fortuitously...without the guidance and direction of any mind or understanding, or else that God himself doth all immediately, and as it were with his own hands, form the body of every gnat and fly, insect and mite."[115]

A key concept in Cudworth's thought is the eternity and immutability of morality and his firm belief that things exist as they are, not by will but by nature.[116] God does not act arbitrarily, but according to objective standards of goodness and justice.[117] Thus moral good and evil have a real existence; they are not merely arbitrary.[118] Cudworth's prime target here was Calvinist theology, which asserted that whatever God wills is good, rather than it being good because God wills it. He feared that such a view would invariably lead to skepticism and even atheism, as the voluntarist God could quickly become an arbitrary tyrant, and humans would have no firm standard of truth, justice, or morality by which to live. Descartes' voluntarism was another target for the same reason, and Cudworth attacked Descartes' belief that "all truth and falsehood do depend upon the arbitrary will and power of God."[119] He also attacked Hobbes for placing emphasis upon the arbitrary will of sovereigns.[120] Instead, Cudworth insisted that science, mathematics, and metaphysics all depend on the true and objective natures of things. If all things depend only on arbitrary will, then "Truth and Falsehood would be only names."[121] However, Cudworth adopted Descartes' belief in the clarity of our conceptions and of reasoning, claiming that reason cannot act unreasonably and that understanding and "clear perceptions" can never err.[122] Indeed, will and understanding are effectively one, as the soul is "reduplicated" upon itself.[123]

Cudworth died on June 28, 1688, at his home in Cambridge, and his body was interred in the chapel of Christ's College. His influence on later philosophy is noteworthy. His impact on Newton has already been mentioned, and his influence on other philosophers such as Bishop George Berkeley and Richard Price was marked. There is an even clearer case for his influence on John Locke. Locke praised *True Intellectual System* as a book "wherein that very learned author, hath with such accurateness and judgement, collected and explained the opinions of the Greek philosophers."[124] Locke's moral philosophy was also arguably derived from Cudworth's views, as was his definition of volition and eternal and immutable morality.[125] Locke's emphasis on the link between reason and revelation is particularly evident in his *Reasonableness of Christianity* (1695), written during the last decade of his life when he lived in the house of Cudworth's daughter and her husband. Damaris, a student of philosophy instructed by her father, was Locke's intellectual companion and supporter during the long progress of the work. Locke maintained that both reason and revelation "together witness to come from God the great law-maker."[126] The result was a defense of a "plain, simple, reasonable" Christianity, the eirenic, tolerant tone of which was closely in keeping with the Cambridge Platonists' own ideas.[127] Locke's emphasis on a "pure heart," rather than on outside ritual and ceremony, is similar to Cudworth's emphasis on the divine life and an "honest and good heart."[128]

Nathaniel Culverwell (1618?–51)

Nathaniel Culverwell remains the most mysterious of the Cambridge Platonists. Few details are known about his life. It seems he lived a life of relative seclusion within Emmanuel College, Cambridge. Culverwell was born in London in January 1619 and attended St. Paul's School.[129] He entered Emmanuel College in 1640, and by 1642 he held a fellowship there. However, his early death (at thirty-two) of a distressing and mysterious complaint—perhaps even some kind of mental disorder—meant that his influence was limited to the views expressed in his only work, posthumously published, *An Elegant and Learned Discourse of the Light of Nature* (1652).[130] Part of the work—"Spiritual Opticks"— was originally preached in Emmanuel Chapel in July 1641. It was published with the rest of the discourses under the title *Discourse*, which was prepared for publication in 1652 by the master of Emmanuel at the time, William Dillingham.[131]

Culverwell's thought diverged somewhat from that of his Cambridge Platonist contemporaries; his sources were Scholastics such as Aquinas and Francisco Suarez.[132] For this reason there has been debate whether Culverwell was enough of a Platonist to be considered a Cambridge Platonist. Indeed, the sources of the humanism espoused by Culverwell (and Whichcote) are dedicated to a conception of reason whose roots, strictly speaking, are more Aristotelian, Stoic, and Scholastic than Platonic.[133] However, D. W. Dockrill defends Culverwell's position in the group by maintaining that, although Culverwell may not really have been a Platonist, the tag is useful in describing him.[134] Yet we believe Culverwell's Platonist outlook has been underestimated. The term *Cambridge Platonism* is, after all, an umbrella for many different influences and different focal points in thought, which nevertheless share an allegiance to the Platonic outlook of toleration; optimism regarding human potential; the goodness of inquiry; the sovereignty of the good, the true, and the beautiful; and the rationality and essential goodness of God. In this way, the tone of Culverwell's thought is very similar to that of the other Cambridge Platonists.

Although Culverwell allows that there are some principles *within* soul, including justice and other moral principles, he differs from all the Cambridge Platonists (except Cudworth) in claiming that these principles were not present with the soul at its creation.[135] Instead, he tends toward the Aristotelian claim that there were no "signatures in his minde till some outward objects had made some impression."[136] In Aristotle's refutation of connate ideas, he sees a "Sun in the firmament that was set to rule the day of knowledge."[137] The influence of the empirical philosophy of Francis Bacon can be seen in Culverwell's value of the sensory and in his declaration that "the rise of knowledge is from the observing and comparing of objects."[138] Yet, there still remain some innate, though not connate, principles within the soul;[139] inside the soul are "scatter'd...some seeds of light" that then fruitfully bring forth "numerous and sparkling posterity of secondary Notions."[140]

Reason is fundamentally entwined with the law of nature, and indeed is the "Pen by which *Nature* writes this Law of her own composing."[141] Divine Reason, or Recta Ratio, issues forth the law of nature, which is the "fountain of wisdom" of all creatures.[142] God's law is therefore an awakening of reason. Culverwell emphasizes that sensory knowledge is ultimately shadowy, and that it must move closer to God and gain greater clarity.[143] Yet there is a distinction, according to Culverwell, between mere precepts discovered by reason in the nature of things, and the laws of nature prescribed for agents possessing free will and intellect. In this way he sought to steer between the antinomian and voluntarist position, and the realist tradition.[144] He was also accommodating his natural-law theory, adopted from Aquinas, and in so doing he was building on the philosophy of Francisco Suarez, who claimed that the moral law depends on God's commands and yet is also inherent within Creation. For Culverwell, final causes have a key place within Creation, as knowledge of these causes— and thus God's purpose—forms the basis for human knowledge's access to divine law.[145] The end of all beings is union with God, and as every being naturally longs for its perfection, therefore every rational nature must "breathe and pant after God."[146] In the same way, not unlike the other Cambridge Platonists, Culverwell believed that the human will only attains true freedom when it moves toward God.[147]

Culverwell offers a sustained defense of the rationality of religion. For him, Recta Ratio is not an innate light, and the Platonists vainly persisted in claiming that it was lit from Creation.[148] Rather, it can be descried as simply "the power of knowing and reasoning, or even the understanding."[149] Culverwell maintained that Right Reason is different and superior to empirical reasoning (although that too has its lesser role). The existence of eternal and immutable Recta Ratio is so crucial that it forms the basis of all truth. Without it, "what difference between sobriety and madnesse?"[150] In the midst of all the contemporary religious radicalism, the excesses and "enthusiasms" of many different sects posed a clear threat to this Recta Ratio, or the "candle of the Lord."[151] However, this candle of Right Reason is vital in attaining some idea of the divine, as the pleasures of purely natural reason are "but husks in comparason of those Gospel-delights, those mysterious pleasures that lie hid in the bosome of Christ."[152] Like Whichcote, Culverwell employed the idea of the divine candle of Reason on many occasions. As early as 1641 he declared that the "Spirit of a Man...is the candle of the Lord."[153] He also claimed that it was "first lighted at a Sun-beam," and is a "lamp" within the Rational nature, guiding it "in the name of God" so that the soul and God "become perfect Unisons."[154] The soul's union with God is made possible by its unique deiformity—its capability as "the image of God"—an idea similar to that espoused by Whichcote. It is important to note that the lamp of reason is not restricted to Christians and Jews only but can also be seen "shining from the candle of an Heathen."[155] All should be thankful for their candles of the Lord, "not to mock and delude them, but to deal truly and faithfully with them."[156]

It is not true that reason jeopardizes faith, for "The light of Reason doth no more prejudice the light of faith, then the light of a Candle doth extinguish the light of a Star."[157] Countering those who maintained that the "over-praise of Reason" must of necessity have "at least a thousand heresies coucht in it," Culverwell argued, "Is it not better to enjoy the faint and languishing light of this candle of the Lord, rather than to be in palpable and disconsolate darkness?"[158] However, with the exception of Peter Sterry, Culverwell was a stronger Calvinist than the other Cambridge Platonists.[159] He therefore placed greater emphasis upon the inferiority of reason to faith. With his Calvinist belief in the ultimate subservience of reason in the face of revelation, Culverwell maintained Recta Ratio's limits—the soul even in its full brightness is still "but the candle of the Lord."[160] Reason is unable to "pierce into [God's] mysterious and unsearchable wayes."[161] Even at the height of reason, it is unable to "spy out such profound and mysterious excellencies, as faith beholds in one twinkling of her eye."[162] Yet Culverwell maintains the importance of reason's role in faith and claims that this candle still has a vital role to play. He is particularly wary, like his Platonist contemporaries, that extreme Calvinists should not profess the weakness of reason so much that they risk caving in to enthusiasm or worse, as even this logical argumentation "in some measure comes from Reason."[163] Instead, there ought to be a complementary relationship between reason and religion, so that "Reason and Faith may kisse each other."[164] "Right Reason" can never oppose "one jot or apex of the word of God,"[165] since to obey Right Reason is to be "persuaded by God himself."[166]

Realizing the tendency of extreme Calvinism to concentrate on the power and wrath of God, Culverwell, like the other Cambridge Platonists, counseled that God is not a God of fear but of love.[167] Religion should not be merely dry ritual, as the Arminians prefer, but a sacrament of heart and feeling; it is not enough that faith should only "warme [the] mouth" with words and external observances, or even "scholastic riddles," but it should "melt the heart" as well.[168] Amid continuing religious division and following the bitterly fought civil war, Culverwell advocates toleration and Christian unity in words painfully relevant today. He is shocked that so many Christians are apparently unaffected by the horrific slaughter of the civil war.[169] The schisms and divisions among Christians merely "give great advantage to the enemies," and Culverwell mourns the factionalism between those who maintain, "I am of Calvin, and another, I am of Luther."[170] He is convinced that believers should be unified in Christ's love and meet together "in the Name of Christian."[171] He places his hope in divine reason, which should form the basis of toleration, "sheath up many a sword...(and) quench many a flame."[172]

John Smith (1618–52)

John Smith's *Select Discourses* contain some of the most beautiful thought and expression in all of Cambridge Platonism and truly exhibit the "richest and most beautiful mind" of the movement.[173] Their author was born in Achurch, near Oundle, Northamptonshire, in 1618, to aged parents. He entered Emmanuel College eighteen years later, where his tutor was Benjamin Whichcote, to whom for his "Directions and Encouragement of him in his Studies, his seasonable provision for his support and maintenance when he was a young scholar... [Smith] did ever express a great and singular regard."[174] By 1644, Smith had graduated with a master's degree, which led to a fellowship at Queen's College from 1644 to 1652. Tragically, he died at thirty-five of consumption.[175] It seems he was a man of integrity, a truly good and devout Christian with "love bubling *[sic]* and springing up in his Soul," someone with whom it was always a delight to meet.[176] His faith made him "Godlike" and he "lived by faith in the Son of God."[177] Also a man of great learning, he was described in a funeral oration by his friend Simon Patrick as a "living library...a walking study."[178] His magnificent library of over five hundred volumes was bequeathed to Queen's College.

None of his work was published in his lifetime, as Smith intended it to be delivered orally, though his *Select Discourses* were eventually edited and prepared for publication by John Worthington (1618–89), who was the master of Jesus College until the Restoration.[179] Six of the discourses were from an unfinished scheme of work, and the remaining four were selected by Worthington from Smith's miscellaneous writings.[180] The *Select Discourses* focus on knowledge of the divine, the nature of God and God's works, and arguments for the immortality of the soul. It is important to emphasize the fact that, despite his early death, Smith's influence extended far beyond his own time. Some of his discourses were extracted for inclusion in John Wesley's *Christian*

Library (1749), while Samuel Taylor Coleridge also commented on Smith in his *Aids to Reflection* (1825) and *Literary Remains* (1836).

Smith's attack on atheism took a form unlike the arguments of Cudworth and More; his concern was not explicitly with contemporary atheism but with the atheism of Democritus, Epicurus, and Lucretius.[181] However, he was also knowledgeable about contemporary philosophy and personally espoused Cartesian mechanism. His "unqualified acceptance" marked a departure from the other Cambridge Platonists, who viewed Descartes' philosophy as a fundamental threat to theism.[182] To the contrary, in Cartesian dualism Smith found contemporary support for the philosophy of Plotinus.[183] He denies the existence of the lower, "plastic" part of the soul, affirming instead the purgation and separation of the soul from the body, for the "inward sweetness and deliciousness" in divine truth cannot be relished by any "sensual mind."[184] The "more deeply our Souls dive into our Bodies," the more the Recta Ratio becomes muddied.[185] Consequently, Smith departs from some of the other Cambridge Platonists' more affirmative view of the body; he advocates complete withdrawal from all bodily things, so as "to set our Souls as free as may be from its miserable slavery to this base flesh."[186] Unlike More, for whom the vital bond between soul and body is much harder to break, the "mechanical" union between soul and body is easily dissolved.[187]

The genius of Smith's theology lies in his ability to maintain both God's transcendence and God's immanence. He was particularly keen to emphasize this worldly immanence in response to the claim that a great gulf lies between God and the world, an image particularly common among Calvinists.[188] In Plotinian language, Smith describes how each person should aim at "knitting his owne centre...unto the centre of Divine Being."[189] Smith, like Whichcote and others, underscores the need for deiformity—the need to "polish and shape our Souls into the clearest resemblance of Him."[190] "Indeed, it is impossible to enjoy God without an "assimilation and conformity of our Natures to [God] in a way of true goodness and Godlike perfection."[191] Smith makes a compelling claim for God's immanence within the individual through the image of an "infant Christ" within the soul.[192] This is a presence best discerned by an "intellectual touch" of him.[193] Professing a religion of power and experience, Smith describes in beautiful prose how reason, once raised by the Holy Spirit into converse with God, "is turn'd into Sense."[194] What before was only faith now becomes vision.[195]

Smith's innatism finds its origin in Cicero. He believes that the common notions of God and virtue upon the soul "are more clear and perspicuous than any else."[196] This is so despite the fact that all too often such notions are "smother'd, or tainted with a deep dye of mens [sic] filthy lusts."[197] He insisted upon the need to flee from earthly things to the world beyond through a practice of contemplation deeply influenced by Plotinus and Proclus. Indeed, God has imprinted something divine on the soul so "that man by reflecting into himself might behold there the glory of God."[198] For there is still need for some "interpreter within," or candle of the Lord—that divine 'Right Reason' in which the soul partakes.[199] Therefore, as with the rest of the Cambridge group, God and reason are inextricably entwined, and "they that live most in the exercise of Religion shall find their Reason most enlarged."[200]

Despite this focus on reason, Smith's is no cold, rational faith—instead, he declares that *both* reason and the heart witness to God's existence. Goodness and a holy life are important, as is the simplicity and power of worship. True religion does not exist merely in books and writings—indeed, to search only there for it is to "seek the living among the dead."[201] Neither is religion found in the mere external trappings of ritual, as its "main business" is to "purge and reform" hearts of all evil.[202] Smith evokes Whichcote in the primacy he places on a good heart and religious action.[203] Religion for him is first a "Divine life, then a Divine Science."[204] It is a "Godlike frame of Spirit, discovering itself in Serene and Clear Minds."[205] In an image taken from Plotinus, as the eye cannot see the sun until it is sunlike, neither can the human soul behold God "unless it be Godlike."[206]

Smith beautifully amplifies the central Cambridge Platonist themes of love and toleration. He attacks the focus on hell and the wrathful, tyrannical picture of God that the extreme Calvinists so often conveyed.[207] Instead, he encourages a portrayal of the Deity as "most serene and lovely,"[208] invoking the resplendent image of the "warm sun of the Divine Love" that breaks forth over all Creation "with healing in its wings."[209]

Peter Sterry (1613–72)

Peter Sterry, surely the most mystical of the Cambridge Platonists, has been undeservedly neglected through the years.[210] Yet his writings influenced many contemporaries—including Robert Greville, Lord Brooke (1608-43), and Sir Henry Vane (1613–62)—and with a rare literary force, tackled issues still relevant today, such as the relationship between free will and determinism, reason and faith. Sterry was born in 1613 in Southwark, London. A devout Puritan, he was aptly sent to Emmanuel College in 1629, where he was elected fellow in 1637. While at Emmanuel, he benefited from the teaching of Benjamin Whichcote, who, in one complex conversation on divinity, heard his pupil explain himself with "such Ease and Clearness" that, rising from his seat and embracing him, he cried, "Peter, thou hast overcome me, thou art all pure intellect."[211] On news of Sterry's death in May 1672, Whichcote purportedly claimed that he would be "well contented" to part with half of his wealth, only to obtain "some Hours free conversation with that greatly Enlightened Friend." He "most readily" agreed to preach Sterry's funeral sermon.[212]

At Emmanuel, Sterry also appreciated the society of the like-minded Puritans with whom he met for regular prayer meetings and fasts.[213] Certainly his contemporaries in the college held him in high regard, as attests Samuel Rogers, a fellow godly young Puritan, who exclaimed that by Sterry's presence "the Lord does much good to Emanuel Colledge [sic]."[214] Why, or precisely when, Sterry resigned his fellowship is unclear.[215] His post as chaplain to the important Parliamentary leader Robert Greville, Lord Brooke, at Warwick Castle, was surely a welcome entrance into the wider Puritan network that was active in Warwickshire at that time, of which Lord Brooke and Warwick Castle formed the center.[216] No doubt the Platonist Lord Brooke delighted in the society of the man, claimed by one source, along with John Sadler, as the first to make a public profession of Platonism within Cambridge.[217] By

1638 there is a record of Sterry dining in Warwick Castle with Lord and Lady Brooke and other local ministers.[218] It was during his time as chaplain to Lord Brooke that the civil war broke out and Sterry found himself engaged in Parliamentary political intrigue against the king; there is evidence that he aided Lord Brooke's covert links to the Scottish rebels in 1641.[219]

Sterry's time as Lord Brooke's chaplain was a period of important theological and literary development. His subsequent early millenarian zeal most likely gained momentum from Brooke's example as a godly militant. It is also highly probable that Sterry helped compose Lord Brooke's 1642 Platonist work *The Nature of Truth*. Of the "lofty and glorious language" and "divers acute and learned Criticismes" with which his work had been adorned, Lord Brooke was anxious to admit that: "none of these are mine."[220] Certainly, numerous passages in the work, as well as many of the ideas, bear the stamp of Peter Sterry. W. R. Sorley's comment that in Lord Brooke "the Puritan temper was combined with the mystic"[221] applies as aptly to the Cambridge Platonist as it does to his aristocratic patron. Thus Sterry's influence is discernable at the origins of Platonist/Puritan thought.

Sterry married Frances Ashworth in 1641.[222] From his private letters of later years, now stored in the library of his old Cambridge college, we can catch a glimpse of his deep devotion to his family.[223] In 1661 he wrote to his daughter Frances, "One of the great pleasures which I have in life is to think of our meeting in the next world, when we shall be forever with each other, and forever with the Lord in one another."[224] His son, Peter, however, caused the godly Puritan a great deal of heartache. Peter's love of wine, women, and gambling led Sterry to exclaim in anguish, "Now I mourn over you as dead in the worst sense; dead in sin."[225] Yet Sterry persisted in exhorting his wayward son to godliness.

By 1643 Lord Brooke had died while commanding a Parliamentary army at Lincoln, and Sterry and his family were living in London. He was swiftly appointed to the Westminster Assembly of Divines. Two years later Sterry was invited to preach before Parliament.[226] In 1649 his firm alliance with the Parliamentarians was sealed by his appointment as chaplain to the Council of State. He became one of Oliver Cromwell's personal chaplains during the Interregnum, an exceedingly influential position at a time when religion and politics were closely intertwined; the historian Blair Worden claims that Sterry's impact on politics was greater than has been believed and that he "exercised much influence at Cromwell's court."[227]

It was during this time that Sterry may have come to know the poet John Milton, who was acting as Latin secretary to Cromwell. In language his hearers in Parliament could easily understand, Sterry enthusiastically extolled the work of Providence in history:[228] "Who taught that New army of Raw Souldiers to fight so, that a Royall army was broken by them at Naseby? Was it not thou, O God?"[229]

Perhaps influenced by prominent millenarians such as the Cambridge fellow Joseph Mede, Sterry became one of the "foremost Interregnum spokesmen" for eschatological theology, which proclaimed that the kingdom of God was at hand.[230] As the scriptures—particularly Daniel and Revelation—had decreed, the kingdom would be preceded by signs such as the collapse of the papacy, the conversion of the Jews to Christianity, and the reign of King Jesus on earth. Sterry's sermons to Parliament were robustly, even militantly, millenarian during the late 1640s and early 1650s, often laden with tortuous calculations regarding the Second Coming.[231] Yet his political millenarianism soon ended in disillusionment; as Sterry turned with increasing interest to the writings of Jacob Boehme, he grew more contemplative and mystical, with "his eyes fixed on the world beyond."[232]

After the Restoration, Sterry's fortunes declined dramatically. He became an unfashionable and unwelcome reminder of the Cromwellian era and was forced to retreat from public life. Yet after his pardon from Charles II on November 9, 1660, he became chaplain to the nonconformist Philip Sidney, Viscount Lisle, and formed a nonconformist religious community at West Sheen in Surrey.[233] He wrote extensively for nonconformists during an era of persecution and consequent lack of higher education, and he must surely be numbered among the founders of the "nonconformist conscience" in England.[234] His works include many sermons, most of which were published during his lifetime, as well as three books, all posthumously published from his manuscripts.

Throughout Sterry's work, the influences of Plotinus, Origen, and Ficino are consistently evident.

Within his thought there is a good deal of tension regarding the role of reason in religion. Sterry clearly perceived the dangers of giving prominence to the rationality of religion at the expense of revelation (as with deism), for divine truths would become "no more Divine, but human truths."[235] Heavenly things would lose their majesty and grow "weak and contemptable" when demonstrated by reason alone, becoming "apish, mimicall imitations" of themselves, like the "Mistresse in her Cook-maid's clothes."[236] Reason cannot attain the highest mysteries of religion without the aid of a divine light.[237] As a stronger Calvinist than many of the Cambridge Platonists—thus presumably a believer in the election of the godly minority—Sterry struggled with the claim that the "candle of the Lord" was within everyone's grasp. This tension is never fully reconciled in his thought, although his belief in apocatastasis and regenerated Right Reason should be seen as a partial attempt to bridge the gap. In this way all people are eventually saved, and yet God's grace alone remains the necessary catalyst. Right Reason—a divine seed ever present in the soul, which needs God's grace to attain partial knowledge of the mysteries of Christ—combines will, desire, heart, and spiritual understanding in perfect unity.[238] Thus reason and mysticism become one.

Sterry's most important work, *A Discourse of the Freedom of the Will* (1675), proclaimed something very akin to Cudworth's "self-determination," and similar to Cudworth, declared that the will and the understanding form a unity. The will "comprehends Reason or Understanding in its essential Form."[239] In an Augustinian-Thomist vein, Sterry believed that the will is determined to the good and is intricately bound to love.[240] Therefore, true liberty of will consists in the "free-springing, flourishing and fruitfulness of...[the will] in all good"[241] and because the will is united to the understanding, it is unable to do just as it pleases.[242] Neither does predestination nullify the point of laws in society; indeed, laws would be pointless if the will were not determined to be good. For "what effect hath the sense of Good and Evil seated in our Understanding, if the Will be guided by an absolute ungoverned arbitrariness, without Order...without respect to the dictates of the Understanding?"[243] Sterry asks: "Would any wise Workman, who had absolute power over his work...frame a work in which the great end of the principal part and of the whole, should be undetermined?"[244] Predestination is also a sign of a benevolent, caring God. Intellectual creatures are not so unimportant to God that they are "left outside his contrivance, to mere chance and indeterminateness." Thus in Sterry's unified and benign view of Creation, there is a joining of liberty and determinism.

Sterry's fundamental belief in the unity of all things and denial of the real existence of evil led him toward a monist outlook, in which he declared: "This world hath nothing real. It is all a Shadow."[245] With the philosopher's help, the soul can always live above the body in the "knowledge of the universal natures of things."[246] Yet, like Anne Conway, Sterry manages to preserve the significance of the incarnation by focusing on the "Word made flesh" and Christ as mediator.[247] For through Christ alone spirit and matter are intimately linked and, with Pythagorean overtones, Christ's divine harmony unites all things together "as links in a golden Chain."[248] Such unity also results in a kind of deiformity, as the glory of a saint lies not in simply conforming the will to God's, but rather in "transforming his will into that [of the Divine], in feeding, and feasting his understanding and will upon the Excellencies and Delicacies of the Divine Wisdom and Will."[249] As in the case of John Smith, Sterry manages to proclaim both God's immanence (He is "in All, through All, on every side, beneath, above, beyond All...Whose center is everywhere"), and also his transcendence, as "in such an excess of Glory, [he] ascends them all, transcends them all."[250]

Sterry's love of unity in all things meant that he espoused the Platonic-Cabbalistic belief in the preexistence of the soul and (singularly among his Cambridge colleagues, apart from Anne Conway) Origen's unorthodox doctrine of apocatastasis, or universal salvation.[251] The latter was a result of Sterry's emphasis on the love of God. Like his fellow Cambridge Platonists, he feared the dangers of espousing the image of the tyrannical God of Calvinism, the "hard taskmaster" of cruelty and wrath pictured by some. Instead, he was keen to stress the benignity of God's nature, and he stated that anyone who hates God, hates a false image.[252]

Strongly influenced by Augustine, Sterry claims that the key attribute of God is love. From God spring "purity, simplicity, sovereignty, the Wisdom, the Almightiness, the Unchangeableness, the Infiniteness, the eternity of Divine Love."[253] It is "love...which runs through the whole work of God."[254]

There is no doubt that it is in the beautiful lines of his preface to *A Discourse of the Freedom of the Will* that the "writer's inmost heart leaps up."[255] Sterry pleads: "Let no difference of Principles or Practices divide thee in thy affection from any person. He who seems to me as a Samaritan to a Jew, most worthy of contempt and hatred, most apt to wound or kill me, may hide under the shape of a Samaritan, a generous, affectionate Neighbour, Brother and Friend."[256] Even at his most militantly millenarian, Sterry bravely advocates a religion of love and an end to bloodshed.[257] Mourning the thousands slain in the civil war in the name of religion, he sadly remarked in a 1645 sermon to Parliament: "Lord we have sin'd, we should have kept these people as their shepherds, but we have procur'd their woe."[258] Peter Sterry claimed that in divine contemplation the soul can soar above the body and, reminiscent of Plato's *Phaedrus*, is carried upon "two soaring wings, as the wings of an Angel, quite out of the sight of sense, above all the tumult of individuals and particulars, to the invisible Glories, and Harmonies of universal Forms."[259] In the same manner, Sterry's own beautiful, poetic, and lyrical mysticism in many ways rises above all differences, so that in the end, all that is important is the unity of all things in the boundless love of God.

Anne Conway (1630–79)

Anne Conway (nee Finch) was born in December 1631 into an affluent London household and grew up in Kensington House (later Kensington Palace, the childhood home of Queen Victoria). Her father, who had died a week before Anne was born, had been speaker of the House of Commons, recorder of London, and a staunch friend of Francis Bacon. Unfortunately (though somewhat unsurprisingly considering the age she lived in), Anne was granted no formal education, although she eagerly studied as much as she could on her own, quickly mastering French and Latin and discovering her love of philosophy. Conway found much intellectual stimulation through her deep devotion to her beloved half-brother John Finch (1626–82). It was through him that she was brought into contact with Henry More, John's tutor at Christ's College, Cambridge. Their first correspondence occurred in 1650, when Anne, curious about Cartesianism, was eager to converse with the quiet Platonist who was so knowledgeable about the fascinating new Cartesian philosophy. However, neither could have foreseen the enduring nature of their friendship and correspondence, which were to last until Anne's death in 1679. The correspondence comprised a total of 179 letters. She became More's "heroine pupil," and his affection and deep respect for her personality and intellect are plainly evident in their correspondence. On one occasion, on a visit to the Conway estate in Ireland in 1664, she affectionately wrote, "If I live so long, there is nobody [in England] I shall have so great a passion to see as yourself."[260]

In 1652 Anne married Edward Conway, later the third Viscount Conway and Killultagh.[261] He too had an alert mind, was interested in philosophy, and welcomed Henry More on his frequent visits to their home, Ragley Hall, in Warwickshire. In later years, from her sickbed in Ragley, her letters to Conway, her "dearest dear," immersed in politics in London, abundantly prove their enduring mutual affection. In 1658 their only son, Heneage Edward, was born; sadly, he lived for just over two years before succumbing to smallpox. His loss caused his mother the greatest sadness of her life, and she desolately wrote to More that her little son's death "hath extorted from me a griefe proportionable to so great a loss."[262]

Suffering from debilitating headaches all her adult life, Conway resorted to many desperate attempts to cure herself, enlisting the scientist William Harvey, the Irish healer Valentine Greatrakes, who, though unsuccessful in helping Conway, was able to cure Ralph Cudworth's son, and the medicines of Francis Mercury Van Helmont.[263] Additionally, she visited Bath to take the waters and resorted to bloodletting and the even more desperate steps of allowing the opening of an artery and the taking of mercury, which led to her near death from poisoning.[264] All were sadly to no avail. The headaches progressively worsened; by 1669 her illness had increased so much that there were times she felt unable to read or even to be read to.[265] Yet amid all, Conway characteristically and devoutly resigned herself to God's will, praying for the "patience to bear whatsoever my sad fate hath designed for me."[266]

Francis Mercury Van Helmont, who was to act as Conway's physician for the final nine years of her life, first arrived in England in 1670 on behalf of Princess Elizabeth of the Palatinate, a grandchild of James I, for whom he was attempting to gain a pension. The son of the alchemist Jean Baptiste Van Helmont, Francis was born in what now is Belgium in 1614. He had an interesting life, wandering through many countries, meeting different people, including philosophers, scientists, and royalty. It was Henry More who first introduced Van Helmont to Anne Conway, in hope that the European chemist's knowledge would provide a cure for his friend.[267] Although Van Helmont's medical ability was powerless in the face of Conway's suffering, his influence proved itself in other ways. He was delighted to find that despite her illness Conway's understanding "continued quick and sound, and it had the greatest Facility imaginable for any, either Physical, Metaphysical, or Mathematical speculations."[268] Van Helmont thus acted in some way as a "catalyst" in Conway's decision to turn away from the dualism of her Platonist background and ultimately to adopt Quakerism.[269] In addition, as a friend of the distinguished Christian Cabbalist Knorr von Rosenroth (1636–89), Van Helmont had a good knowledge of the Lurianic Cabbala.[270] He introduced the viscountess to these esoteric Jewish mystical teachings.[271] Cabbalistic doctrines with their so-called unwritten account of Mosaic revelation (as compared with the scriptural, written account) appeared to have a certain affinity with the *prisca theologia*, the Renaissance idea referred to by the other Cambridge Platonists.[272]

Van Helmont's even greater influence on Conway was with regard to Quakerism. The Society of Friends originated during the Commonwealth period from a variety of different influences including the mysticism of Jacob Boehme (1575–1624), the English Lollards, and other groups such as the Baptists and Seekers.[273] By the 1670s the Society of Friends was holding meetings close to Ragley, and they awakened the interest of Van Helmont. From the mid 1670s many prominent Quaker leaders (as they were then known) visited Ragley, including George Keith from 1675, and George Fox in 1678. By November 1675 Conway was able to tell More that the reading of the Quakers' books recently "had in great measure freed me from former prejudicate [sic] opinions, but their conversation doth much more reconcile me to them."[274] Van Helmont's own conversion in early 1676 could only have aided such a change in the convictions of the viscountess.[275] By 1677 all her maids were from the Society of Friends. Some of Lady Conway's affinity with the Quakers was a consequence of her extreme suffering, which she felt that only the silent Friends could entirely understand, for they too had suffered greatly.[276] As she explained to More in 1676: "The weight of my affliction lies so very heavy upon me, that it is incredible how very seldom I can endure anyone in my chamber, but I find them so still and very serious, that the company of such of them as I have hitherto seene, will be acceptable to me, as long as I am capable of enjoying any."[277] The Quaker aim of yielding one's inner struggles and self-will to God and of waiting in silence and simple devotion to be led by God's pure light was one with which, in her acute suffering, Conway's own resigned, rather melancholic temperament could empathize.[278] Nevertheless, her eventual conversion to Quakerism in 1677 was both a courageous and a rather shocking act at the time, particularly for a woman occupying such an elevated place in society. It was also courageous in an age that considered Quakers, with their enthusiasm for the inward spirit rather than external ceremony, ritual, and sacrament, as little better than the antinomian Ranters or any of the other extreme religious sects of the day. The Quakers refused to respect the social hierarchy, called everyone "thee" and "thou," ignored the custom of doffing the hat to a superior, and refused to recognize all titles. Their refusal to pay tithes to the state church, alongside their allowing women to preach, gave the movement the appearance of a subversive sect. Henry More allegedly received the news of Conway's conversion to Quakerism in 1677 "with Tears, and labour'd, all that a Faithful Friend could do, to set her right."[279] Although he had made an effort to befriend individual Quakers and to see Conway's point of view—and even conceded that "there be some amongst them good and sincere-hearted Men"[280]—he was still wary of their orthodoxy, claiming that he thought it "not so far from the spirit of a real Quaker to burn the Bible, when...the letter of it is so little believed by them."[281] More's suspicion of Quakerism placed a decided strain on the friendship, although it was never entirely to break it. Yet in Conway's last, painful years, More found himself more and more excluded from Conway's company. Despite the fact that he stayed at Ragley all one summer, More "did not see her above twice or thrice."[282]

The Principles of the Most Ancient and Modern Philosophy, found after Lady Conway's death in one of her notebooks, had been written sometime during the mid 1670s, after Van Helmont's arrival at Ragley and before Conway's conversion to Quakerism, since the treatise lacks any references to the movement. Translated into Latin, probably by Henry More, and with a preface jointly composed by More and Van Helmont, it was taken to Holland by the latter, where it appeared originally as one of three Latin treatises in the collection *Opuscula philosophica* (1690). Two years later it was retranslated back into English.

It has been claimed that Conway's *Principles* is "truer to the Platonic tradition" than either More or Conway, although "more sweeping" in its rejection of Cartesianism.[283] The work is certainly a fascinating, original piece. On the whole, it is clear that Conway's thought was "impregnated" with the spirit of Cambridge Platonism.[284] Her emphasis on toleration, realism, and free will, and her attack on Hobbes, Spinoza, and Descartes, all point to the Cambridge Platonists, particularly to her teacher, Henry More.[285]

Cambridge Platonism's themes of love and toleration are apparent in the manner in which Conway believes that not every sin is punished in hell, since God is not a "cruel tyrant" over his creatures, but instead, a "benign father" whose aim is that punishments should be primarily to purify and restore.[286] Instead of the Calvinist voluntarist, tyrannical God, Lady Conway espouses quite the opposite and plays down the "fire and brimstone" idea of eternal hell by stressing its purgative, restorative faculty.[287] She stresses the benevolent love of God, which humans would be aware of "if our souls could inwardly feel and taste him."[288]

The point on which Conway shows her independence and pointedly diverges from her teacher, Henry More, concerns her monist philosophy of substance. Although she believes, like More, that spirit is extended, she criticizes the dualism found in More's work.[289] She dislikes More's "vital congruity" or "plastic power" uniting matter and soul, because she believes that the union of the two must be more fundamental. If matter and spirit are so opposed to another, why are they so united?[290] More's "vital congruity" between soul and body seems to make no sense, because he cannot tell "in what this affinity consists." Body, according to More, is dead matter, and thus, maintains Conway, there could be no affinity at all between it and the substance of the soul.[291] The question of pain is understandably on her mind. Why, if the dualist argument is to be believed, does the spirit or soul suffer so much from bodily pain?[292] Conway believes that such difficulties can only be done away with if one admits that the soul is of one nature and substance with the body.[293] She stresses instead a vitalist and monist theory of substance, in which every creature contains infinitesimal spirits and bodies, or "monads."[294] Every spirit is a body, differing only from a material body in that the latter is darker and less refined.[295] The further that substances are from God, the darker and more "gross" they are. Therefore, the only difference between body and spirit is "modal and incremental, not essential and substantial."[296] Species do not differ in substance or essence but only in certain attributes; for example, an entity (such as water) does not change in essence, but only in its mode of being, when it freezes and becomes ice.[297] Every being (excepting God) is joined in a great chain of being: "All creatures from the highest to the lowest are inseparably united one to another by their subtler mediating parts, which come between them and which are emanations from one creature to another."[298] On the ontological scale, by virtue of a plastic nature of the soul, "there occurs a transmutation from one species to another either by ascending from a lower or by descending in the opposite way."[299] Such a reincarnation clearly steps into heterodoxy and exhibits the greatest influence that Van Helmont and the Cabbala had on Conway's thought. However, such unorthodoxy is limited; Christ is the key medium in Conway's philosophy, since Christ is in a unique position between creatures and spirit, as a unifying, mediating principle who can raise all things, by his action, into union with God.[300]

There is much debate over the influence of Conway on Leibniz.[301] Because Van Helmont took the *Principles* to Holland in 1690, Leibniz would certainly have had access to Conway's treatise. Conway's influence on Leibniz is very possible, and even likely. Did Leibniz, writing in 1690, acquire the term *monad* from Conway and Van Helmont?[302] It has been argued that the withholding of Conway's name from the Latin edition of the *Principles* prevented her from achieving the recognition she deserved in the development of Leibniz's thought.[303] Leibniz himself wrote the English clergyman Thomas Burnet in 1697 that his philosophical views "approach somewhat closely those of the late Countess of Conway."[304] Although Lady Conway's precise influence on Leibniz may be difficult to estimate accurately, it is true that at the very least she had a "significant imput" in the philosopher's thought, right up to his writing of the 1714 *Monadology*.[305]

Anne Conway, arguably the most original and remarkable seventeenth-century female philosopher, died on February 23, 1679, "giving up her spirit very peaceably without any perceivable motion and keeping a very sweet face."[306] According to her own wishes, she was buried in the village church at Arrow, Warwickshire, without ceremony or splendor, with only her husband, More, and Van Helmont present. On the leaden cover of her coffin were scratched the words "Quaker Lady."[307] On hearing of her death, her heartbroken teacher and friend for nearly thirty years could yet reflect proudly on her as follows: "My Lady Conway was my Lady Conway to her last Breath; the greatest Example of Patience and Presence of Mind, in highest Extremities of Pain and Affliction....Scarce any thing to be found like her, since the Primitive times of the Church."[308]

Part Three
An Overview of the Political and Religious Context of Cambridge Platonism

The Cambridge Platonists lived at a time when politics and religion were intricately linked, so it is impossible to talk about the one without the other. The English Civil War and Interregnum were exceedingly turbulent times, and the Cambridge Platonists could have been forgiven for having "partisanship and prejudice bred in their bones."[309] Amazingly, the opposite was true.[310] In this context we can see an explanation for the Cambridge Platonists' focus on reason and toleration; this alone, they believed, could bring an end to the interminable cycle of sectarianism, war, and persecution. What follows is a compact account of the salient events of their day, intended to provide essential background for appreciating Cambridge Platonism.

Throughout the sixteenth-century Reformation, Protestantism challenged Roman Catholic authority. In England, under the rule of Henry VIII, the Reformation heralded a dramatic split from Rome. In the 1534 Act of Supremacy the monarch became head of the Church of England. However, a broad uniformity of religion between Roman Catholicism and Protestantism was carefully maintained under the Protestant Queen Elizabeth I (1558–1603). As Elizabeth's reign went on, war with Catholic Spain contributed to increasing distrust and persecution of Roman Catholics.[311] Between 1590 and 1603, eighty-eight Catholics (including fifty-three priests) were executed in England. Finally the Catholics' disillusionment culminated in the unsuccessful Gunpowder Plot of 1605, when King James I was on the throne.

The main troubles in early seventeenth-century England were religious ones involving two branches of Protestantism. Even in Queen Elizabeth's reign there had been a group of more extreme Protestants—abusively termed *Puritans* since the 1560s—that disliked the liturgy and formality in church services and protested at having to kneel for communion. They emphasized the importance of sermons over liturgy.[312] This group became far more vocal in James I's reign, and in 1603 they presented a Millenary Petition, demanding various reforms in religion. The Puritans pleaded for a reformed theology that would make the Church of England more on the lines of the new reformed churches on the Continent. In response, James I arranged the Hampton Court Conference a year later. The only concessions granted to the Puritans were a new version of the Bible and a pledge to reduce the number of pluralist clergy, whom they had accused of neglecting their parishioners.[313]

By the late 1620s and early 1630s, the Puritans were increasingly disturbed by the "dramatic shift" exhibited by the court toward Arminianism, a movement within Protestantism that held an optimistic view of human abilities, the grace of God available to all, and the role of good works in leading to salvation.[314] These beliefs clearly differed from those of the Calvinists, who, in contrast, stressed human depravity, predestination, and total reliance on the grace of God. Calvinists regarded the Arminian view on good works as close to the position of the so-called papists. The Arminians also loved ritual and beauty in worship, and they highlighted the sacraments, as opposed to the Calvinists, for whom scripture and sermons were central.[315] The *Book of Sports* in 1618 and the decidedly Arminian *Directions to Preachers* (1622), along with proposals for a Spanish Catholic wife for Prince Charles, further incensed the Puritans.[316]

King Charles's reign began badly, with economic and political crises due to a war first waged against Spain and later France. His 1628 appointment of Richard Montague as Bishop of Chichester left no doubt about his Arminian sympathies.[317] Moreover, William Laud, appointed Bishop of London in 1628, became Archbishop of Canterbury in 1633 and, in addition, the 1629 republishing of the Elizabethan "Thirty-nine Articles" contained a new preface blatantly favoring Arminianism. Then, incensed by Parliament's grievances over religion and taxation, Charles resolved in 1629 to rule without Parliament. Yet the matter that roused the godly Puritans most was the reissuing of the "monstrous and prodigious" *Book of Sports* in 1633, which allowed lawful recreation to take place on Sundays—something that the sabbatarian Puritans could never agree to.[318] In addition, in the same year, preaching was more stringently regulated and a decree was issued that railed communion tables were to be placed north-south against the east wall of churches. This may seem relatively trivial to us now, but in the early seventeenth century such an action, with its "papist" theological implications, raised strong feelings among the "godly." Some who attacked the king's religious policy were very severely dealt with; a classic example of this is William Prynne, whose 1637 punishment for writing Puritan tracts against the church was the loss of both his ears, a branding on his cheeks with the letters "S. L." (for "seditious libeller"), a fine of five thousand pounds, and a sentence to life imprisonment. Not surprisingly, his health was broken as a result.

This increase in Arminianism in England, or Laudianism, as it came to be called, led to the establishment of Puritan colonies in America.[319] The first emigration had taken place in 1620, when the Pilgrim Fathers settled in Plymouth, New England, but the exodus was to increase dramatically in the 1630s, with a remarkable one-third of the clergy emigrating from the Puritan stronghold of Emmanuel College, Cambridge. During the 1630s as many as fifteen thousand of the "godly" forsook the country with "sighs and farewell tears" for the New World, repulsed by the bishops' tyrannous behavior and other Laudian innovations.[320] It was alleged that were it not for the 1633 *Book of Sports,* many would have remained in their homeland.[321] Leading Puritans such as Lord Brooke were involved in the formation of the Massachusetts Bay Company and the planting of new colonies such as Saybrook in Connecticut; the establishment of Harvard College in Cambridge, Massachusetts, in 1637, was for the express purpose of educating learned Puritan ministers.

Laudianism was to cause even more trouble for King Charles, and his attempts to introduce it in Scotland were even less successful than in England. In fact, his attempt to have the Scottish Prayer Book read in Edinburgh in 1637 led to riots, as the Scots feared a plot to convert them to Catholicism. Thereafter the rebels in Scotland moved fast; by 1638 they had abolished episcopacy. Charles's reaction was to order the counties of England to raise forces against the Scots, so that by 1639 several thousand Englishmen were poised ready to fight on the Scottish border. However, despite an eventual settlement, the Scots refused either to reinstate episcopacy or to disband their army. For the first time since the eleven years of his personal rule without Parliament, a desperate Charles, running short of money with which to fight the rebels, was forced to call Parliament in 1640. Nevertheless, he had to dissolve it amid increasing Puritan complaints and obstructions. Then, the churchmen of Convocation, without Parliament, passed the "Etcetera oath," which meant that clergy would never be allowed to alter the episcopal structure of the church, another move worrying and offensive to the Puritans. Meanwhile, the Presbyterian Scottish and English Puritan MPs realized that they had much in common in their grievances against Laudianism, and there is evidence of secret communications between them before the Scots' invasion of northeast England necessitated the recall of Parliament.[322]

In order to pacify Parliament, Charles was forced to sacrifice his closest advisers, including Archbishop Laud, who was sent to the Tower at the end of 1640. Some extreme Puritans then carried out a radical program of destruction of religious images within churches, smashing stained glass and statues and whitewashing ancient wall paintings. Parliamentary commissioners were sent to college chapels to remove monuments of superstition and idolatry, although they found, in contrast to many colleges, that on entering Puritan Emmanuel College, they had nothing to do.[323]

More problems faced Charles I with the outbreak of the Irish rebellion in 1641, when around three thousand Protestants were killed in Ireland by the Catholics of Ulster. Suspicions and rumors abounded that it was all a Roman Catholic plot, and even that Charles had been behind it all. Angry MPs continued to oppose the king by producing the document known as the "Grand Remonstrance," which declared that he should only appoint ministers first approved by Parliament. At the same time, furious crowds obstructed the bishops from occupying their seats in the House of Lords. At the beginning of 1642 Charles panicked and entered the House of Commons with an armed force to arrest Parliamentary ringleaders, only to discover that they had already escaped; sensibly or not, Charles then quickly fled London, fearing for the safety of his family, and in doing so left the capital at the mercy of the advancing Parliamentarians. Finally, the king's raised standard at Nottingham in August 1642 signaled the start of the bloody civil war.

The Parliamentarians' "Solemn League and Covenant" of 1643 declared that religion was to be according to that of the Reformed churches; despite the tension between Presbyterians and Independents, the Parliamentary alliance with the Scottish Presbyterians led to the Westminster Assembly, begun in 1643.[324] This aimed to reorganize the Church of England more along the lines of Scottish Presbyterianism, though it met with very limited success.[325]

One of the effects of the civil war was to increase social mobility. The highly effective, nationally organized Parliamentarian New Model Army marched up and down the country, "mixing up population in a way previously unknown."[326] The civil war as a whole was to claim thousands of lives—as much as 3.6 percent of the population.[327] It deeply affected those who lived though it and witnessed the destruction, not only of family and friends, but also of houses, towns, and villages throughout the country. After numerous battles over four years, the king was forced to admit defeat, and on May 5, 1646, he surrendered to the Scots. Thereafter he signed the "Engagement" with the Scots, in which he promised to introduce Presbyterianism into England within three years in return for their military support of Charles's cause against the Parliamentarians; however, the resulting Scottish invasion on his behalf was easily defeated.

Even before the famous Pride's Purge of December 1648, in which Royalist sympathizers were forcibly expelled from Parliament by the army, several hundred clergy had already been dismissed and the Book of Common Prayer made illegal.[328] Charles I's days were also numbered. Refusing to yield any more of his royal prerogative, King Charles's dramatic trial before the High Court of Justice ended in his execution on January 30, 1649. It was an action considered deeply shocking to many in the country and in Europe as a whole. Yet Oliver Cromwell, one of the main commissioners hearing Charles's case, was one of those who had come to the decision that it was God's will that the "sinful" monarch should be sacrificed for the good of the country, and he also supported the abolition of the House of Lords the following month. Now, without obstruction, "godly" reform could begin.

The 1650 Engagement Act, which required obedience to the new Commonwealth, was passed by the Rump Parliament, which was increasingly dependent on the army to crush rebellions by the Scots and to deal devastating blows to the rebels in Ireland.[329] Moreover, in 1651 Cromwell's army defeated another invasion from Scotland led by Charles I's son, Charles Stuart (recognized as Charles II by the Scots), at the Battle of Worcester.[330] Yet the Scots and Irish were not the only problems for the Rump Parliament; a 1649 uprising by the Levellers also demanded attention. The Levellers were one of a number of more radical groups that arose during these turbulent years, having benefited from the increased freedom of the press after 1641 and from the support of the radical Agitators in the army in the late 1640s. Their most radical document, "The Agreement of the People" (October 1647), demanded various social and political reforms, including the widening of the franchise, increased liberty in religious matters, and equality in education. However, by 1649 the Levellers were feeling betrayed at the lack of democratic reform instituted by the Rump Parliament and constant dismissal of their revised agreement. As a result of the defeat of the sympathetic army Agitators, and the imprisonment of main Leveller leaders, the movement faded.

The Levellers were not the only radical group in England at this time, and many other political and religious groups were springing up all over the country. Various sects such as the Seekers, Muggletonians, and Grindletonians existed, but they posed little threat to social order. Apart from the Levellers, the most significant radical political group was the True Levellers or Diggers. This was a more extreme and more "communist" version of the Levellers. It gained its nickname by digging up the common land and pressing for more political reforms to obtain social and economic equality, such as universal male suffrage. Another religious sect, the Fifth Monarchists, were particularly influential in the army. With their militaristic millenarianism, they "seemed to be really in expectation every day [that] Christ should appear"[331] and the reign of the Fifth Monarchy would begin on earth.[332] However, the Ranters were perhaps the most notorious sect at this time; pantheist and materialist, they declared the Bible an allegory and maintained that there was no such thing as sin. Not surprisingly, immorality and debauchery were the results of such antinomianism. The Society of Friends or Quakers, as they were more commonly known, were considered by some to be as disgraceful as the Ranters, although their beliefs were quite different and basically orthodox. Yet with their emphasis upon the "inner light" and silent worship, and their disregard of social hierarchy, they attracted great persecution from 1652 onward. Indeed, the Cromwellian Protectorate attacked one radical Quaker, James Naylor, for blasphemously riding into Bristol on an ass in the way Christ had ridden an ass into Jerusalem. Naylor's subsequent extreme punishment, ordered by Parliament and harsher than Cromwell and his chaplain Peter Sterry would have wished,[333] was to have his tongue bored through and to suffer branding, flogging, and imprisonment. However, despite such persecution, by 1670 there were around seventy thousand Quakers in Britain.

In 1650 the Rump Parliament initiated various acts aiming at creating a "godly society," such as the Adultery and the Blasphemy Acts. These acts attacked various doctrines including free will and universal salvation, while the Toleration Act, also of 1650, was less stringent and merely demanded attendance at some form of religious service once a week. Despite these measures, though, as a whole the period of the Rump Parliament's rule was rather ineffectual, being preoccupied with high taxes and war against the Dutch over trade.

In April 1653 an exasperated Oliver Cromwell along with thirty other soldiers dissolved the Rump Parliament and established the Nominated Assembly, more frequently known as the Barebones Parliament, a Parliament with a sizeable number of radical members intent on initiating the longed-for "godly reformation" effectively. However, the unpredictable Barebones Parliament simply increased dissatisfaction with the general uncertainty of government and stimulated the increasingly strong desire in the country for stability. The subsequent "Instrument of Government" officially established Cromwell as Lord Protector and, in contrast to the more cautious wishes of most of the government, proclaimed toleration for everyone except Roman Catholics and the "licentious." However, it was not so much tolerance as the strong influence of millenarianism that led to the formation of a committee on which some of the Cambridge Platonists served,[334] along with others, such as merchants, to discuss whether or not to readmit the Jews to England, an occurrence that happened in 1654.[335]

Keen to continue the "godly reformation" in England, Cromwell employed triers and ejectors in 1654 both to vet and to improve the standard of clergy.[336] Upon the same lines, the following year the brief and extremely unpopular rule of the Major-Generals operated in ten regions of England, attempting to maintain order and reduce bad behavior of various kinds. Despite his pious intentions and concern about divine will and providence, Cromwell feared the lack of God's favor as a consequence of the failure of the fleet sent in 1655 to protect English merchants' religious rights in Spanish ports. A similar regard for providence and the will of God led to Cromwell refusing the title of king in "The Humble Petition and Advice" of 1657, claiming that he "would not set up that that providence hath destroyed and laid in the dust."[337] Just over a year later, on September 3, 1658, Cromwell was dead.

After the brief and ineffectual chaos of Richard Cromwell's Protectorate, the return of the Rump Parliament and the reversal of Pride's Purge led to a renewed desire for permanent stability and for the restoration of the monarchy. Thus it happened that Charles II's "Declaration of Breda" proclaimed "liberty to tender consciences," and the crown and Parliament agreed to work together once again. Perhaps such an Anglican Restoration occurred peaceably because throughout the war and Interregnum the Anglican liturgy was secretly, even openly, read with great devotion throughout the country.[338] In any case, throughout the Restoration many Puritans were quite happy to attend both chapel and the parish church.

However, not all Puritans were prepared to attend Church of England services. Within a few years it was clear that those who strongly objected to the 1662 Prayer Book were to be excluded from the Church of England. In the end, about 960 clergy were removed from their livings as a result of the demands of the 1662 Act of Uniformity and the requirements to use the new Book of Common Prayer and renounce the Solemn League and Covenant.[339] Between 1660 and 1662, forty-two were ejected from Cambridge university, including six heads of colleges, thirty-two fellows, seven students, and two college chaplains.[340]

In the early 1660s the Clarendon Code aimed at suppressing dissenters by means of repressive measures such as the 1664

Conventicle Act and the 1665 Five Mile Act, which attempted to prevent the meetings of nonconformists. Such "sporadic persecution"[341] culminated in the 1672 Declaration of Indulgence, which allowed freedom of worship so long as a license had first been obtained to declare sectarian status. Around fifteen hundred Independents and Baptists hurried to obtain their licenses, only to find the Indulgence canceled the following year! Yet the king was bent on increased religious toleration, and the Puritans were not to be the only beneficiaries. By 1676 there were around fourteen thousand Roman Catholics in England and Wales,[342] and a few years later the monarch's long-suspected bias toward Catholicism was clear. By 1685 his brother, now James II, issued another Declaration of Indulgence, this time including Catholics. Yet England's insecurity increased, this time not about Puritanism but about Catholicism.[343] Finally, the flight and abdication of James II and the consequent, peaceful Glorious Revolution of 1688 firmly established the Protestant King William and Queen Mary on the throne in a balanced constitution of monarch, Lords, and Commons, and the 1689 Toleration Act established liberty of worship for all Protestant Trinitarian Christians. It seemed that peace and stability had arrived at long last.

Conclusion

The long-term influence of Cambridge Platonism may be found in the background of much post-seventeenth-century theology that articulates, even celebrates, the "sweet reasonableness" of Christian faith. As the spirituality of the Cambridge Platonists is throughout informed by the vital union of faith and reason, they may be seen in solidarity with some of the core teachings of Christians as diverse as Cardinal Newman and C. S. Lewis. Cambridge Platonism has had its champions, though it has also had detractors. For example, Evelyn Underhill in *Mystics of the Church*, dismisses Cambridge Platonism in a brief paragraph:

The Platonists were highly cultivated and spiritually susceptible men. They knew and admired Plotinus,

Dionyisus the Areopagite, and many of the classics of medieval mysticism, which were at this period republished and widely read, influencing numerous religious writers who could not properly be described as mystics. But they show us, as St. Augustine had said long ago of their predecessors, "the vision of the land of peace—but not the road thereto."[344]

The entry "Anglican Spirituality" in the authorative *World Spirituality: Encyclopedic History of the Religious Quest*, offers a different picture. The author, Walter Wakefield, concedes that the Cambridge Platonists "are certainly no mystics in the sense that the term is used of Teresa and John of the Cross. There are no paroxysms of love or dark nights of sense or soul. Yet Union with God is for them the goal of philosophy and faith."[345] Wakefield goes on to summarize plausibly their contribution to Western spirituality with wonderful simplicity: "Religion for the Platonists is a joyful thing, at times rapturous. Holiness is happiness, a share in the happiness of God."[346]

As we mentioned in the Foreword and Acknowledgments, we believe that our present era marks a time when Cambridge Platonist spirituality is of enormous value. Like us, they lived through profound political, religious, and social conflict. And yet they saw both "the vision of the Land of peace" and the road thereto through tolerant love, the concord of intellect and faith, joy, and moral life, the recognition of the goodness of Creation, the sovereignty of truth, goodness, and beauty; and the calling to participate in the very life of God through Christ. On this last theme the Cambridge Platonists not only show us a road but also give us a report on what a life unified with God is like. In all, they witnessed to an abiding, wise joy in God's love at a time of fierce division and confusion.

I

A Sermon Preached before the Honorable House of Commons at Westminster, March 31, 1647

Ralph Cudworth

To the Honorable House of Commons

The scope of this sermon, which not long since exercised your patience, worthy Senators, was not to contend for this or that opinion, but only to persuade men to the life of Christ, as the pith and kernel of all religion; without which, I may boldly say, all the several forms of religion in the world, though we please ourselves never so much in them, are but so many several dreams. And those many opinions about religion, that are everywhere so eagerly contended for on all sides, where this does not lie at the bottom, are but so many shadows fighting with one another: so that I may well say of the true Christian, that is indeed possessed of the life of Christianity, in opposition to all those that are but lightly tinctured with the opinions of it. Therefore I could not think anything else either more necessary for Christians in general or more seasonable at this time than to stir them up to the real establishment of the righteousness of God in their hearts and that participation of the divine nature which the apostle speaks of. That so they might not content themselves with mere fancies and conceits of Christ, without the Spirit of Christ really dwelling in them and Christ himself inwardly formed in their hearts. Neither would they satisfy themselves with the mere holding of right and orthodox opinions, as they conceive, while they are utterly devoid within of that divine life, which Christ came to kindle in men's souls, and therefore are so apt to spend all their zeal upon a violent obtruding of their own opinions and apprehensions upon others, which cannot give entertainment to them. Which, besides its repugnancy to the doctrine and example of Christ himself, is similar to the bellows that will blow a perpetual fire of discord and contention in Christian commonwealths, while in the meantime these hungry and starved opinions devour all the life and substance of religion, as the lean cows, in Pharaoh's dream did eat up the fat. Lastly, they please themselves only in the violent opposing of other men's superstitions, according to the genius of the present times, without substituting in the room of them an inward principle of spirit and life in their own souls. For I fear many of us that pull down idols in churches may set them up in our hearts and, while we quarrel with painted glass, make no scruple at all of entertaining many foul lusts in our souls and committing continual idolatry with them.

I present this sermon that you may, by your kindly influence, effectually encourage all goodness, and by virtue of your power and authority (to use the phrase of Solomon) "scatter away all evil with your eye" as the sun by his beams scatters the mists and vapors (Prov 20:8). That from you "judgment may run down like waters, and righteousness like a mighty stream" to refresh this whole land that thirsts after them; which, while you distribute them plentifully to others, will bestow both strength and honor to yourselves. For justice and righteousness are the establishment of every throne, of all civil power and authority, and if these should once forsake it, though there are lions to support it, it could not stand long. These, together with a good peace, well settled in a commonwealth, are all the outward felicity we can expect till that happy time come, which the prophet foretells, and is therefore more than a Platonic idea, when "the wolf shall dwell with the lamb, and the leopard shall lie down with the kid, and the calf, and the young lion, and the fatling together, and a little child lead them," and when "the sucking child shall play on the hole of the asp, and the weaned child shall put his hand on the cockatrice den," when "they shall not hurt nor destroy in all God's holy mountain; for the earth shall be full of the knowledge of the Lord, as the waters cover the sea" (Isa 11:19).

I have but one word more, if you please to give me leave, that after your care for the advancement of religion and the public good of the commonwealth, you would think it worthy of you to promote ingenuous learning and cast a favorable influence upon it. I mean not only that which furnishes the pulpit, which you seem to be very regardful of, but that which is more remote from such popular use, in the several kinds of it, which yet are all of them both very subservient to religion and useful to the commonwealth. There is indeed, as the apostle instructs us, a knowledge falsely so called, which deserves not to be pleaded for. But the noble and generous improvement of our understanding faculty, in the true contemplation of the wisdom, goodness, and other attributes of God, in this great fabric of the universe, cannot easily be disparaged without a blemish cast upon the Maker of it. Doubtless we may as well enjoy that which God has communicated of himself to the creatures, by this larger faculty of our understandings, as by those narrow and low faculties of our senses; and yet nobody counts it to be unlawful to hear a lesson played upon the lute or to smell a rose. And these raised improvements of our natural understandings may be as well subservient and subordinate to a divine light in our minds, as the natural use of these outward creatures here below to the life of God in our hearts. No, all true knowledge does of itself naturally tend to God, who is the fountain of it, and would ever be raising our souls up upon its wings there, did we not detain it and hold it down in unrighteousness, as the apostle speaks. All philosophy to a wise man, to a truly sanctified mind, as he in Plutarch speaks, is but matter for Divinity to work on.[347] Religion is the queen of all those inward endowments of the soul, and all pure natural knowledge, all virgin and undeflowered arts and sciences, are her handmaids, that rise up and call her blessed. I need not tell you how much the skill of tongues and languages, besides the excellent use of all philology in general, is conducive to the right understanding of the letter of sacred writings, on which the spiritual notions must be built; for none can possibly be ignorant of that which have but once heard of a translation of the Bible. The apostle exhorts private Christians to whatsoever things are lovely, whatsoever things are of good report, if there is any virtue, if there is any praise, to think on those things (Phil 4:7–9), and therefore it may well become you, noble gentlemen, in your public sphere to encourage so noble a thing as knowledge is, which will reflect so much luster and honor back again upon yourselves. That God would direct you in all your counsels, and still bless you and prosper you in all your sincere endeavors for the public good is the hearty prayer of

Your Most humble Servant,
RALPH CUDWORTH

Sermon

And hereby we do know that we know him, if we keep his commandments. He that says, I know him, and keeps not his commandments, is a liar, and the truth is not in him.   —1 John 2:3–4

We have much inquiry concerning knowledge in these latter times. The sons of Adam are now as busy as he ever was about the tree of knowledge of good and evil, shaking the boughs of it, and scrambling for the fruit, while, I fear, many are too unmindful of the tree of life. And though there now are no cherubim with their flaming swords to frighten men away from it, yet the way that leads to it seems to be solitary and untrodden, as if there were only a few that had any mind to taste the fruit of it. There are many that speak of new glimpses and discoveries of truth, of dawnings of gospel light, and no question but God has reserved much of this for the evening and sunset of the world, for in the latter days knowledge shall be increased. But yet I wish we could in the meantime see that day to dawn, which the apostle speaks of, and that day-star to arise in men's hearts (2 Pet 1:19). I wish, while we talk of light and dispute about truth, we could walk more as children of the light. Whereas, if St. John's rule be good here in the text, that no man truly knows Christ but he that keeps his commandments, it is much to be suspected that many of us who pretend to light have a thick and gloomy darkness within, overspreading our souls.

A SERMON BEFORE THE HOUSE OF COMMONS

There are now many large volumes and discourses written concerning Christ, thousands of controversies discussed, infinite problems determined concerning his divinity, humanity, union of both together, and what not, so that our bookish Christians, that have all their religion in writings and papers, think they are now completely furnished with all kinds of knowledge concerning Christ; and when they see all their leaves lying about them, they think they have a good stock of knowledge and truth and cannot possibly miss the way to heaven—as if religion were nothing but a little book-craft, a mere paper skill.

But if St. John's rule here is good, we must not judge our knowing of Christ by our skill in books and papers, but by our keeping of his commandments. And that, I fear, will show many of us (notwithstanding all this light which we boast of around us) to have nothing but Egyptian darkness within our hearts.

The vulgar sort think that they know Christ enough out of their creeds and catechisms and confessions of faith, and if they have but a little acquaintance themselves with these, and like parrots conned the words of them, they don't doubt that they are sufficiently instructed in all the mysteries of the kingdom of heaven. Many of the more learned, if they can only wrangle and dispute about Christ, imagine themselves to be grown greatly proficient in the school of Christ.

The greatest part of the world, whether learned or unlearned, think that there is no need of purging and purifying their hearts for the right knowledge of Christ and his gospel; but though their lives are never so wicked, their hearts never so foul within, yet they may know Christ sufficiently out of their treaties and discourses, out of their mere systems and bodies of divinity, which I deny not to be useful in a subordinate way. However, our Savior prescribes his disciples another method to come to the right knowledge of divine truths, by doing God's will, "He that will do my Father's will (he says) shall know of the doctrine, whether it is of God" (John 7:17). He is a true Christian indeed, not he that is only book taught, but he that is God taught; he that has an unction from the Holy One (as our apostle calls it) that teaches him all things, he that has the Spirit of Christ within him, that searches out the deep things of God: "For as no man knows

59

the things of a man, save the spirit of man, which is in him; even so the things of God knows no man, but the Spirit of God" (1 Cor 2:10–11).

Ink and paper can never make us Christians, can never make a new nature, a living principle in us, can never form Christ, or any true notions of spiritual things in our hearts. The gospel, that new law which Christ delivered to the world, is not merely a letter without us, but a quickening spirit within us. Cold theorems and maxims, dry and jejune disputes, lean syllogistical reasonings could never yet of themselves beget the least glimpse of true heavenly light, the least sap of saving knowledge in any heart. All this is but the groping of the poor dark spirit of man after truth, to find it out with his own endeavors, and feel it with his own cold and benumbed hands. Words and syllables, which are but dead things, cannot possibly convey the living notions of heavenly truths to us. The secret mysteries of a divine life, of a new nature, of Christ formed in our hearts, cannot be written or spoken—language and expressions cannot reach them, neither can they ever be truly understood, except the soul itself be kindled from within and awakened into the life of them. All the skill of cunning artisans and mechanics cannot put a principle of life into a statue of their own making. Neither are we able to enclose in words and letters the life, soul, and essence of any spiritual truths, and, as it were, to incorporate it in them.

Some philosophers have determined that virtue cannot be taught by any certain rules or precepts. Men and books may propound some direction to us, that may set us in such a way of life and practice, as in which we shall at last find it within ourselves and be experimentally acquainted with it, but they cannot teach it to us like a mechanic art or trade. No, surely, "there is a spirit in man, and the inspiration of the Almighty gives this understanding" (Job 32:8). But we shall not meet with this spirit anywhere but in the way of obedience. The knowledge of Christ, and the keeping of his commandments, must always go together and be mutual causes of one another.

"Hereby we know that we know him, if we keep his commandments" (1 John 2:2–4). "He that says, I know him, and keeps not his Commandments, is a liar, and the truth is not in him" (1 John 2:4).

I come now to these words themselves, which are so pregnant that I shall not need to force out anything at all from them. I shall therefore only take notice of a few observations which drop from them of their own accord, and then conclude with some application of them to ourselves.

I. First, then, if this is the right way and method of discovering our knowledge of Christ, by our keeping of his commandments, then we may safely draw conclusions concerning our state and condition from the conformity of our lives to the will of Christ.

So that we know whether we know Christ aright, let us consider whether the life of Christ is in us. He that has not the life of Christ in him, he has nothing but the name, nothing but a fancy of Christ, has not the substance of him. He that builds his house upon this foundation, not an airy notion of Christ swimming in his brain, but Christ really dwelling and living in his heart, as our Savior himself witnessed, he "built his house upon a rock," and when the floods come, and the winds blow, and the rain descends, and beats upon it, it shall stand impregnably (Matt 7:24). But he that builds all his comfort upon an ungrounded persuasion, that God from all eternity has loved him and absolutely decreed him to life and happiness, and seeks not for God really dwelling in his soul, he builds his house upon quicksand, and it shall suddenly sink and be swallowed up: "His hope shall be cut off, and his trust shall be a spider's web; he shall lean upon his house, but it shall not stand; he shall hold it fast but it shall not endure" (Job 8:14–15).

We are nowhere commanded to pry into these secrets, but the wholesome counsel and advice given us is this: "to make our calling and election sure" (2 Pet 1:10). We have no warrant in scripture to peep into these hidden rolls and volumes of eternity, and to make it our first thing that we do when we come to Christ, to spell out our names in the stars, and to persuade ourselves that we are certainly elected to everlasting happiness, before we see the image of God, in righteousness and true holiness, shaped in our hearts. God's everlasting decree is too dazzling and bright an object for us at first to set our eye upon. It is far easier and safer for us to look upon the rays of his goodness and holiness as they are reflected in our own hearts, and there to read the mild and gentle characters of God's love to us in our love to him and our hearty compliance with his heavenly will; as it is safer for us, if we see the sun, to look upon it here below in a pail of water than to cast up our daring eyes upon the body of the sun itself, which is too radiant and scorching for us. The best assurance that anyone can have of his interest in God is undoubtedly the conformity of his soul to him. Those divine purposes, whatever they are, are altogether unsearchable and unknowable by us. They lie wrapped up in everlasting darkness, and covered in a deep abyss. Who is able to fathom the bottom of them?

Let us not therefore make this our first attempt toward God and religion, to persuade ourselves strongly of the everlasting decrees; for if at our first flight we aim so high, we shall happily scorch our wings, and be struck back with lightning, as those giants of old were, that attempted to invade and assault heaven. And it is indeed a most gigantic attempt to thrust ourselves so boldly into the lap of heaven; it is the prank of a Nimrod, of a mighty hunter thus rudely to deal with God, and to force heaven and happiness before his face, whether he will or not. The way to obtain a good assurance indeed of our title to heaven, is not to clamber up to it by a ladder of our own ungrounded persuasions, but to dig as low as hell by humility and self-denial in our own hearts. And though this may seem to be the furthest way about, yet it is indeed the nearest and safest way to it. We must, as the Greek epigram speaks, ascend downward and descend upward, if we would indeed come to heaven, or get any true persuasion of our title to it.

The most gallant and triumphant confidence of a Christian rises safely and surely upon this low foundation, that lies deep underground, and there stands firmly and steadfastly. When our heart is once tuned into a conformity with the word of God, when we feel our will perfectly to concur with his will, we shall then presently perceive a spirit of adoption within ourselves, teaching us to cry, Abba, Father. We shall not then care for peeping into those hidden records of eternity, to see whether our names be written there in golden characters; no, we shall find a copy of

God's thoughts concerning us written in our own breasts. There we may read the characters of his favor to us; there we may feel an inward sense of his love to us, flowing out of our hearty and unfeigned love to him. And we shall be more undoubtedly persuaded of it than if any of those winged watchmen above, that are privy to heaven's secrets, should come and tell us that they saw our names enrolled in those volumes of eternity. Whereas, on the contrary, though we strive to persuade ourselves never so confidently that God from all eternity has loved us and elected us to life and happiness, if we do yet, in the meantime, entertain any iniquity within our hearts and willingly close with any lust, do what we can, we shall find many a cold qualm every now and then seizing upon us at approaching dangers. And when death itself shall grimly look us in the face, we shall even feel our hearts die within us and our spirits quite faint away, though we strive to raise them and recover them never so much with the strong waters of our own ungrounded presumptions. The least inward lust willingly continued will be like a worm, fretting the gourd of our jolly confidence and presumptuous persuasion of God's love, and always gnawing at the root of it; and though we strive to keep it alive, and continually sprinkle it with some dews of our own, yet it will always be dying and withering in our bosoms. But a good conscience within will be always better to a Christian than "health to his navel, and marrow to his bones"; it will be an everlasting cordial to his heart, it will be softer to him than a bed of down, and he may sleep securely upon it in the midst of raging and tempestuous seas, when the winds bluster, and the waves beat round about him (Prov 3:80). A good conscience is the best looking glass of heaven, in which the soul may see God's thoughts and purposes concerning it, as so many shining stars reflected to it. "Hereby we know that we know Christ, hereby we know that Christ loves us, if we keep his commandments" (1 John 2:3).

II. Secondly, if hereby only we know that we know Christ, by our keeping his commandments, then the knowledge of Christ does not consist merely in a few barren notions in a form of certain dry and sapless opinions.

Christ did not come into the world to fill our heads with mere speculations, to kindle a fire of wrangling and contentious dispute among us and to warm our spirits against one another with nothing but angry and peevish debates, while in the meantime our hearts remain all ice within toward God and have not the least spark of true heavenly fire to melt and thaw them. Christ came not to possess our brains only with some cold opinions that send down nothing but a freezing and benumbing influence upon our hearts. Christ was a teacher of life, not of school, and he is the best Christian whose heart beats with the truest pulse toward heaven, not he whose head spins out the finest cobwebs.

He that really endeavors to mortify his lusts and to comply with that truth in his life which his conscience is convinced of, is nearer a Christian, though he never heard of Christ, than he that believes all the vulgar articles of the Christian faith and plainly denies Christ in his life.

Surely the way to heaven that Christ has taught us is plain and easy, if we only have honest hearts. We need not many criticisms, many school distinctions, to come to a right understanding of it. Surely Christ came not to ensnare us and entangle us in with captious niceties, or to puzzle our heads with deep speculations and lead us through hard and craggy notions into the kingdom of heaven. I persuade myself that no man shall ever be kept out of heaven for not comprehending mysteries that were beyond the reach of his shallow understanding, if he had but an honest and good heart that was ready to comply with Christ's commandments. "Say not in your heart, Who shall ascend into heaven?"— that is, with high speculations, to bring down Christ from there; or "Who shall descend into the abyss beneath?"—that is with deep searching thoughts to fetch up Christ from there; but look, "The word is near you, even in your mouth, and in your heart" (Rom 10:6–8).

But I wish it were not the distemper of our times, to scare and frighten men only with opinions and make them only solicitous about the entertaining of this and that speculation, which will not render them anything better in their lives, or the closer to God; while in the meantime there is no such care taken about keeping of Christ's commandments and being renewed in our minds according to the image of God in righteousness and true holiness. We say, "Lo, here is Christ" and, "Lo, there is Christ" in these and these opinions, whereas in truth Christ is neither here nor there nor anywhere, but where the Spirit of Christ, there the life of Christ is (Matt 24:23; Mark 13:21).

Do we not nowadays open and lock up heaven with the private key of this and that opinion of our own, according to our several fancies, as we please? And if anyone observes Christ's commandments never so sincerely, and serves God with faith and a pure confidence, that yet haply skills not of some contended-for opinions, some darling notions, he has not the right shibboleth,[348] he has not the true watchword, he must not pass the guards into heaven. Do we not make this and that opinion, this and that outward form, to be the wedding garment, and boldly sentence those to outer darkness that are not so invested? Whereas, every true Christian finds the least dram of hearty affection toward God to be more cordial and sovereign to his soul than all the speculative notions and opinions in the world; and though he also studies to inform his understanding aright, and free his mind from all error and misapprehensions, yet it is nothing but the life of Christ deeply rooted in his heart which is the chemical "elixer" that he feeds upon. He had "all faith that he could remove mountains" (as St. Paul speaks), he had "all knowledge, all tongues and languages," yet he prizes one dram of love beyond them all. He accounts him that feeds upon mere notions in religion to be but an airy and chameleon-like Christian (1 Cor 13:12). He finds himself now otherwise rooted and centered in God than when he did before merely contemplate and gaze upon him. He tastes and relishes God within himself, he has a certain favor of him, whereas before he did only rove and guess at random at him. He feels himself safely anchored in God and will not be dissuaded from it, though perhaps he is not skilled at many of those subtleties, which others make the *alpha* and *omega* of their religion. Neither is he scared with those childish frights with which some would force their private conceits upon him. He is above the superstitious dreading of mere speculative opinions as well as the superstitious reverence of outward ceremonies. He cares not so much for subtlety as for soundness and health of mind. And, indeed, as it was well spoken by a noble philosopher, that "without purity and virtue, God is nothing but an empty name;" so it is as true here, that without obedience to Christ's commandments, without the life of Christ dwelling in us, whatever opinions we entertain of him, Christ is only named by us, he is not known.

I do not speak here against a free and ingenuous inquiry into all truth, according to our several abilities and opportunities; I plead not for the captivating and enthralling of our judgments to the dictates of men; I do not disparage the natural improvement of our understanding faculties by true knowledge, which is so noble and gallant a perfection of the mind. But the thing which I aim against is the dispiriting of the life and vigor of our religion by dry speculations, and making it nothing but a mere dead skeleton of opinions, a few dry bones without any flesh and sinews, tied up together, and the misplacing of all our zeal upon an eager prosecution of these, which should be spent to better purpose upon other objects.

Knowledge indeed is a thing far more excellent than riches, outward pleasures, worldly dignities, or anything else in the world besides holiness and the conformity of our wills to the will of God; but yet our happiness consists not in it, but in a certain divine temper and constitution of soul which is far above it.

But it is a piece of that corruption that runs through human nature that we naturally prize truth more than goodness, knowledge more than holiness. We think it a gallant thing to be fluttering up to heaven with our wings of knowledge and speculation, whereas the highest mystery of a divine life here, and of perfect happiness hereafter, consists in nothing but mere obedience to the divine will. Happiness is nothing but that inward sweet delight that will arise from the harmonious agreement between our wills and God's will.

There is nothing contrary to God in the whole world, nothing that fights against him, but self-will. This is the strong castle that we all keep garrisoned against heaven in every one of our hearts, which God continually lays siege unto; and it must be conquered and demolished, before we can conquer heaven. It was by reason of this self-will that Adam fell in paradise, that those glorious angels, those morning stars, kept not their first station, but dropped down from heaven like falling stars, and sank into this condition of bitterness, anxiety, and wretchedness in which now they are. They all entangled themselves with the length of their own wings, they willed more and otherwise than God would will in them, and going about to make their wills wider and to enlarge them into greater amplitude, the more they struggled, they found themselves the faster pinioned, and crowded up into narrowness and servility; insomuch that now they are not able to use any wings at all, but, inheriting the serpent's curse, can only creep with their bellies upon the earth. Now, our only way to recover God and happiness again is, not to soar up with our understandings, but to destroy this self-will of ours; and then we shall find our wings grow again, our plumes fairly spread, and ourselves raised aloft into the free air of perfect liberty, which is perfect happiness.

There is nothing in the whole world able to do us good or hurt, but God and our own will. Neither riches nor poverty, nor disgrace nor honor, nor life nor death, nor angels nor devils, but willing or not willing, as we ought to do. Should hell itself cast all its fiery dart against us, if our will be right, if it be informed by the divine will, they can do us no hurt. We have then (if I may so speak), an enchanted shield that is impenetrable and will bear off all. God will not hurt us and hell cannot hurt us if we will nothing but what God wills. No, then we are acted by God himself, and the whole divinity flows in upon us; and when we have cashiered this self-will of ours, which shackled and confined our souls, our wills shall then become truly free, being widened and enlarged to the extent of God's own will. Hereby we know that we know Christ indeed, not by our speculative opinions concerning him, but by our keeping of his commandments.

III. Thirdly, if hereby we are to judge whether we truly know Christ, by our keeping of his commandments, so that he that says he knows him and keeps not his commandments is a liar; then this was not the plot and design of the gospel, to give the world an indulgence to sin, upon whatever pretense.

Though we are too prone to make such misconstructions of it, as if God had intended nothing else in it but to dandle our corrupt nature and contrive a smooth and easy way for us to come to happiness, without the toilsome labor of subduing our lusts and sinful affections. Or, as if the gospel were nothing else but a declaration to the world, of God's engaging his affections from all eternity on some particular persons in such a manner as that he would resolve to love them and dearly embrace them, though he never made them partakers of his image in righteousness and true holiness; and though they should remain under the power of all their lusts, yet they should still continue his beloved ones, and he would, notwithstanding, at last bring them undoubtedly into heaven—which is nothing else but to make the God we worship, the God of the New Testament, an acceptor of persons, and one that should encourage that in the world which is diametrically opposite to God's own life and being.

And, indeed, nothing is more ordinary than for us to shape out such monstrous and deformed notions of God to ourselves, by looking upon him through the colored medium of our own corrupt hearts, and having the eye of our soul tinctured by the suffusions of our own lusts. And therefore because we mortals can fondly love and hate, and sometimes hug the very vices of those to whom our affections are engaged, and kiss their very deformities, we are so ready to shape out a deity like ourselves, and to fashion out such a God as will, in Christ at least, hug the very wickedness of the world; and in those that are once his own, by I know not what fond affection, appropriated to himself, connive at their very sins, so that they shall not make the least breach between himself and them. Truly I know not which of the two be the worse idolatry and of the deeper stain, for a man to make a god out of a piece of wood, and fall down unto it and worship it, and say, "Deliver me, for you are my God," as it is expressed in the prophet Isaiah, or to set up such an idol-god of our own imagination as this is, fashioned out according to the similitude of our own fondness and wickedness (Isa 44:15–17). When we should paint out God with the liveliest colors that we can possibly borrow from any created being, with the purest perfections that we can abstract from them, [we] draw him out thus with the blackest coal of our own corrupt hearts, and to make the very blots and blurs of our own souls to be the letters which we spell out his name by. Thus do we, that are children of the night, make black and ugly representations of God to ourselves, as the Ethiopians were inclined to do, copying him out according to our own likeness, and setting up that to ourselves for a god which we love most dearly in ourselves, that is, our lusts.

But there is no such God as this anywhere in the world, but only in some men's false imaginations, who know not all this while, that they look upon themselves instead of God, and make an idol of themselves, which they worship and adore for him; being so full of themselves, that whatever they see round about them, even God himself, they color with their own tincture. This is like him that Aristotle speaks of, that wherever he went and whatever he looked upon, he saw still his own face, as in a glass, represented to him.[349] And therefore it is no wonder, if men seem naturally more devoutly affected toward such an imaginary god as we have now described, than to the true real God, clothed with his own proper attributes; since it is nothing but an image of themselves, which, Narcissus-like, they fall in love with. No wonder if they kiss and dandle such a baby-god as this, which, like little children, they have dressed up out of the clouts of their own fond fancies, according to their own likeness, of purpose that they might play and sport with it.

But God will ever dwell in spotless light, however we paint him and disfigure him here below; he will still be circled about with his own rays of unstained and immaculate glory. And though the gospel be not God as he is in his own brightness, but God veiled and masked to us, God in a state of humiliation and condescension, as the sun in a rainbow, yet it is nothing else but a clear and unspotted mirror of divine holiness, goodness, purity in which attributes lie the very life and essence of God himself. The gospel is nothing else but God descending into the world in our form, and conversing with us in our likeness; that he might allure and draw us up to God, and make us partakers of his divine form (as Athanasius speaks),[350] "God was therefore incarnated and made man, that he might deify us"—that is (as St. Peter expresses it), make us partakers of the divine nature (2 Pet 1:4). Now, I say, the very proper character and essential tincture of God himself is nothing else but goodness. Now, I may be bold to add that God is therefore God, because he is the highest and most perfect good, and good is not therefore good because God out of an arbitrary will of his would have it so. Whatever God does in the world, he does as is suitable to the highest goodness: the first idea, and fairest copy of which is his own essence.

Virtue and holiness in creatures, as Plato well discourses in his *Euthyphro*, are not therefore good because God loves them and will have them be accounted such, but rather God therefore loves them because they are in themselves simply good.[351] Some of our own authors go a little further yet, and tell us that God does not fondly love himself because he is himself, but therefore he loves himself because he is the highest and most absolute goodness; so that if there could be anything in the world better than God, God would love that better than himself. But because he is essentially the most perfect good, therefore he cannot but love his own goodness infinitely above all other things. And it is another mistake, which sometimes we have of God, by shaping him according to the model of ourselves, when we make him nothing but a blind, dark, impetuous self-will running through the world, such as we ourselves are furiously acted with, that have not the ballast of absolute goodness to poise and settle us.

That I may therefore come nearer to the thing in hand: God, who is absolute goodness, cannot love any of his creatures and take pleasure in them, without bestowing a communication of his goodness and likeness upon them. God cannot make a gospel to promise men life and happiness hereafter, without being regenerated and made partakers of his holiness. As soon may heaven and hell be reconciled together and lovingly shake hands with one another, as God can be fondly indulgent to any sin, in whoever it be. As soon may light and darkness be espoused together, and midnight be married to the noonday, as God can be joined in a league of friendship to any wicked soul.

The great design of God in the gospel is to clear up this mist of sin and corruption which we are here surrounded with, and to bring up his creatures out of the shadow of death to the region of light above the land of truth and holiness. The great mystery of the gospel is to establish a Godlike frame and disposition of spirit, which consists in righteousness and true holiness in the hearts of men. And Christ, who is the great and mighty Savior, came on purpose into the world, not only to save us from fire and brimstone but also to save us from our sins. Christ has therefore made an expiation of our sins by his death upon the cross, that we, being thus delivered out of the hands of these our greatest enemies, might serve God without fear, in holiness and righteousness before him all the days of our life. This grace of God, that brings salvation, has therefore appeared to all men, in the gospel, that it might teach us to deny ungodliness and worldly lusts, and that we should live soberly, righteously, and godly in this present world; looking for that blessed hope, and glorious appearing of the great God and our Savior Jesus Christ, who gave himself for us, that he might redeem us from all iniquity, and purify to himself a particular people, zealous of good works. These things I write to you (says our apostle a little before my text) that you sin not; thus expressing the end of the whole gospel, which is not only to cover sin by spreading the purple robe of Christ's death and sufferings over it, while it still remains in us with all its filth and noise unremoved; but also to convey a powerful and mighty spirit of holiness, to cleanse us and free us from it (Titus 2:11–14). And this is a greater grace of God to us than the former, which still both go together in the gospel: besides the free remission and pardon of sin in the blood of Christ, the delivering of us from the power of sin by the Spirit of Christ dwelling in our hearts.

Christ came not into the world only to cast a mantle over us, and hide all our filthy sores from God's avenging eye with his merits and righteousness, but he came likewise to be a physician of souls, to free us from the filth and corruption of them, which is more grievous and burdensome, more noisome to a true Christian, than the guilt of sin itself.

Should a poor wretched and diseased creature, that is full of sores and ulcers, be covered all over with purple or clothed with scarlet, he would take but little contentment in it while his sores and wounds remain upon him; and he had much rather be arrayed in rags, so he might obtain only soundness and health within. The gospel is a true Bethesda, a pool of grace, where such poor, lame, and infirm creatures as we are, upon the moving of God's Spirit in it, may descend down, not only to wash our skin and outside, but also to be cured of our diseases within (John 5:1–5). And whatever the world thinks, there is a powerful Spirit that moves upon these waters, the waters of the gospel, for this new creation, the regeneration of the souls; the very same spirit, that once moved upon the waters of the universe at the first creation and, spreading its

71

mighty wings over them, hatched the newborn world into this perfection. I say, the same almighty spirit of Christ still works in the gospel, spreading its gentle, healing, quickening wings over our souls. The gospel is not like Abana and Pharphar, those common rivers of Damascus, that could only cleanse the outside, but it is a true Jordan, in which such leprous Naamans as we all are, may wash and be clean (2 Kgs 5). Blessed indeed are they whose iniquities are forgiven, and whose sins are covered. Blessed is the man to whom the Lord will not impute sin; but yet rather blessed are they whose sins are removed like a morning cloud, and quite taken away from them. Blessed, three times blessed are they, that hunger and thirst after righteousness, for they shall be satisfied. Blessed are the pure in heart, for they shall see God (Matt 5:6).

God sent his own Son (says St. Paul) in the likeness of sinful flesh, and by a sacrifice for sin condemned sin in the flesh that the righteousness of the law might be fulfilled in us, who walk not after the flesh, but after the spirit (Rom 8:3–4).

The first Adam, as the scripture tells us, brought in a real defilement, which, like a noisome leprosy, has overspread all mankind. Therefore, the second Adam must not only fill the world with a conceit of holiness and mere imaginary righteousness, but he must really convey such an immortal seed of grace into the hearts of true believers as may prevail still more and more in them, till it have at last quite wrought out that poison of the serpent.

Christ was nothing but divinity dwelling in a tabernacle of flesh, and God himself immediately acting a humane nature, he came into the world to kindle here that divine life among men, which is certainly dearer to God than anything else whatever in the world, and to propagate this celestial fire from one heart still to another until the end of the world. Neither is he, nor was he, ever absent from this spark of his divinity kindled among men, wherever it be, though he seem bodily to be withdrawn from us. He is the standing, constant, inexhausted fountain of this divine light and heat, that still touches every soul that is enlivened by it with an outstretched ray, and freely lends his beams and disperses his influence to all, from the beginning of the world to the end of it. We all receive of his fullness grace for grace as all the stars in heaven are said to light their candles at the sun's flame. For though his body is withdrawn from us, yet by the lively and virtual contact of his Spirit he is always kindling, cheering, quickening, warming, and enlivening hearts. No, this divine life, begun and kindled in any heart, wherever it be, is something of God in flesh, and, in a sober and qualified sense, Divinity incarnate, and all particular Christians, who are really possessed of it, so many mystical Christs.

And God forbid that God's own life and nature, here in the world, should be forlorn, forsaken, and abandoned of God himself. Certainly wherever it is, though never so little, like a sweet, young, tender babe, once born in any heart, when it cries to God the father of it, with pitiful and bemoaning looks imploring his compassion, it cannot choose but move his fatherly bowels, and make them yearn and turn toward it, and by strong sympathy draw his compassionate arm to help and relieve it. Never was any tender infant so dear to those bowels that begat it as an infant newborn Christ, formed in the heart of any true believer, to God the father of it. Shall the children of this world, the sons of darkness, be moved with such tender affection and compassion toward the fruit of their bodies, their own natural offspring? Shall God, who is the father of lights, the fountain of all goodness, be moved with no compassion toward his true spiritual offspring, and have no regard to those sweet babes of light engendered by his own beams in men's hearts, that, in their lovely countenances, bear resemblance of his own face, and call him their father? Shall he see them lie fainting and gasping and dying here in the world, for lack of anything to preserve and keep them, but an influence from him who first gave them life and breath? No, hear the language of God's heart, hear the sounding of his bowels toward them: Is it Ephraim, my dear Son? Is it that pleasant child? Since I spoke of him, I do earnestly remember him; my bowels are troubled for him; I will surely have mercy upon him, says the Lord (Jer 31:20). If those expressions of goodness and tender affection here among creatures are but drops of that full ocean that is in God, how can we then imagine that this father of our spirits should have so little regard to his own dear offspring, I do not say our souls, but that which is the very life and soul of our souls, the life of God in us (which is nothing else but God's own self communicated to us, his own Son born in our hearts), as that he should suffer it to be cruelly murdered in its infancy by our sins, and like young Hercules, in its very cradle to be strangled by those filthy vipers, that he should see him to be crucified by wicked lusts, nailed fast to the cross by invincible corruptions, pierced and gored on every side with the poisoned spears of the devil's temptations, and at last to give up the ghost. Yet does his tender heart not at all relent nor be at all this while impassionated with so sad a spectacle? Surely we cannot think he has such a flinty nature, as this is.

What then? Must we say that though indeed he be willing, yet he is not able to rescue his crucified and tormented Son now bleeding upon the cross, to take him down from there and save him? Then must sin be more powerful than God, that weak, crazy, and sickly thing more strong than the Rock of ages, and the devil, the prince of darkness, more mighty than the God of light. No, surely, there is a weakness and impotency in all evil, a masculine strength and vigor in all goodness; and therefore doubtless the highest good is the strongest thing in the world. God's power, displayed in the world, is nothing but this goodness strongly reaching all things from heights to depth, from the highest heaven to the lowest hell, and irresistibly imparting itself to everything, according to those several degrees in which it is capable of it.

Have the fiends of darkness, then, those poor forlorn spirits that are fettered and locked up in the chains of their own wickedness, any strength to withstand the force of infinite goodness, which is infinite power? Or do they not rather skulk in holes of darkness, and fly, like bats and owls, before the approaching beams of this Sun of Righteousness? Is God powerful to kill and to destroy, to damn and to torment, and is he not powerful to save? No, it is the sweetest flower in all the garland of his attributes, it is the richest diamond in his crown of glory, that he is mighty to save; and this is far more magnificent for him than to be styled mighty to destroy (Isa 63:1). For that, except it be in the way of justice, speaks no power at all, but mere impotency; for the root of all power is goodness.

Or must we say, lastly, that God indeed is able to rescue us out of the power of sin and Satan, when we sigh and groan toward him, but yet sometimes, to exercise his absolute authority, his uncontrollable dominion, he delights rather in plunging wretched souls down into infernal night and everlasting darkness? What shall we then make of the God of the whole world? Nothing but a cruel and dreadful *Erynnis*, with curled fiery snakes about his head and firebrands in his hands, thus governing the world? Surely this will make us either secretly think that there is no God at all in the world, if he must be such, or else to wish heartily there were none. But, doubtless, God will at last confute all these our misapprehensions of him; he will unmask our hypocritical pretenses, and clearly cast the shame of all our sinful deficiencies upon ourselves, and vindicate his own glory from receiving the least stain or blemish by them. In the meantime, let us know that the gospel now requires far more of us than ever the law did, for it requires a new creature, a divine nature, Christ formed in us.[352] But yet withal, it bestows a quickening spirit, an enlivening power, to enable us to express that which is required of us. Whoever therefore truly knows Christ, the same also keeps Christ's commandments. But he that says, I know him, and keeps not his commandments, is a liar, and the truth is not in him.

I have now done with the first part of my discourse, concerning those observations which arise naturally from the words and offer themselves to us. I shall, in the next place, proceed to make some general application of them all together.

Now therefore, I beseech you, let us consider whether or not we know Christ indeed, not by our acquaintance with systems and models of divinity, not by our skill in books and papers, but by our keeping of Christ's commandments. All the books and writings which we converse with can but represent spiritual objects to our understandings, which yet we can never see in their own true figure, color, and proportion, until we have a divine light within to irradiate and shine upon them. Though there are never such excellent truths concerning Christ and his gospel set down in words and letters, yet they will be but unknown characters to us until we have a living Spirit within us, that can decipher them; until the same Spirit, by secret whispers in our hearts, does comment upon them, which did at first indict them. There are many that understand the Greek and Hebrew of the scripture, the original languages in which the text was written, that never understood the language of the Spirit.

There is a flesh and a spirit, a body and a soul in all the writings of the scriptures. It is but the flesh and body of divine truths that are printed upon paper, which many moths of books and libraries do only feed upon; many walking skeletons of knowledge, that bury and entomb truths in the living sepulchers of their souls, do only converse with—such as never did anything else but pick at the mere bark and rind of truths, and crack the shells of them. But there is a soul, a spirit of divine truths, that could never yet be congealed into ink, that could never be blotted upon paper; by secret traduction and conveyance, it passes from one soul to another, being able to dwell and lodge nowhere but in a spiritual being, in a living thing, because itself is nothing but life and spirit. Neither can it, where indeed it is, express itself sufficiently in words and sounds, but it will best declare and speak itself in actions, as the old manner of writing among the Egyptians was not by words but things. The life of divine truths is better expressed in actions than in words, because actions are more living things than words. Words are nothing but the dead resemblances and pictures of those truths which live and breathe in actions; and the kingdom of God (as the apostle speaks) consists not in word but in life and power. Sheep do not come and bring their fodder to their shepherd, and show him how much they eat, but inwardly concocting and digesting it, they make it appear by the fleece which they wear upon their backs and by the milk which they give (1 Enoch 46). And let not us Christians affect only to talk and dispute of Christ, and so measure our knowledge of him by our words; but let us show our knowledge concocted into our lives and actions, and then let us really manifest that we are Christ's sheep indeed, that we are his disciples, by that fleece of holiness which we wear, and by the fruits that we daily yield in our lives and conversations: for *herein* (says Christ) is my Father glorified, that you bear much fruit; so shall you be my disciples (John 15:8).

Let us not, I beseech you, judge of our knowing Christ by our ungrounded persuasions that Christ from all eternity has loved us and given himself particularly for us, without the conformity of our lives to Christ's commandments, without the real partaking of the image of Christ in our hearts. The great mystery of the gospel does not lie only in Christ without us (though we must know also what he has done for us), but the very pith and kernel of it consists in Christ inwardly formed in our hearts.

Nothing is truly ours but what lives in our spirits. Salvation itself cannot save us as long as it is only without us, no more than health can cure us and make us sound, when it is not within us but somewhere at distance from us, no more than arts and sciences, while they lie only in books and papers without us, can make us learned. The gospel, though it be a sovereign and medicinal thing in itself, yet the mere knowing and believing of the history of it will do us no good; we can receive no virtue from it, till it be inwardly digested and concocted into our souls, till it be made ours and becomes a living thing in our hearts. The gospel, if it be only without us, cannot save us, no more than that physician's bill could cure the ignorant patient of his disease, who, when it was commended to him, took the paper only and put it up in his pocket, but never drank the potion that was described in it.

All that Christ did for us in the flesh, when he was here upon earth, from his lying in a manger when he was born in Bethlehem to his bleeding upon the cross on Golgotha, will not save us from our sins unless Christ by his Spirit dwells in us. It will not avail us to believe that he was born of a virgin unless the power of the Most High overshadows our hearts and begets him there likewise. It will not profit us to believe that he died upon the cross for us unless we are baptized into his death by the mortification of all our lusts, unless the old man of sin is crucified in our hearts. Christ indeed has made an expiation for our sins upon his cross, and the blood of Christ is the only sovereign balsam to free us from the guilt of them; but yet, besides the sprinkling of the blood of Christ upon us, we must be made partakers also of his spirit. Christ came into the world as well to redeem us from the power and bondage of our sins as to free us from the guilt of them. You know (says St. John) that he was manifested to take away our sins; whosoever therefore abides in him, sins not; whosoever sins, has not seen or known him (1 John 3:5–6). Lo, the end of Christ's coming into the world! Lo, a design worthy of God manifested in the flesh!

Christ did not take all those pains to lay aside his robes of glory, and come down here into the world, to enter into a virgin's womb, to be born in our human shape, and to be laid a poor crying infant in a manger, and having no form nor comeliness at all upon him, to take upon him the form of a servant, to undergo a reproachful and ignominious life, and at last to be abandoned to shameful death, a death upon the cross. I say, he did not do all this merely to bring a notion into the world, without producing any real and substantial effect at all, without the changing, mending, and reforming of the world; so that men should still be as wicked as they were before, and as much under the power of the prince of darkness, only they should not be thought so; they should still remain as full of all the filthy sores of sin and corruption as before, only they should be accounted whole. Shall God come down from heaven and pitch a tabernacle among men? Shall he undertake such a huge design and make so great a noise of doing something, which, when it is all summed up, shall not at last amount to a reality? Surely Christ did not undergo all this to so little purpose; he would not take all these pains for us, that he might be able to last put into our hands nothing but a blank. He was with child, he was in pain and travail, and has he brought forth nothing but wind? Has he been delivered of the east wind (Isa 26:18)? Is that great design, that was so long carried in the womb of eternity, now proved abortive, or else nothing but a mere windy birth? No surely, the end of the gospel is life and perfection—it is a divine nature, it is a Godlike frame and disposition of spirit, it is to make us partakers of the image of God in righteousness and true holiness, without which salvation itself were but a notion.

Christ came indeed into the world to make an expiation and atonement for our sins; but the end of this was that we might eschew sin, that we might forsake all ungodliness and worldly lusts. The gospel declares pardon of sin to those that are heavy laden with it and willing to be disburdened, to this end, that it might quicken and enliven us to new obedience. Whereas otherwise the guilt of sin might have detained us in horror and despair, and so have kept us still more strongly under the power of it, in sad and dismal apprehensions of God's wrath provoked against us and inevitably falling on us. But Christ has now appeared like a day-star with most cheerful beams; no, he is the Sun of Righteousness himself, which has risen upon the world with his healing wings, with his exhilarating light, that he might chase away all those black despairing thoughts from us. But Christ did not rise that we should play and sport and wantonize with his light, but that we should do the works of the day in it; that we should walk (as the apostle speaks) not in our nightclothes of sinful deformity, but clad all over with the comely garments of light (Rom 13:13). The gospel is not big with child of fancy, of a mere conceit of righteousness around us, hanging at distance over us, while our hearts within are nothing but cages of unclean birds, and like houses continually haunted with devils, no, the very rendezvous of those friends of darkness.

Holiness is the best thing that God himself can bestow upon us, either in this world or the world to come. True evangelical holiness, that is, Christ formed in the hearts of believers, is the very cream and quintessence of the gospel. And were our hearts sound within, were there not many thick and dark fumes that did arise from there and cloud our understandings, we could not easily conceive the substance of heaven itself to be anything else but holiness, freed from those encumbrances that did ever clog it and cloy it here; neither should we wish for any other heaven besides this. But many of us are like those children whose stomachs are so vitiated by some disease that they think ashes, coal, mud wall, or any such trash to be more pleasant than the most wholesome food. Such sickly and distempered appetites have we about these spiritual things, that hanker after I know not what vain shows of happiness, while in the meantime we neglect that which is the only true food of our souls, that is able solidly to nourish them up to everlasting life.

Grace is holiness militant, holiness encumbered with many enemies and difficulties, which it still fights against, and manfully quits itself of; and glory is nothing else but holiness triumphant, holiness with a palm of victory in her hand, and a crown upon her head: God himself cannot make me happy, if he is only outside me, unless he give in a participation of himself and his own likeness into my soul. Happiness is nothing but the releasing and unfettering of our souls from all these narrow, scant, and particular good things, and the espousing of them to the highest and most universal good, which is not this or that particular good, but goodness itself—and this is the same thing that we call holiness. Which, because we ourselves are so little acquainted with (being for the most part ever courting a mere shadow of it), therefore we have such low, abject, and beggarly conceits thereof, whereas it is in itself the most noble, heroical, and generous thing in the world. For I mean by holiness nothing else but God stamped and printed upon the soul. And we may please ourselves with what conceits we will, but so long as we are void of this, we only dream of heaven, and I know not what fond paradise; we only blow up and down an airy bubble of our own fancies, which rises out of the froth of our vain hearts; we do but court a painted heaven, and woo happiness in a picture, while in the meantime a true and real hell will suck our souls into it, and soon make us sensible of a solid woe and substantial misery.

Divine wisdom has so ordered the frame of the whole universe, so that everything should have a certain proper place that should be a receptacle for it. Hell is the sink of all sin and wickedness. The strong magic of nature pulls and draws everything continually to that place which is suitable to it, and to which it belongs; so all these heavy bodies press downward, toward the center of our earth, being drawn in by it. In like manner hell, wherever it is, will by strong sympathy pull in all sin and magnetically draw it to itself; as true holiness is always breathing upward and fluttering toward heaven, striving to embosom itself with God; and it will at last undoubtedly be conjoined with him. No dismal shades of darkness can possibly stop it in its course or beat it back.

No, we do only deceive ourselves with names. Hell is nothing but the orb of sin and wickedness, or else that hemisphere of darkness in which all evil moves. Heaven is the opposite hemisphere of light, or else, if you please, the bright orb of truth, holiness, and goodness, and we do actually in this life instate ourselves in the possession of one or other of them. Take sin and disobedience out of hell, and it will presently clear up into light, tranquility, serenity, and shine out into a heaven. Every true saint carries his heaven about with him in his own heart; and hell, that is without him, can have no power over him. He might safely wade through hell itself, and like the three children, pass through the middle of that fiery furnace and yet not at all be scorched by the flames of it; he might walk through the valley of the shadow of death and yet fear no evil (Dan 3:19; Ps 23:4).

A SERMON BEFORE THE HOUSE OF COMMONS

Sin is the only thing in the world that is contrary to God. God is light, and that is darkness. God is beauty, and that is ugliness and deformity. All sin is direct rebellion against God; and with whatsoever notions we may sugar it and sweeten it, yet God can never smile upon it. He will never make a truce with it. God declares open war against sin and bids defiance to it, for it is a professed enemy to God's own life and being. God, who is infinite Goodness, cannot but hate sin, which is purely evil. And though sin be in itself but a poor, impotent, and crazy thing, nothing but straightness, poverty, and nonentity, so that of itself it is the most wretched and miserable thing in the world and needs no further punishment besides itself, yet divine vengeance beats it off still farther and farther from God, and wherever it is, will be sure to scourge it and lash it continually. God and sin can never agree together.

That I may therefore come yet nearer to ourselves, this is the message that I have now to declare unto you, that God is light, and in him is no darkness at all. If we say that we have fellowship with him, and walk in darkness, we lie, and do not tell the truth (1 John 1:5–6). Christ and the gospel are light, and there is no darkness at all in them. If you say that you know Christ and his gospel, and yet do not keep Christ's commandments but dearly hug your private darling corruptions, you are liars and the truth is not in you—you have no acquaintance with the God of light, or with the gospel of light. If any of you say that you know Christ, and have an interest in him, and yet (as I fear too many do) still nourish ambition, pride, vainglory within your breasts, harbor malice, revengefulness, and cruel hatred to your neighbors in your hearts, eagerly scramble after this worldly self, and make the strength of your parts and endeavors serve that blind mammon, the god of this world; if you wallow and tumble in the filthy puddle of fleshly pleasures, or if you aim only at yourselves in your lives and make yourself the compass by which you sail and the star by which you steer your course, looking at nothing higher and more noble than yourselves, do not deceive yourselves, you have neither seen Christ nor known him. You are deeply incorporated (if I may so speak) with the spirit of this world, and have no true sympathy with God and Christ, no fellowship at all with them.

And, I beseech you, let us consider: be there not many of us that pretend much to Christ, that are plainly in our lives as proud, ambitious, vainglorious as any others? Are there not many of us that are as much under the power of unruly passions, as cruel, revengeful, malicious, censorious as others? That have our minds as deeply engaged in the world, and as much enslaved to riches, gain, profit, those great admired deities of the sons of men, and their souls, as much overwhelmed and sunk with the cares of this life? Do not many of us (as much) give ourselves to the pleasures of the flesh, and though not without regrets of conscience, yet ever now and then secretly soak ourselves in them? Are there not many of us that have as deep a share likewise in injustice and oppression, in vexing the fatherless and the widows? I wish it may not prove some of our cases at that last day, to use such pleas as these to Christ on our behalf: Lord, I have prophesied in your name, I have preached many a zealous sermon for you, I have kept many a long fast, I have been very active for your cause in church, in state—no, I never made any question, but that my name was written in your book of life. When yet, alas! We shall receive no other return from Christ but this: I know you not. Depart from me, you workers of iniquity (Luke 13:27). I am sure there are too many of us, that have long pretended to Christ, who make little or no progress in true Christianity, that is, holiness of life; that ever hang hovering in a twilight of grace, and never seriously put our selves forward into clear daylight, but esteem that glimmering starlight which we are in, and like that faint twilight better than broad open day. Whereas the path of the just (as the wise man speaks) is as the shining light, that shines more and more until the perfect day (Prov 4:18). I am sure there are many of us that are perpetual dwarfs in our spiritual stature, like those silly women (that St. Paul speaks of) laden with sins, and led away with diverse lusts, that are ever learning and never able to come to the knowledge of the truth; that are not now one jot taller in Christianity than we were many years ago, but have still as sickly, crazy, and unsound a temper of soul as we had long before (2 Tim 3:6–7).

Indeed, we seem to do something; we are always moving and lifting at the stone of corruption that lies upon our hearts, but yet we never stir it notwithstanding, or at least never roll it off from us. We are sometimes a little troubled with the guilt of our sins, and then we think we must thrust our lusts out of our hearts; but afterward we sprinkle ourselves over with I know not what holy water, and so are contented to let them still abide quietly within us. We every day truly confess the same sins, and pray against them, and yet still commit them as much as ever, and lie as deeply under the power of them. We have the same water to pump out in every prayer, and still we let the same leak in again upon us. We make a great deal of noise, and raise a great deal of dust with our feet, but we do not move from off the ground on which we stood, we do not go forward at all; or if we do sometimes make a little progress, we quickly lose again the ground which we had gained, like those upper planets in the heaven, which (as the astronomers tell us) sometimes move forward, sometimes quite backward, and sometimes perfectly stand still and have their stations and retrogradations as well as their direct motions. As if religion were nothing else but a dancing up and down upon the same piece of ground, and making several motions and friskings on it, and not a sober journeying and traveling onward toward some certain place. We do and undo; we weave sometimes a web of holiness, but then we let our lusts come, and undo and unravel all again. Like Sisyphus in the fable, we roll up a mighty stone with much ado, sweating and tugging up the hill, and then we let it go, and tumble down again to the bottom—and this is our constant work. Like those Danaides which the poets speak of, we are always filling water into a sieve, by our prayers, duties, and performances, which still runs out as fast as we pour it in.[353]

What is it that thus cheats us and gulls us of our religion, that makes us thus constantly to tread the same ring and circle of duties, where we make no progress at all forward, and the further we go are still never the nearer to our journey's end? What is it that thus starves our religion, and makes it look like those cows in Pharaoh's dream, ill-favored and lean fleshed, that it has no color in its face, no blood in its veins, no life nor heat at all in its members (Gen 41:4)? What is it that does thus bedwarf us in our Christianity? What low, sordid, and unworthy principles do we act by, that thus hinder our growth, and make us stand at a stay, and keep us always in the very porch and entrance where we first began? Is it a sleepy, sluggish conceit that it is enough for us if we are but once in a state of grace; if we have but once stepped over the threshold, we need not take such great pains to travel any further? Or is it another damping, choking, stifling opinion, that Christ has done all for us already without us, and nothing need more to be done within us? No matter how wicked we are in ourselves, for we have holiness without us, no matter how sickly and diseased our souls are within, for they have health without them? Why may we not as well be satisfied and contented to have happiness without us too to all eternity, and so ourselves forever continue miserable? Little children, let no man deceive you; he that does righteousness is righteous, even as he is righteous; but he that commits sin is of the devil (1 John 3:17). I shall therefore exhort you in the wholesome words of St. Peter: Give all diligence to add to your faith, virtue, and to virtue, knowledge, and to knowledge, temperance, and to temperance, patience, to patience, godliness, and to godliness, brotherly kindness, and to brotherly kindness, charity. For if these things are in you and abound, they make you, that you shall neither be barren nor unfruitful in the knowledge of our Lord Jesus Christ. (The apostle still goes on, and I cannot leave him yet): But he that lacks these things is blind, and cannot see far off, and has forgotten that he was once purged from his old sins. Wherefore rather brethren, give diligence to make your calling and election sure; for if you do these things, you shall never fall (2 Pet 1:6–10). Let us not only talk and dispute of Christ, but let us indeed put on the Lord Jesus Christ. Having those great and precious promises which he has given us, let us strive to be made partakers of the divine nature, escaping the corruption that is in the world through lust; and being begotten again to a lively hope of enjoying Christ hereafter, let us purify ourselves as he is pure.

Let us really declare that we know Christ, that we are his disciples, by our keeping of his commandments; and, among the rest, that commandment especially, which our Savior Christ himself commends to his disciples in a peculiar manner: This is my commandment, that you love one another, as I have loved you; and again: These things I command you that you love one another (John 15:12). Let us follow peace with all men, and holiness, without which no man shall see God (Heb 12:14). Let us put on, as the elect of God, holy and beloved, bowels of mercies, kindness, humbleness of mind, meekness, long-suffering—forbearing one another, and forgiving one another, if any man have a quarrel against any, even as Christ forgave us. Above all these things let us put on charity, which is the bond of perfectness (Col 3:12–19). Let us in meekness instruct those that oppose themselves; if God peradventure will give them repentance to the acknowledging of the truth, that they may recover themselves out of the snares of the devil, that are taken captive by him at his will (2 Tim 2:24–26). Beloved, let us love one another, for love is of God, and whosoever loves is born of God and knows God (1 John 4–7).

O divine Love! The sweet harmony of souls! The music of angels! The joy of God's own heart! The very darling of his bosom! The source of true happiness! The pure quintessence of heaven! That which reconciles the jarring principles of the world, and makes them all chime together! That which melts men's hearts into one another! See how St. Paul describes it, and it cannot choose but enamor your affections toward it: Love envies not, it is not puffed up, it does not behave in an unseemly manner, and seeks not her own, is not easily provoked, thinks no evil, rejoices not in iniquity; it bears all things, believes all things, hopes all things, endures all things (1 Cor 13:4–7). I may add, in a word, it is the best-natured thing, the best-complexioned thing in the world. Let us express this sweet harmonious affection in these jarring times, that so, if it is possible, we may tune the world at last into better music. Especially in matters of religion, let us strive with all meekness to instruct and convince one another. Let us endeavor to promote the gospel of peace, the dovelike gospel with a dovelike spirit. This was the way by which the gospel at first was propagated in the world: Christ did not cry, nor lift up his voice in the streets; he did not break a bruised reed, and he did not quench the smoking flax, and yet he brought forth judgment into victory (Isa 42: 2–3). He whispered the gospel to us from Mount Sion, in a still voice, and yet the sound thereof went out quickly throughout all the earth. The gospel at first came down upon the world gently and softly like the dew upon Gideon's fleece, and yet it quickly soaked quite through it (Judg 10). And doubtless this is still the most effectual way to promote it further. Sweetness and ingenuity will more powerfully command men's minds than passion, sourness, and severity; as the soft pillow sooner breaks the flint than the hardest marble. Let us follow truth in love—and of the two indeed, be contented rather to miss the conveying of a speculative truth than to part with love. When we would convince men of any error by the strength of truth, let us pour the sweet balm of love upon their heads. Truth and love are two of the most powerful things in the world, and when they both go together, they cannot easily be withstood. The golden beams of truth and the silken cords of love, twisted together, will draw men on with a sweet violence, whether they will or no.

Let us take heed we do not sometimes call that zeal for God and his gospel, which is nothing else but our own tempestuous and stormy passion. True zeal is a sweet, heavenly, and gentle flame, which makes us active for God, but always within the sphere of love. It never calls for fire from heaven to consume those that differ a little from us in their apprehensions. It is like that kind of lightning which the philosophers speak of, that melts the sword within, but does not singe the scabbard; it strives to save the soul, but does not hurt the body.[354] True zeal is a loving thing, and makes us always active to edification and not to destruction. If we keep the fire of zeal within the chimney, in its own proper place, it never does any harm—it only warms, quickens, and enlivens us; but if once we let it break out, and catch hold of the thatch of our flesh, and kindle our corrupt nature, and set the house of our body on fire, it is no longer zeal, it is no heavenly fire, it is a most destructive and devouring thing. True zeal is a soft and gentle flame, that will not scorch one's hand; it is no predatory or voracious thing. But carnal and fleshly zeal is like the spirit of gunpowder set on fire, that tears and blows up all that stands before it. True zeal is like the vital heat in us that we live upon, which we never feel to be angry or troublesome, but though it gently feed upon the radical oil within us, that sweet balsam of our natural moisture, yet it lives lovingly with it, and maintains that by which it is fed. But that other furious and distempered zeal is nothing but a fever in the soul. To conclude, we may learn what kind of zeal it is that we should make use of in promoting the gospel by an emblem of God's own, given us in the scripture, those fiery tongues that upon the day of

Pentecost, sat upon the apostles (which sure were harmless flames, for we cannot read that they did any hurt or that they did so much as singe a hair of their heads) (Acts 10).

I will therefore finish this with that of the apostle: Let us keep the unity of the Spirit in the bond of peace (Eph 4:3). Let this soft and silken knot of love tie our hearts together though our heads and apprehensions cannot meet, as indeed they never will, but always stand at some distance off from one another. Our zeal, if it is heavenly, if it is true vestal fire kindled from above, will not delight to tarry here below, burning up straw and stubble and such combustible things, and sending up nothing but gross earthly fumes to heaven. But it will rise up and return back pure as it came down, and will be ever strong to carry up men's hearts to God along with it. It will be only occupied about the promoting of those things which are unquestionably good, and when it moves in the irascible way, it will quarrel with nothing but sin. Here let our zeal busy and exercise itself, every one of us beginning first at our own hearts. Let us be more zealous than ever we have yet been in fighting against our lusts, in pulling down those strongholds of sin and Satan in our hearts. Here let us exercise all our courage and resolution, our manhood and magnanimity.

Let us trust in the almighty arm of our God, and not doubt that he will as well deliver us from the power of sin in our hearts as preserve us from the wrath to come. Let us go out against these uncircumcised Philistines (I mean our lusts) not with shield or spear, not in any confidence of our own strength, but in the name of the Lord of Hosts, and we shall prevail, we shall overcome our lusts: For greater is he that is in us, than he that is in them. The eternal God is our refuge, and underneath are the everlasting arms; he shall thrust out these enemies from before us, and he shall say: Destroy them (Deut 33:27). We shall enter the true Canaan, the good Land of Promise, that flows with milk and honey, the land of truth and holiness (Deut 31:20). Therefore take unto you the whole armor of God, that you may be able to withstand. Let your loins be girt about with truth, have on the breastplate of righteousness, and let your feet be shod with the preparation of the gospel of peace. Above all, take the shield of faith, whereby you shall be able to quench all the fiery darts of the wicked; and take the helmet of salvation, and the sword of the Spirit, which is the word of God (Eph 6:13–17). And lastly, be sure of this, that you be strong only in the Lord, and in the power of his might (Eph 6:10).

Let us take heed that we are not discouraged, and before we begin to fight, despair of victory. But to believe and hope well in the power of our God and his strength will be half a conquest. Let us not think holiness in the hearts of men here in the world is a forlorn, forsaken, and outcast thing from God that he has no regard of. Holiness, wherever it is, though it is never so small, if it is but hearty and sincere, it can no more be cut off, and discontinued from God, than a sunbeam here upon Earth can be broken off from its intercourse with the sun and be left alone amid the mire and dirt of this world. The sun may as well discard its own rays and banish them from itself into some region of darkness far remote from it, where they shall have no dependence at all upon it, as God can forsake and abandon holiness in the world, and leave it a poor orphan thing that shall have no influence at all from him to preserve and keep it. Holiness is something of God, wherever it is; it is an efflux from him that always hangs upon him and lives in him, as the sunbeams, though they guild this lower world and spread their golden wings over us, yet they are not so much here, where they shine, as in the sun, from where they flow. God cannot draw a curtain between himself and holiness, which is nothing but the splendor and shining of himself. He cannot hide his face from it, he cannot desert it in the world. He that is once born of God shall overcome the world and the prince of this world too, by the power of God in him. Holiness is no solitary, neglected thing—it has stronger confederacies, greater alliances than sin and wickedness. It is in league with God and the whole universe; the whole creation smiles upon it. There is something of God in it, and therefore it must necessarily be a victorious and triumphant thing.

Wickedness is a weak, cowardly, and guilty thing, a fearful and trembling shadow. It is the child of ignorance and darkness; it is afraid of light, and cannot possibly withstand the power of it, nor endure the sight of its glittering armor. It is allied to none, but wretched, forlorn, and apostate spirits, that do what they can to support their own weak and tottering kingdom of darkness, but are only strong in weakness and impotency. The whole polity and commonwealth of devils is not so powerful as one child of light, one babe in Christ; they are not all able to quench the least smoking flax, to extinguish one spark of grace. Darkness is not able to make resistance against light, but, ever as it comes, flies before it. But if wickedness invites the society of devils to it (as we learn by the sad experience of these present times, in many examples of those that were possessed with malice, revengefulness, and lust), so that those cursed fiends do most readily apply themselves to it, and offer their service to feed it, and encourage it, because it is their own life and nature, their own kingdom of darkness, which they strive to enlarge and to spread the dominions of; shall we then think that holiness, which is so nearly allied to God, has no good genius at all in the world, to attend upon it, to help it and encourage it? Shall not the kingdom of light be as true to its own interest, and as vigilant for the enlarging of itself, as the kingdom of darkness? Holiness is never alone in the world, but God is always with it, and his loving Spirit associates and joins itself to it. He that sent it into the world is with it as Christ speaks of himself: The Father has not left me alone, because I do always those things that please him (John 8:29). Holiness is the life of God, which he cannot but feed and maintain wherever it is; and as the devils are always active to encourage evil, so we cannot imagine but that the heavenly host of blessed angels above are as busily employed in the promoting of that which they love best, that which is dearest to God whom they serve, the life and nature of God. There is joy in heaven at the conversion of one sinner, heaven takes notice of it; there is a choir of angels, that sweetly sings the epithalamium of a soul divorced from sin and Satan, and espoused into Christ (Luke 15:7). What therefore the wise man speaks concerning wisdom (Prov 4:13, 23), I shall apply to holiness: Take fast hold of holiness, do not let her go, keep her, for she is your life. Keep your heart with all diligence, for out of it are the issues of life, and of death, too. Let nothing be esteemed of greater consequence and concern to you than what you do and act and how you live. Nothing outside us can make us either happy or miserable; nothing can either defile us, or hurt us, but what goes out from us and what springs and bubbles up, out of our own hearts. We have dreadful apprehensions, of the flames of hell outside us; we tremble and are afraid when we hear of fire and brimstone, while in the meantime we securely nourish within our own hearts, a true and living hell. The dark fire of our lusts consumes our bowels within, and miserably scorches our souls, and we are not troubled at it. We do not perceive how hell steals upon us while we live here. And as for heaven, we only gaze abroad, expecting that it should come in to us from without, but never look for the beginnings of it to arise within, in our own hearts.

But lest there should yet happily remain any prejudice against that which I have all this while heartily commended to you—true holiness and the keeping of Christ's commandment—as if it were a legal and servile thing that would subject us to a state of bondage, I must here add a word or two either for the prevention or removal of it. I do not therefore mean by holiness the mere performance of outward duties of religion, coldly acted over as a task, or our habitual prayings, hearing, fastings, multiplied one upon another (though these are all good, as subservient to a higher end), but I mean an inward soul and principle of divine life, that spirits all these that enliven and quicken the dead carcass of all our outward performances whatsoever. I do not here urge the dead law of outward works, which indeed if it is alone, subjects us to a state of bondage, but the inward law of the gospel, the law of the Spirit of life, than which nothing can be more free and ingenuous. For it does not act us by principles outside us, but is an inward self-moving principle living in our hearts. I do not urge the law written upon tables of stone outside us (though there is still a good use of that too) but the law of holiness written within, upon the fleshly tables of our hearts (2 Cor 3:3).

The first, though it works us into some outward conformity to God's commandments, and so has a good effect upon the world, yet we are all this while but like dead instruments of music, that sound sweetly and harmoniously when they are only struck and played upon from without, by the musician's hand, who has the theory and law of music living within himself.

But the second, the living law of the gospel, the law of the Spirit of life within us, is as if the soul of music should incorporate itself with the instrument and live in the strings and make them of their own accord, without any touch or impulse from without, dance up and down, and warble out their harmonies.

They that are acted only by an outward law are but like those little puppets that skip nimbly up and down, and seem to be full of quick and sprightly motion, whereas they are all the while moved artificially by certain wires and strings from without, and not by any principle of motion from themselves within; or else like clocks and watches that go pretty regularly for a while, but are moved by weights and plummets or some other artificial springs that must be ever now and then wound up, or else they cease.

But they that are acted by the new law of the gospel, by the law of the Spirit, have an inward principle of life in them, that from the center of itself puts itself forth freely and constantly into all obedience to the will of Christ. This new law of the gospel is a kind of musical soul informing the dead organ of our hearts, that makes them of their own accord delight to act harmoniously according to the rule of God's word.

The law that I speak of is a law of love, which is the most powerful law in the world. Yet it frees us in a manner from all law without us, because it makes us become a law to ourselves. The more it prevails in us, the more it eats up and devours all other laws without us; just as Aaron's living rod, swallowed up those rods of the magicians, that were only made to counterfeit a little life (Exod 7:12).

Love is at once a freedom from all law, a state of purest liberty, and yet a law too of the most constraining and indispensable necessity.

The worst law in the world is the law of sin, which is in our members, which keeps us in a condition of most absolute slavery, when we are wholly under the tyrannical commands of our lusts. This is a cruel Pharaoh indeed, that sets his hard taskmasters over us, and makes us wretchedly drudge in mire and clay.

The law of the letter outside us sets us in a condition of a little more liberty, by restraining of us from many outward acts of sin; but yet it does not disenthrall us from the power of sin in our hearts.

But the law of the Spirit of life (Rom 8:1–3), the gospel law of love, puts us into a condition of most pure and perfect liberty; and whoever really entertains this law, has quite thrust out Hagar, and has cast out the bondwoman and her children (Gen 2:8–10);

henceforth, Sarah the free woman, shall live forever with him, and she shall be to him a mother of many children; her seed shall be as the sand of the seashore for number, and as the stars of heaven (Gen 21:12, 22:17). Here is evangelical liberty, here is gospel freedom, when the law of the Spirit of life in Christ Jesus has made us free from the law of sin and death, when we have liberty from sin, and not a liberty to sin; for our dear Lord and Master has told us, that whoever commits sin, he is the servant of it (John 8:34).

He that lies under the power and vassalage of his base lusts, and yet talks of gospel freedom, is but like a poor condemned prisoner who in his sleep dreams of being set at liberty and of walking up and down wherever he pleases, while his legs are all the while locked fast in fetters and irons. To please ourselves with a notion of gospel liberty while we do not have a gospel principle of holiness within us to free us from the power of sin, is nothing else but to gild over our bonds and fetters and to fancy ourselves to be in a golden cage. There is a straightness, slavery, and narrowness in all sin. Sin crowds and crumples up our souls, which, if they were freely spread abroad, would be as wide, and as large as the whole universe.

No man is truly free, but he that has his will enlarged to the extent of God's own will, by loving whatever God loves, and nothing else. Such a one does not fondly hug this and that particular created good thing, and enslave himself to it; but he loves everything that is lovely, beginning at God, and descending down to all his creatures, according to the several degrees of perfection in them. He enjoys a boundless liberty and a boundless sweetness, according to his boundless love. He enclasps the whole world within his outstretched arms; his soul is as wide as the whole universe, as big as yesterday, today, and forever (Heb 13:8). Whoever is once acquainted with this disposition of spirit never desires anything else, and he loves the life of God in himself, dearer than his own life. To conclude this, therefore: If we love Christ, and keep his commandments, his commandments will not be grievous to us; his yoke will be easy, and his burden light: it will not put us into a state of bondage, but of perfect liberty (Matt 11:30). For it is most true of evangelical obedience—that the wise man speaks of wisdom, her ways are ways of pleasantness, and all her paths are peace; she is a tree of life to those that lay hold upon her, and happy are they that retain her (Prov 3:17–18).

I will now finish up all with one or two considerations, to persuade you farther to the keeping of Christ's commandments.

First, from the desire which we all have of knowledge: If we would indeed know divine truths, the only way to come to this is by keeping of Christ's commandments. The grossness of our apprehensions in spiritual things, and our many mistakes we have about them, proceed from nothing but those dull and soggy steams which rise up from our foul hearts and cloud our understandings. If we did only heartily comply with Christ's commandments, and purge our hearts from all gross and sensual affections, we should not then look about for truth wholly without ourselves, and enslave ourselves to the dictates of this and that teacher, and hang upon the lips of men; but we should find the great eternal God, inwardly teaching our souls, and continually instructing us more and more in the mysteries of his will, and out of our bellies should flow rivers of living waters (John 7:38). Nothing puts a stop and hindrance to the passage of truth in the world but the carnality of our hearts, the corruption of our lives.

It is not wrangling disputes and syllogistical reasonings that are the mighty pillars that underprop truth in the world. If we would only underset it with the holiness of our hearts and lives, it should never fail. Truth is a prevailing and conquering thing that would quickly overcome the world, did not the earthiness of our dispositions and the darkness of our false hearts hinder it. Our Savior Christ bids the blind man wash off the clay that was upon his eyes in the pool of Siloam, that he should see clearly; intimating this to us, that it is the earthiness of men's affections that darkens the eye of their understandings in spiritual things (John 9:1). Truth is always ready and near at hand, if our eyes were not closed up with mud, that we could only open them to look upon it. Truth, always waits upon our souls and offers itself freely to us, as the sun offers its beams to every eye that will but open and let them shine in upon it. If we could only purge our hearts from that filth, and defilement, which hangs about them, there would be no doubt at all truths prevailing in the world. For truth is great, and stronger than all things. All the earth calls upon truth and the heaven blesses it; all works shake and tremble at it. The truth endures and is always strong; it lives and conquers forevermore. She is the strength, kingdom, power, and majesty of all ages. Blessed be the God of truth.

Last of all, if we desire a true reformation, as we seem to do, let us begin here in reforming our hearts and lives, in keeping of Christ's commandments. All outward forms and models of reformation, though they are never so good in their kind, yet are of little worth to us without this inward reformation of the heart. Tin, or lead, or any other baser metal, if it is cast into never so good a mold, and made up into never so elegant a figure, yet is but tin or lead still; it is the same metal that it was before. And if we are molded into never so good a form of outward government, unless we mold our hearts anew within too, we are but a little better than we were before. If adulterate silver, that has much alloy or dross in it, has never so current a stamp put upon it, yet it will not pass notwithstanding, when the touchstone tries it. We must be reformed within, with a spirit of fire and a spirit of burning, to purge us from the dross and corruption of our hearts, and refine us as gold and silver (Prov 25:4); and then we shall be reformed truly, and not before. When this once comes to pass, then shall Christ be set upon his throne indeed, then the glory of the Lord shall overflow the land; then we shall be a people acceptable to him, and as Mount Sion, which he dearly loved.

II

THE JOY WHICH THE RIGHTEOUS HAVE IN GOD

Benjamin Whichcote (1650)

Rejoice in the Lord, O ye righteous, for praise is comely for the upright.
—Psalm 33:1

The remarkable providences, and happier dispensations of God, call upon us to be glad in the Lord, and thankful for his benefits. God has not only given us leave to rebuild our ruins, and repair our waste places, but he has been with us, and given us encouragement to this good undertaking. We read that the Jews, when they returned out of captivity, and rebuilt their walls, had meetings of joy and triumph (as you find it among other places, Ezra 3:2 and 6:16 and Neh 11:27). And this is not only pious, but a transcendent act of faith and confidence in God, upon such occasions to bless him, to rejoice in him, and to praise him. And they are of the basest and most sordid temperaments that are not affected with the expressions of the divine goodness and kindness. And truly if we do not do the former duty of the text, we shall fail in the latter; if we be not glad and rejoice in the Lord, we shall never be thankful or bless his holy name. For (pray) what thankfulness when the heart is possessed with melancholy, and the spirit full of heaviness? Besides this, it is the general direction of wisdom, to acknowledge God in all our ways; therefore in things remarkable, so much the more, and it is the effect of religion to do it, for what is religion but a participation, imitation, and resemblance of the divine goodness, both in the temper of the subject, and in its expressions of gratitude, ingenuity, acknowledgment, and the like? I know no other result of religion but this. And surely were religion estimated by this, we should endeavor after it, and all be good friends, and he would be accounted the best man, that is most free and ingenuous in the sense of divine goodness. At least let us not neglect to make acknowledgments to God upon those eminent advantages that the course of his providence affords; such as eminent successes in our undertakings, and happy recoveries from any trouble and calamity, and giving us to see light after darkness. Such opportunities as these, pious souls have wanted to close. And it is noted of one, a very good person, and king of great fame, as a thing that was very unnatural and unbecoming him, and very ill resented by God, that he did not render to the Lord according to the great benefits that were bestowed upon him (thus it is reported of Hezekiah, 2 Chr 32:21). But his heart was lifted up. Now pride is opposite to the acknowledgment of God and giving thanks to him. He that has his heart lifted up, will arrogate and assume to himself, and this seems to have been his fault, for which wrath was upon him, and the Israel of God. Now let such failings as these were, though in former ages, be for our admonition, as the apostle tells us, that things before us were for our example, upon whom the ends of the world are come (1 Cor 10:2). If God had not taken pleasure in us and in this great undertaking, to restore and rebuild this ancient city, he might have obstructed and prohibited the same; as Joshua cursed anyone that undertook rebuilding of Jericho. You shall find the curse (Josh 6:26) and in effect (1 Kgs 16:34). Therefore we have cause to be sensible of the divine goodness, in that his good hand of providence has been over us and given success to our endeavors, and scattered our fears and sad apprehensions, and given us to see so much of restoration as at this day, as this place gives testimony of.

In the text we have two things:
I. The duty; and
II. The reason of it.

I. The duty is expressed in two words, rejoice in the Lord, and praise him: and the reason in these words, for it is seemly to do so.

THE JOY WHICH THE RIGHTEOUS HAVE IN GOD

Rejoice in the Lord. Then certainly religion is not such a thing as it is represented to the world by many men. For it is looked upon as a doleful, troublesome, melancholy thing, hurtful to the body and disquieting to the souls of men. But see whether this is true. Look upon religion in its actions and employment: and what are they? Rejoice and give thanks. Are not these actions grateful and delightful? What transcends divine joy and ingenuous acknowledgments? But to continue.

II. The reason. It is seemly. Whatever is the true product of religion is graceful, beautiful, and lovely. There is nothing in religion that is dishonorable, selfish, particular, and narrow-spirited. No, it is a principle of the greatest nobleness and generousness in the world. They are worldly spirits that are low, narrow, and contracted: the truly religious are most noble and generous, and are the freest from narrowness, discontent, and selfishness. There is the most solid peace, and most grounded satisfaction found in it.

I. Rejoice in the Lord.

1. For himself; because of his own goodness.

2. In other things, with respect to him.

1. For himself. First, God is the most excellent object in the world. And second, what he is in himself, he is to the righteous who have interest in him, and who are in reconciliation with him. It is vanity and emptiness to glory in men and ordinary things, and where there is no property; though things are excellent yet there is no glory in that case. Men are prone to envy, therefore it is requisite to glorying that men have property, that men think upon God as their own; for where men have no property, they are apt to say, what am I the better? The devilish nature delights in God the less, because of his goodness; for the more good God is, the further is he removed from their degenerate temper. It is our unsuitableness and unlikeness to God, that hinders our delight and satisfaction in him. It is a great saying, Whosoever is pleased with God, pleases God.[355] Whoever, I say, is pleased with that which God is pleased with, is pleasing unto God. But they that are in an unsuitable temper and disposition (as the unregenerate man and sensual spirit, as the atheistical and profane, and those that are malicious and devilish), they are in a spirit opposite to the Spirit of God, and therefore they are offended with God, as well as God is

offended with them; but, whoever are pleased with God, God is pleased with them, but to the wicked and unregenerate, God himself (as good as he is) is a burden, for it is the temper of wickedness to say unto God, Depart from us, for we do not desire the knowledge of your ways (Job 21:14). For it is universally true that things are to persons, according as they are in state, spirit, and temper. Let men pretend love to the things of God ever so much, for they will not relish them, unless they are born of God. It is them that are naturalized to heaven, that relish and savor divine things. That which is born of the world is enmity against God. But

2. Our rejoicing must be with some respect to God, and though it be in other things, yet it must be in the Lord: and this is done, when

- We acknowledge God originally, as the fountain from where all good things come, and the first cause of all good. When we are aware that we receive from him and hold of him, and have what we enjoy, from his bounty.
- When we account God better than all other enjoyments whatever, and have all things in subordination to him.
- When we look upon all our enjoyments as fruits of the divine goodness, and consider them as enjoyments,

First, to endear God to us, and

Second, of obliging us to God. For you know, a courtesy is accounted as lost if the party does not gain the goodwill and affection of the person to whom he has shown kindness. Even so, it is in respect of God; if God be not endeared to us by his kindness, and we thus obliged to him for his goodness, all is lost. But

- We then may be said to rejoice in the Lord, when we make God the final end, and make all things subservient to his glory, and account ourselves bound to dispose of what he gives us according to his appointment, and for the ends of virtue. And to this purpose, that we may rejoice in the good things, that through providence we do enjoy, with some respect to God, two things are necessary:

1. It is necessary to give God place in the world.

2. That we take pleasure in the works of his providence. For there is nothing that God does, or that he permits to be done, but it offers to the intelligent mind some notion from God, and causes some observance of God in the world; and gives advantage to

some divine contemplation, and so puts the soul upon some action of acknowledgment and adoration of God....

II. Praise is comely for the upright. First: These words you see are exegetical to rejoicing. Rejoice in the Lord, for praise is comely....And then, secondly: Uprightness is exegetical to righteousness. Rejoice in the Lord, O ye righteous, for praise is comely for the upright. By uprightness is here meant our sincerity and integrity, our honest meaning and true intention, which through God's gracious acceptance is our righteousness. We are, none of us, at all better than we mean; our gracious God takes us by what we understand, intend, and mean, and the truth is here, there is no dispensation for failure in intention. For misapprehension, God grants allowance, and dispenses with human frailties, but for a failing of intention there is no dispensation. Fail here, and you are hypocrites, and false-hearted, and therefore, uprightness is our perfection, and our righteousness. For either you intend well, or you do not; if you do, you are upright, if you do not, you are hypocrites. It goes mighty far in religion, that a man simply, honestly, and in plainness of heart, means and intends God and goodness, righteousness, and truth. He is upright that means well. Though he be in many particulars mistaken and incumbred [sic] with weakness, yet he is righteous in the sight of God, through God's gracious acceptance. Therefore it becomes us to be highly charitable, one toward another, since God is so gracious, and sets such a value upon our good meanings and sincere intentions, as to account of this for righteousness, either in practice or opinion. If a man, in the integrity of his heart, honestly means God, goodness, righteousness, and truth, God will receive him. Every man's mind is himself, and a man is what he means and intends; and what a man means not, that he is not, that he does not. And this I have said because in the text there are two words made exegetical, praise and rejoicing, righteousness and uprightness. Rejoice in the Lord, O ye righteous, for praise is comely for the upright.

This remains to be spoken to, and it is a gallant notion in this age that tends so much to atheism.

Praise is comely. This is spoken by way of argument, and it is no argument, if this be not true, that there is a reason for what we do, from the things themselves. I mean this, and if you grant by this, that there is that which of itself is good and comely, just and right, and there is that which of itself is sinful and abominable; we exclude atheism out of the world, and this must be acknowledged, otherwise there is no argument in these words, for praise is comely. If all things are alike, and no difference of things, one thing is no more comely than another. Now because this is an excellent rule, and a way to exclude atheism out of the world, I will show you that this notion is abundant in scripture: that goodness and truth are first in things, and though they are so in men's apprehensions secondarily, yet they are so first in themselves; and that men live in a lie, and are in a lie, if their apprehensions are not conformed to things in their reality and existence.

The reason for things is that law and truth which none must transgress. I say, the reason for things is a law and truth which none, either by power or privilege, may transgress. And for this I will give you such arguments for conviction, that greater cannot be given, for I tell you, it is a law in heaven, and that which God takes notice of in all his dispensations to his creatures. It is that which God will give an account of himself by, to the understandings of his creatures. For this I will produce many scriptures: Righteousness and judgment are the habitation of his throne (Ps 97:2). Can any man understand this to be nothing but what is arbitrary? Will he by power pervert that which is right? Is there unrighteousness with God? God forbid (Rom 9:14). How insignificant are all these expressions, if all things be alike and arbitrary, if the difference of things be nothing else but fantastical and conceited? And yet this and much more must the atheist say, or else his opinion is worth nothing. For if there be a difference in things, he will be self-condemned. I could quote you hundreds of places for this—all the ways of God are ways of truth of righteousness and of judgment (Deut 32:4). Can any man imagine that this signifies no more but that things are as will would have them. Therefore I tell you (and it is that by which you and all the world shall be judged) that these are not bare words and titles, not shadows and imaginations. There is that which is decent and fitting to be done, or that which is equal, that which is fair, that which is comely and seemly: there is that which holds of itself, and is decent, comely, and fitting. Truth and goodness are first in things, then in persons, and it is our duty to observe them and our uprightness to comply with them. All things are not arbitrary and positive constitution, but there is that which is lovely and comely in itself, and there is that which is impure and ugly in its own nature and quality, and if any man meddles with it, let him be sure it will disparage him, and render him contemptible, vile, and base. There is also that which is generous, noble, and worthy, and will gain repute and credit to him that uses it. It is not all one from an intelligent and voluntary agent, to do one thing or another; for there are rules of right wherewith all intelligent agents must comply, and they do righteously when they do, and sinfully when they do not. There is such a turpitude in some things, that there is no privilege or protection; nothing that can be alleged that will gain a man liberty to do them, for they have an intrinsic malignity and impurity; and these things are a disparagement to any person whatsoever. And there are things that are just and righteous, worthy and generous, that will recompense the person that is exercised in them.

And then God made man with a judgment of discerning, and it is expected that man should judge and discern and reason concerning things. And this is not so much our privilege, as our charge and trust, to observe the difference of things. The whole motion of the world below men is nulled upon a moral consideration, and no morality is to be found in any agent below man. The motions of all else are no better than mechanic. Now this is the foundation of scripture, exhortation, and admonition. We are to examine by reason and by argument, because God applies to reason and judgment, and to understanding, which is inseparable from choice and resolution.

In short, a man is accomplished by two things. First, by being enlightened in his intellectual faculties; second by being directed in his morals to refuse evil, and to do good; and to choose and determine things according to the difference of them. The first is the perfection of a man's understanding. The second is the goodness of his mind: Work out your salvation with fear, for it is God that worketh in you (Phil 2:13). This supposes a judgment of discerning, and then consequently, that God expects that a man, according to his apprehension and judgment, should choose, resolve, and determine. Now where we are called upon to work in the affair of salvation, see how cautiously the scripture speaks of it:

Work out your own salvation, for it is God that worketh in you, both to will and to do of his own good pleasure (Phil 2:12). From here nobody should be discouraged from the sense of his own disability, nor arrogate to himself, or be presumptuous, for God works in him to will and to do of his own good pleasure. If this notion were only well observed, a great part of some controversies, at this day, would be resolved; for scripture attributes to us that which God does with us. That which we do is attributed to God, and that which God does by us is both ascribed to God, and to us; we work, and God works, we are awakened, directed, and assisted by him....

We see there is a direct and exact government in heavenly bodies. Whenever did the sun fail? It were prodigious if it should. Why should not we, who are guided by principles of reason and illumination (which is a far greater communication from God), why should we be so irregular and inconsistent, since the lower creation is so regular and uniform? For there is nothing of conflagration in the heavenly motions, because there are no oppositions, and if we were uniform to principles of reason and right understanding, all motions with us would be so, and tend to mutual information and edification, but not at all to provocation, and exasperation, one of another.

Pray let me leave this notion with you, that there is a difference in things. There is that which is comely, that which is regular, decent, and directed according to rule, and the standing principle of God's creation. You see how much time I have spent in the notion, or that which is the force of the argument; we are to rejoice and give thanks, because it is comely. The reason lies in the quality of the thing, which supposes that there is a difference in things; by which the atheist is excluded from the world and men's liberties restrained to that which is right. It is no rule to a man's actions, to do that which he may maintain by power and privilege, but to do that which is fit to be done, just and right: to comply in all things with the reason of things, and the rule of right, and in all things to be according to the nature, mind, and will of God, the law of justice, the rule of right, the reason of things. These are the laws, by which we are to act and govern our lives; and we are all born under the power of them. If this be not true, this argument of the psalmist is insignificant, praise ye the Lord, for it is comely (Ps 147:1). The reason of things, therefore, is our rule, both in religion and converse, one with another, and though these are different forms of speech, yet they are always in conjunction. The reason of the mind is by these to be directed; and indeed, all principles of religion are founded upon the surest, most constant, and highest reason in the world. There is nothing so intrinsically rational as religion is; nothing so self-evident, nothing that can so justify itself, or that has such pure reason to commend itself, as religion has; for it gives an account of itself to our judgments and to our faculties. But so much for the notion that there is a difference in things, that good and evil are first in things; right and wrong first in things themselves. This is not arbitrary, nor imagined, nor determined by power and privilege, but there is good and evil, comely and uncomely in things themselves. A word of this particular case, and I have done.

Praise is comely. It is nature's sense, it is the import of any man's reason. Every man's mind tells him that this is decent, and no man can have peace, quiet, and satisfaction in the contrary; unless he is sunk down into baseness and degenerated into a sordid temper, he will acknowledge the kindness of his benefactor. Now, because God infinitely transcends all the benefactors in the world, if any man does not acknowledge his goodness, and praise him for his benefits, he is sunk down into baseness, and fallen beneath his creation and nature.

God loves us, and therefore he does us good. We love God because we are partakers of his benefits. Now praise and thanksgiving are all the return that our necessity and beggary are capable of, and it is very comely for us, that are so much beholden to the divine goodness, to make our due acknowledgments, and therefore it is observed that in ingratitude there is a connection of all vice. All disingenuity and baseness are concentred in the depths of ingratitude. He that will not be engaged by kindness, no cords of man will hold him. It is observed both by God and man, as degeneracy in its ultimate issue, the greatest depravation that nature is capable of, to be insensible of courtesies, and not to make due acknowledgments. How often did David complain of those persons, that were obliged to him by kindness, that they turned

103

into his enemies. How is he represented by him, as a most sordid wretched person, one that was degenerated to the fullest degree? and then God himself complains (Deut 34:15). Jeshurun waked fat and kicked, he forsook God that made him, and lightly esteemed the rock of his salvation (Deut 32:15). God and man complain of the ungrateful, because all favors and courtesies are lost. Yes, it is well observed that it is the only way to make a desperate enemy, to bestow kindness upon an unthankful person. And this is too well known that those who have been made friends by courtesy, proving false, have been the greatest betrayers. Therefore, of all persons and tempers, the insensible and ungrateful are the worst, yes, truly, these are the very pests of the world, the enemies of human nature; they harden men's hearts, who otherwise were free to do courtesies, because they do not know that they may make an enemy. I will make this out (the baseness of ingratitude) in these two words:

1. Because nothing is more due to God than our gratitude, for he loads us with his benefits and is pleased to please us and does many things to gratify us.

2. By this we give testimony of our minds to God for we have nothing at all to sacrifice to God but the consent of our minds, an ingenious acknowledgment. We have nothing to bring him but the consent of our minds, and this the grateful person does, and by this he signifies that if it were within his compass, he would requite the divine goodness; for it is not so much the gift, as the mind of the giver. He that is unthankful is most full of himself and apt to think that all the world was made for him, and that all men are bound to be his servants, and to attend his purpose, that he may serve himself of all men's parts, powers, privileges, and opportunities; but he himself is exempt from all men, so that he is an enemy to God and men.

III

THE MORAL PART OF RELIGION REINFORCED BY CHRISTIANITY

Benjamin Whichcote (1651)

*For the grace of God, that bringeth salvation, hath appeared
to all men; teaching us, that denying ungodliness and worldly
lusts, we should live soberly, righteously, and godly in this
present world.*

—Titus 2:11–12

I have made it appear that all of us owe our hope of happiness to the grace and goodness of God, according to the terms of
the gospel, and that the gospel requires of us avoidance of ungodliness and worldly lusts, and positively (which amounts to the
same) to live soberly, righteously, and godly.…

I. To be sober in ourselves: of good minds, of the very complexion of virtue—not vainly fraught and possessed, not giddily
minded and intoxicated, not having over-weaned thoughts of ourselves, but modest and humble.

For the other part, not sensual and brutish, abusing our bodies by an excess, but governing them as the mansions of our souls,
and as tools and instruments of virtue. Now if anyone fails in this he
cannot go further, or make any progress in the business of religion.
For he that is inept in vain goes out to any attempt, for conceit spoils
the ingenuity of the mind, and intemperance spoils the temper of
the body.

II. To be righteous toward others. When well constituted in
ourselves, then we go forth to act, and the first thing we meet with

abroad is our neighbor....With all we must deal justly, equally, and fairly, and do to them as we would have them do to ourselves....

And whoever he is you have to do with, though he is a person whom you never saw before and are not likely to see again, yet be sure in all things to do him right, so that when he leaves you he may say he met with a man, and with a Christian, and be encouraged to travel further, because you who are a stranger to him do well by him. And yet further, if this man who you thus meet requires anything of you, where you can do him good and not hurt yourself, plainly tell him the truth, that he may go away well instructed; and if he commits anything to you, do not deceive him, or restore to him what he commits to you when he calls for it. And if he does on his part that which is disproportionate, be slow to resent it, but mend it by fair interpretation, and so shall he reflect upon himself, and see his own baseness. And thus having brought it home to all particular occasions of life, the universal benevolence that spirits the intellectual world, requires these mutual and interchangeable offices universally toward one another. And for a lower participation of it, you have in the inferior world a fitness and disposition in one thing to serve another, where being nothing in nature, but as it is conservative in its being and natural perfection, so also is it accommodated to serve another. Thus we may conclude that treachery and all sorts of falseness are prodigious in the world, and tend to the defacement of the institution of God.

III. And now I come to the third: to live godly, to perform all duty toward God your Creator. And this I am sure you will acknowledge to be godliness and included in Christianity, and more than a heathen virtue, to perform all duty toward God, which includes these eight things:

1. Reverence and regard of the divine majesty. Now this depends upon great and worthy apprehensions of the divine excellencies and perfections, and expresses itself by prostration before God, and sense of our inferiority and distance from him.
2. Submission to him, and obedience to his commands. And this is founded in our relation to him: this is our state, and God's due, if he is our maker....

3. Reference of ourselves to him, and dependence upon his pleasure, for we are best in his hands. This supports placing a trust...and confidence in him, otherwise we shall never refer ourselves to him.

4. Love and delight in him, harmony and complacence with him. This will make us acquiesce in him—and what is more lovely than the first and chief good? And God is the first and chief good.

5. Thankfulness to him, for his benefits, free communication, and influence; and this is advanced by our sense of our unworthiness, and a sense of our incapacity to make a just retribution.

6. Since he has been faithful to you in all past times of your life, trust him for the time to come.

7. Since he is the center of your soul, rest in him, for the center is the place of rest.

8. Since he is your utmost end; subordinate all things to him. And this is strictly godliness. These things express and declare a man's duty toward God. And we are naturally obliged in all these particulars to our maker. And when you have done all this, then I assure you that you are a godly person, and gone beyond those heathen virtues that fall short of religion. And yet when you have done all, I can still assure you, you have not gone one step beyond true reason, and have done no more than what exactly becomes a moral agent; and none can give an account of the use of his reason, either to God or himself, if he is a stranger to these instances of piety or devotion to God. For were it not for this mighty power of mental contemplation of this excellent object we call God, it hadn't mattered much if instead of the perfection we call *reason* (in the world), there had been only a higher elevation of that which we call sense and imagination. For then in the scale of the creatures the several rounds of that ladder would have been at a more even distance. The reason of our minds is not surer of anything that is in the world, than that there is a God. For thus we know, and every man may know, that God made him, and this is an argument fairly before him: he

that cannot continue himself in being when he has it, certainly he could not bring himself into being, when he was nothing. For that which cannot do the less, cannot do the greater; and it is less to maintain a thing in being when it has a being, than to bring a thing into being when it is quite out of being. We prove a cause antecedent by an effect consequent, and this is the best argument in the world. Now no account is to be given to the reason of a man's mind, of the being of the world, but that there is a God. For thus, if we are intelligent and voluntary agents, God was at least so, or much more, for lower cannot produce higher, nor a weak produce a stronger. If therefore we are intelligent and voluntary agents, he that made the world was much more so.

Now this notion, that there is a God that made the world, has an even proportion to the reason of all ages. All persons of any improvement and indifference (for I abate gross self-neglect and faction) have this notion, that God made the world; this has been laid before all understandings, in all ages and successions of time. And though we cannot comprehend the being of God (for finite cannot comprehend infinite), yet if we do acknowledge God the first and chief goodness, and ascribe all excellency and perfection to him, we do him as much right as we are capable of. And, without doubt, God will take it as well at our hands, because it holds a proportion to our being, as if it were of a thousand times more intrinsic value if we ourselves had been of higher capacities. The knowledge of God that has been universally acquired in the world, and which is most saving to man, is to think that God is righteous, and gracious, and merciful. The one is for your own sake, the other to give God adequate justice.

1. To do God adequate justice, I advise you to think God righteous, or else you do not make him so good as all his creatures ought to be. For this is for certain, the affectation of arbitrariness and independence, the pretense of exorbitance and self-will—*these* are the greatest deformities in the rational commonwealth. Now the scripture declares otherwise concerning God: God will judge the world in righteousness, and All the ways of God are ways of

righteousness, judgment, and truth (Deut 32:4). Therefore, be sure you attribute righteousness to your maker.

2. For your own sake, I advise you that you always think and report of God as gracious and merciful: and so he has declared himself in Jesus Christ. If you do not think that God is gracious and merciful, you ruin yourself, and if you tell it abroad, you do all that lies in you to make all men desperate. So that whoever does not think God righteous and merciful does not do God justice, nor answer the principles of natural light, and is wholly a stranger to gospel revelation.

Then for our duty: that which is properly divinity, ends in two things: a good mind, and a good life. That is the effect of divinity, or that you call religion in us. If it does not bring us into a good frame of mind, a good temper of spirit, into reconciliation with the law of righteousness, and the nature, mind, and will of God, and leading a holy life, our religion evaporates, is but a notion; for that that is sincere and real, and soul-saving religion, finally issues in these two, to bring us to a good mind, and to lead a good life.

Christianity comprehends in it the moral part of religion, as well as the instituted part thereof: going to God in and through Christ. The former of these the apostle represents by living soberly, righteously, and godly, etc. Sobriety, which terminates in ourselves, righteously, which refers to our neighbors, and then godliness, which particularly refers to God, and lies in an inward sense and high esteem of God in our minds, and expresses itself in all acts of devotion and obedience to God. For a man in his acting, carriage, and behavior shows what mind he is of; so those who have a high esteem of God in their thoughts will certainly express themselves in all acts of devotion and obedience toward God; and in these three, the moral part of religion is comprehended.

For the notion and account of morality, you must know, consist in this: the congruity and proportion between the action of an agent and his object. He acts morally who observes the proportion of an action to its object; that is, he acts on its proper object, as I will explain, that you may distinguish between the moral part of religion, the instituted part of religion, and the instrumental part of religion.

For instance, hatred and disrespect toward that being we depend upon for all that we have is an immoral thing, that is, it is an unequal and preposterous thing; it is an action disproportionate, unequal, and unfit.

Again, for a creature to be insolent, and rise up against his creator, is an action unsuitable and disproportionate to an intelligent agent; nothing is more absurd. These things therefore are immoral, because there is unsuitableness between the action and the object of the action.

Misbehavior is in God's family, for God is the governor of the world; and the whole world is his family. Now for anyone to act unduly, to fall to beating his fellow servants—this is misbehavior in God's family. It is undue, unfit, indecent, and uncomely; it is immoral, impure, and unholy in itself. If it is immediately against God, we call it ungodliness, if immediately against a man's neighbor, we call it unrighteousness, and if against a man's self, it is contrary to sobriety.

...Sobriety, righteousness, and godliness are the due perfections of an intellectual nature upon a moral account. These are the things that are good in themselves, and sanctify by their presence, and are necessary and indispensable. They are not means to higher ends, but ends themselves. There cannot be a relaxation or commutation in these particulars, upon any account. But the intellectual nature is necessarily and unavoidably under an obligation to acts of sobriety, to acts of righteousness, and to acts of godliness. Of all the instrumental parts of religion, you cannot say of them, put them together: for all the other things in religion are but in order to these. These are the things that make men Godlike, these are the things that are final and ultimate, these are the things that sanctify human nature by their presence. A hypocrite may pray, and the profane person (when he is in a better fit) may call upon the name of God; but here, neither the hypocrite, nor the profane, have any due reverence of God in their minds, nor submit to him, obey him, depend upon him, delight in him, move to him as a center, nor refer to him as the utmost end. As for the moral part of religion, they have not the least idea of it; for that sanctifies the subject, and makes them really Godlike. These are the things that are necessary at all times, and these are the things that are self-evident; no sooner is a man told of them, but he knows them to be true. All men know that they are to be sober, and that they ought to deal righteously and fairly with others; and all men know they ought to have reverence for deity; he who never thought of them, if he hears them only spoken of, cannot but own them. And by the inherence of these found in him, a man is made as truly holy as a man is sound by health in his body, or strong by strength.

Of these I may say:

1. Some of them are according to the nature of God, as holiness and righteousness.
2. Some are founded in the relation we stand in to God, as his creatures; as reverence, adoration, and submission to God, referring ourselves to him.
3. Some rise out of our capacity. As we are rational, and intelligent, and voluntary agents, so we are under the obligation to all rational acts. Everything must act according to its nature; therefore an intelligent agent is under an obligation to act rationally in what he does.
4. Some of these are requisite in respect of our make and composition of parts: part spirit and part body. In the spirit we communicate with angels; in the lower part, which is body, we descend to the lower world. Hence it follows that the nobler ought to have the advantage and the government of the inferior, and that the state of the foul soul is to be preferred before bodily circumstances.
5. Lastly, some of them are founded upon the relation we stand in to our fellow creatures. For either they are our equals, and then shown all fairness and regard, as we would have them regard us; or else inferiors, and then all shown tenderness and encouragement; or if they are the creatures below us, then shown mercy, for the merciful man is merciful to his beast (Prov 12:10).

So you see of what foundation in religion these are. You must unmake the whole species of creatures, or you cannot take out these principles of righteousness, equity, and fairness; these are principles of piety and devotion.

These things are of certainty to all the world. Whereas, take other things in religion: the immortality of reasonable souls, future rewards and punishments, God pardoning sin to all those that do repent, divine aid and assistance, as it is declared in the gospel—the famous philosophers only hoped these choice points of religion were true, but they were not assured of them. But of all the other they were undoubtedly assured. We indeed have extraordinary assurance, because we have gospel revelation; they are certain to us Christians, but they were only of hope, fair persuasions, and belief to the philosophers who had no scripture. Yet many of them wrote excellently upon these subjects—they hoped all these were true, but we are satisfied and assured. But in the other points, we have the harmony of the whole world; it is the language of everyone's thoughts, it is nature's sense that these things are so. These are things of general obligation, and universal acknowledgment, for they bear a true and even proportion to the common reason of mankind. As to these things we all agree, as well as we agree that the sun enlightens the world.

The test tells us, they are not only acknowledged but further established and settled by the doctrine of the gospel. Therefore these things have a double sanction from God. First, they are the principles of his creation, discoverable and knowable by natural light. Secondly, they are again declared and included in the terms of the covenant of grace, for the text says: The grace of God, which brings salvation, has appeared to all men, teaching us that denying ungodliness and worldly lusts, we should live soberly, righteously, and godly in the present world (Titus 2:11–13). These have all the settlement possible: things settled when God first made man, and further settled by the grace of the gospels.

To secure ourselves from dreams and enthusiasms, let us confine ourselves to the dictates of reason and letter of scripture, which gives joint assurance and acknowledgment to morals. Now, if any man pretends a revelation from heaven and does not show his warrant from holy scripture, which is God's instrument in the world, this we have to say: "You come in the name of God, you say you have a revelation from him, but I must then have a revelation too, before I can believe you." So that if you go to revelation, you must show it to me in scripture. If you pretend anything out of scripture, I must have a revelation also, before I believe it. But in respect of the principles of reason, God speaks generally at once to all; there needs no other assurance in that which is reason.

And then for institutes, which are the voluntary results of the divine will; scripture is so full and clear in them, that of institutes we may say these four things.

1. Nothing of matter of faith but as it is in scripture.
2. Nothing is necessary in way of faith that is otherwise expressed than in scripture.
3. Nothing of faith is certain, as it is further made out, than in scripture.
4. Men may live in Christian love and union, though they do not agree in expressing their faith, in any other words than those that are in scripture.

They are greatly mistaken who oppose matters of reason in religion, and points of faith; and think in religion we are not to know, but only to believe, and think that when morality is spoken of, there is nothing to be understood but some complementary virtue. But here you see what is involved in morality: all reverence of deity, all submission to him, dependence upon him, love and delight in him, thankfulness to him, etc. All righteousness between man and man, fairness, justice, equity, and reasonable dealing, doing to one another as we would have others do to us—all sobriety and self-government, etc. And will any man say that these things are but heathenish virtues? Let us not, therefore, to whom the grace of the gospel is declared, be averse from hearing and practicing those duties and virtues that are founded in our creature state; for you cannot be an intelligent agent, but you are under the obligation to all these. And yet to make you full and complete Christians, I have two things more:

1. Repent of all your sins, failings, and miscarriages.
2. Be to sure to hold the head; make due acknowledgment to the Son of God, whom he has set up to be a prince and a savior, whom God in love and good will has given to us, that we believing in him may be saved. And so now I have brought you through religion, from the beginning of God's creation, from that part of it which is connatural to us, to that which is final in it, God in Christ.

I have but one word more, and that is in the subsequent verse. Looking for the blessed hope and the glorious appearance of the great God and our Savior Jesus Christ (Titus 2:13). These things are consistent with, and connatural, and in order to the blessed hope. Where you may observe:

1. This blessed hope is an argument to all holiness.
2. It is proposed to us in scripture...
3. That we are so to use it. Now, he that has this hope in him, purifies himself, even as he is pure (1 John 3:3). And it is Christ's intent to purify to himself a particular people zealous of good works, which agrees fully with this: that the grace of God which brings salvation, teaches us that, denying ungodliness and worldly lusts, we should live soberly, righteously, and godly in this present world.

From which it is apparent that we are Christians only in external denomination and do not have a principle of divine and heavenly life if we are not reconciled in nature and disposition to the law of righteousness, goodness, and truth.

IV

THAT THOSE WHO ARE TRULY RELIGIOUS WILL BE DELIVERED FROM ALL DANGEROUS ERRORS ABOUT RELIGION

Benjamin Whichcote (1651)

That those who are truly religious will be delivered from all dangerous errors about religion.
—Philippians 3:15–16

I. ...There is that in religion which is necessary and determined; fixed, and immutable; clear, and perspicuous; about which good men, those that are perfect, that is, who are of growth and proficiency, or are sincere and honest, do not differ. The great, momentous, and weighty things of religion are such wherein there is universal consent and agreement. Good men do not differ in things that are (1) perfectly agreeable to the divine nature or (2) in things that are perfectly agreeable to human nature: the great materials of natural light and the great articles of Christian faith.

II. There is also in religion that which is not so necessary and immutable; so clear and plain; in which good men may happen to be otherwise minded, one than another; or otherwise than ought to be. If any be otherwise minded...

Here we may note:

First, the causes and occasions of error and mistake in these things.

Secondly, the preservatives, and security, against the danger of it.

First, the causes and occasions of error and mistake, are these.

1. The creature's fallibility.

2. Accidental prejudices from education; converse: common sense, strong imagination, melancholic temper, weakness of parts, and (which is of greater deformity than all the former) affectation, singularity, worldly interest.

3. The darkness of things themselves: as where there is less of reason to be said for a thing; or where the rule of faith is short. As to that I take the rule to be, so far as God has not determined we are referred to reason, and to the sense of our nature. For God did not make one incapable creature, when he made one that was intelligent. Reason is the first participation from God.

Now, as to certain resolution, where there is neither conviction in the way of reason nor assurance from revealed truth; in this case, our course (after diligent search) will be, stay and expectance, rather than any preemptory conclusion in the point. It is safer to suspend determination, than to be ungroundedly resolved....It is hard to get rid of an error, therefore take heed of admitting one.

In this case, the knowledge of the thing is of less importance, and the ignorance of it is of less danger. An implicit faith in God, without particular knowledge, is safe in this case; and nothing is gained by temerity, rashness, and suddenness of opinion. He that is light of faith, by the same reason, will be light of unbelief; he will as easily disbelieve truth, as believe error. So that he does whatever he does by accident, and chance; he does nothing by a certain rule, so that another may know what he will do next. I do not suppose uncertainty in necessities of faith, or life and practice, but there is darkness in other things.

4. Not improvement of intellectuals is another cause of error. Men are nothing, where they have not thought....A man's temper and improvement make him that which he is. We work out of ourselves. Knowledge is fetched out of us, not brought into us....The understanding is not in habit before it is in act....

There are common principles, which everyone who considers may come to the knowledge of, but before study and thought, the mind is...as white paper, that has nothing written upon it. The principles of reason are as the term of a reasonable soul, and those principles, are principles of action....

It is necessary the mind of man should be enlightened, as to matters of faith, and excited as to other things within its sphere, within the compass of reason....

The materials of knowledge are large and various; many are greatly encumbered with business and have little leisure; and we are not considerable where we have not thought, and examined. None is self-sufficient or born to actual knowledge, but to faculties and possibilities only; we are much more ourselves, where we have taken pains and made inquiry.

5. Another cause of error is want of necessary helps and supplies which others do enjoy, as friends, fitting acquaintance, freedom of converse, liberty of time, and opportunity. It betters men's health and constitutions to live and breathe in a free and open air. Had some but once heard a supposition, or suggestion to the contrary, they had escaped their mistakes. Possibly, if they had once imagined, that other had not so thought, they would have considered, so sensible is modesty and ingenuity.

Men acted by God's spirit, imitate the divine spirit; and come as refiners with fire, to do away man's dross. One who has well considered, consulted, examined is oracular to the ignorant to persons of no vacancy and leisure. These have prepared intellectual dainties, spiritual food for them....

These are the causes and occasions of error and mistake.

Secondly, the preservatives and securities against the danger of error, are,

1. Care of right information. We owe this to ourselves, as of nearer concern than food and raiment. We owe this, as to truth, in respect of its worth and excellency; so to our own souls. Truth is of kin to our souls, and natural to us; error is foreign, and a lie. No truth is so useless and unprofitable, as by any principle we may admit, to be neglected. 'Tis the best apology for a mistake that we did look out after truth.

2. Let the temper of mind be modest and humble. Secure the ornament of a meek and quiet spirit. The meek God will lead in judgment, and he gives grace to the lowly (Ps 25:9). Everyone is encouraged to discover his sense to the candid and ingenuous. This is the learner's temper. It is everyone's duty to give answer to every such inquirer. To be ready always to give answer to every

man that asks a reason of the hope that is in him, with meekness and fear (1 Pet 3:15). But he is not likely to learn, who is not of a teachable spirit.

3. A general intention to entertain and submit to all truth whatsoever, whenever it shall appear; an implicit faith in God, where the sense of any text is not clear. This carries with it a double advantage: it does qualify, prepare, and dispose the mind to be receptive of the highest truth whenever it shall appear; and it is an antidote against the malignity of any error, which, in the meanwhile, anyone may chance to be in. He is in an honest meaning, while in error.

4. Deal ingenuously with truth, and love it for itself, both in respect of the ground upon which you receive it, and of the use you make of it. The certainty and assurance we have that it is truth, we receive from reason and scripture; that it may be out of conscience to God, not out of compliance with humor and lust, nor out of a respect to a party or faction. To compromise, and refer ourselves, is only excusable for a while, as we are yet weak, and in the state of heaven.

Make not truth subservient to base ends. Have religion only to honor God with, to do good to me, to sanctify and save your own soul.

5. See the fatal issue of willfulness or wantonness of opinion, in the shameful miscarriages of those who have given themselves up to dreams and fancies. Of this several histories give an account....We love to hear of dangers, that we may provide against them, and avoid them. As good examples are for our imitation, so the bad are for our admonition and warning. If we are not careful of good security of truth, we give advantage to the devil to put his delusions upon us. We shall be obnoxious to all the cheats and impostors of all counterfeits among men.

Those at Muenster in Germany, much about the time of the Reformation, proved a scandal to the reason of the world, and a reproach to Christianity. So are all those who make religion reprovable by sober reason, or turn the grace of God into wantonness. The Gnostics of old, and the successors in spirit ever since, did this. There is nothing of after-light in God in Christ reconciling, subject to reproof of the former light of God creating.

The uses to be made of this are:

1. Let us live in the sense of our fallibility, being subject to error, liable to mistake. It is safe to know where we are weak—the sense of it will make us lowly, temperate, cautious. Why should not sense of being subject to error make us careful to establish a right throne of judgment in our souls for security against mistakes, as well as sense of weakness makes us watchful against miscarriages in practice? Is a lasting spot...that blemishes the soul's excellency? Is a crooked principle less than a step awry? Especially since the understanding is the leading part of our souls; and all that follows is according to the dictates of mind and understanding, and a good meaning may do harm, if grounded in ignorance and discretion, as occasioning a false zeal, a zeal of God, but not according to knowledge.

2. Although error is nowhere to be countenanced, yet it is not everywhere severely to be challenged. Particular errors and misapprehensions in some things are an incidency to uprightness of heart to honest meaning. Yet the pure in heart have this advantage, from the principles of purity in them, that either their error is not grievous, or they will not long continue it, for they have within them a principle of self-rectification and refinement....

3. Even he that is in a good estate still has work to do: to free his understanding from ignorance and error, to advance knowledge to a just height, then to conform his life and practice to his rule and principle. We have not done our task, nor the work we have to do in the world, till we are well informed in point of judgment concerning right and wrong, true and false, good and evil, till we are suitably refined in spirit, to relish and taste, and reformed in life, to do and practice. When this is done then let a man think of dying, but before he is made ripe for eternity, he is not naturalized in spirit and temper to the employment and society of that heavenly state.

4. The sense of this should make us modest and humble and preserve us from being peremptory and dogmatical; for there is in religion that which is not so necessary and immutable, clear and plain, and in which good men may happen to be otherwise-minded, one than another, or otherwise than ought to be.

III. There is reason to think, that God will bring out of particular mistake, him that is right in the main. God shall reveal even this unto him.

There is otherwise-minded one than another: that where they differ one from another; where one thinks otherwise than others think; perhaps think otherwise than he should, or otherwise than is true. But where men are honest in the main, sincere and upright in the great points of faith, as is before expressed: We are persuaded better things of you, and things that accompany salvation. Where it is thus, God shall reveal.

First, this is a thing likely and credible in respect of something on God's part, and that for three reasons.

1. Because of God's relation to us; his disposition toward us as his creatures and worshipers. God is the father of our spirits, and so it is natural to him to guide our spirits. He teaches man knowledge; the inspiration of the almighty gives understanding. The eyes of all things look up to God for bodily food, mind and understanding look up to God for intellectual communications....God has appointed the material sun to enlighten the world of sense....God intended by himself to enlighten reasonable souls. The spirit of a man is the candle of the Lord. As we are the creatures of God, we are sure of this, and as we are the worshipers of God, we shall be directed and assisted by him.

2. Because God has so declared and promised. The meek will be led in judgment; the meek will he teach his way (Ps 25:9). The disciples of Christ were his special instruments to spread the gospel, by immediate inspiration; the successive generations have it by their writings.

3. Because God begins with us, with intention to go on, if we are not perverse and willful, if we give him not offense, and if a provocation to him does not...put a bar as the murmuring of the Israelites in the wilderness, and their unbelief, obstructed and delayed their entrance into the promised land. It is the account why Moses himself might only see Canaan but might not enter into it. It is said of our Savior, that he could do no miracles there because of their unbelief (Matt 13:58). And that he had many things to say, but they could not hear them then (John 16:12).

Now in the case supposed in the text, God had *begun*, yes he had done greater; they were minded and resolved to press toward the mark, etc. The true effect of God's grace, and the same goodness which moved God to begin, will further engage him. God is not wanting in necessaries, neither as to the beginning, nor as to the progress in goodness, neither to the beginning, nor increase, nor perfecting our faith (Phil 3:13).

It is therefore for these reasons, likely and credible, that God will reveal it to them, if any are otherwise-minded.

Secondly, this is likely and credible, in respect of something on our part. By truth *already* received, we have a double advantage for receiving more:

1. The way to the understanding which was obstructed, is opened; and

2. The mind is brought into a disposition and preparation to receive all divine truth. The mists and fogs of natural ignorance are dispelled; the faculty is initiated to its proper employment; the greatest difficulty is over, which is at the beginning. We are made readily receptive of any truth, being thus sanctified by truth already entertained. We hold the truth virtually implicitly in the preparation of our minds, which we do not actually know when we are thus resolved, ready to receive whatever God shall further or otherwise show, or wherever we may be hereafter informed.

He that is thus only in an error is not in love with any opinion, but upon supposition that it is truth as he is not in danger while he is in a mistake, so whenever he is shown, he presently rectifies his apprehensions, and thanks the discoverer....

Thus in respect of something on our part, it is likely and credible that God will reveal truth unto those who are otherwise-minded.

3. This is likely and credible in respect of something on the part of truth:

1. Because truth is connatural to our souls. The common motions of our minds and truth are not at any odds at all. The mind makes no more resistance to truth than the air does to light—both are thereby beautified and adorned. This is to be understood, *while* the mind retains its primitive temper and con-

121

stitution, and after, when it has recovered it by moral purgation and virtue; but fondness and partiality limit the generousness of heaven-born souls.

2. Because the several truths hang together, they mutually depend on each other. One truth helps on the discovery of another, and each truth is declaratory and convicting of the same error. For instance, if God is a spiritual substance, then his worship chiefly must be mental and intellectual (Ps 93:5). If God is holy, holiness becomes his house, and we must serve him in holiness and righteousness, before him all of our days (Luke 1:75). If he is the first and chief goodness, then he will graciously consider our frame, and remember we are but dust (Ps 103:14). If the spirit of man is the candle of the Lord, the mind and understanding ought to be employed about God (Prov 20:27). If God is the governor of the world, then we are to be of good carriage and behavior in his family, and are not to beat our fellow servants. If God is the first cause, and the last end, then are we to acknowledge him, and finally to refer to him.

If man is made for converse, then we are to do as we would be done by; we are to do righteous things, and to live in love.

If we consist of reasonable souls as well as bodies of earth, then we are to make a sober and moderate use of bodily conveniences, that our minds are not annoyed and disturbed.

Thus it is likely and probably in respect of something on the part of truth, that God will reveal where men are otherwise-minded. If in any thing, if in any other thing, where you hold to the main, to press toward the mark, be right in principles, serious in practice and endeavors, and be otherwise-minded one than another—even this, where you think differently, to him who knows not, or mistakes, God shall reveal.

Here I observe:

1. That *this* is more for the certain guidance of any honest man, than he can in scripture show for infallibility, who abroad usurps the title of the head of the church.

2. That we have warrant enough to think and speak of God, things worthy of him, and tending to our encouragement in good behavior. For I look at this (God shall reveal) as rationally spoken; becomingly in respect of God, charitably in respect of men. There

is no need of the gift of prophecy to declare such a future. It is but the right use of reason, and the true improvement of scripture. I should not doubt to assure men that God will not be wanting to them, while they keep in his ways.

I have given grounds of good persuasion and confidence, that God will reveal, as the apostle here says, but lest I should give any advantage to enthusiasm,[356] the confounder of all reason and religion, I will further insist upon explication, caution, and limitation; to which purpose I shall add four things:

1. ...Thus this of God's revealing supposes we keep within the compass of the case....God's superintendence does neither discharge, nor dispense with our subservience. Faith and repentance on our part are always to be understood in the terms of the new covenant. They put men upon running a desperate hazard, who tell them of absolute promises in this sense, as not inclusive of due qualification on our part, as not supposing our due diligence, careful use of means, consent of our minds....

2. I conceive it antecedent, and necessary to the teaching of God, that we put off pride. Presumption, imagination, and conceitedness wholly indispose men for learning. There are more hopes of a fool, than of such. One that is wise in his own eyes is readier to impose than to receive. Also, who will trouble himself with him? And so he is not like to have anything offered to his consideration. God resists the proud, but gives grace to the humble; the meek he will guide in judgment, and teach his way (Ps 25:9). And not that I have already attained. Why not be wise in your own eyes (Prov 3:7)?

3. This does *not* necessarily import immediate inspiration. God will reveal, one way or other, in the course of his providence; some instrument of God, some lover of truth shall tell him what he is to do, as was the case of the eunuch (Acts 8:35). He shall find it out by some search of scriptures, he shall meet with it comparing places, he shall hear of it in some good company, in the use of ordinary means. As it is true that God feeds us, and clothes us, though he does not send manna from heaven, nor quails, as the Israelites had in the wilderness (Exod 16:12–16); nor does he make coats for us, as he did for Adam and Eve (Gen 3:20–22). So in this case, it is not necessary there should be a voice from heaven, as

there was three times in our Savior's life: at his baptism, transfiguration, and a little before his death. God will teach so far as is necessary to ingenerate piety in us here, and to bring us to safety hereafter.

4. Where knowledge is pursued by practice, there is other expectation than from speculation alone. He that does the will of God shall know of his doctrine (Job 7:17). The Holy Ghost is given to those that obey him. For none can reasonably claim the promise of God or man, who does not come up fully to the terms of him who made such promise (Acts 5:32). Now religion, though it begins at knowledge, proceeds to temper, and ends in practice.

These cautions and limitations to prevent enthusiasm, for nothing is more necessary for the interest of religion than to secure the minds of men against enthusiasm; for through unskillfulness of men, many have been subject to acknowledge more of supernatural assistance in hot, unsettled fancies, and in perplexed melancholy, than in the calm and distinct use of reason.

The inferences I make from here are:

1. The purity of a man's mind, the sincerity of his intention [and] the honesty of his heart is his great security, gives mighty advantage to right understanding [and] orthodox judgment. Of holy things, men of holy hearts and lives speak with great assurance of truth. There is not only the ability of these men's parts (as others have), but there is the naturalness of the subject to their state and temper, especially of the acquaintance they have with it, and the experience they have of it, and God's blessing over and above.

There is a double advantage from the grace of the heart and the goodness of the spirit, for it restores health and soundness after a declination and tendency to discomposure and distemper. It is of a different nature from falsehood and lies, and so has the force of a contrary inclination and bias. In point of misapprehension and failure of judgment, it is a principal light for detecting and discovering; in case of miscarriage in practice, it is sanative and restorative.

2. In ways of uprightness of integrity we may presume God's leading us into all truth. God allows it not to be vainly spoken in his name (God shall reveal unto you). It is congruous and seemly, that the sense of God should walk in all ways of truth. This is in pursuance of the former great work of regeneration and conversion; it is a thing which belongs to them, in respect of their state; it is what God is ready to do for them, at their entreaty. Therefore, depend upon God, seek to him for it, acknowledge him in it, and wholly; lean not to your own understanding. It is true that the blessing of God in every way makes rich, gives issue, makes successful, but remarkably, in this work of illuminating minds and understandings.

3. Give a fair allowance of patience to those who mean well; be ready to show it to them, since there is ground of expectation, that in a little time they will come out of their error. Otherwise persons of good nature, parents, and friends wait and expect while there is any hope. Nothing is desperate in the condition of good men; they will not live and die in any dangerous error. They have a right principle within them, and God's superintendence, conduct, and guidance. The devil is thrown out of his stronghold, where there is holiness of heart; and being dispossessed of his main fort, he will lose all his holds, one after another; all errors and mistakes will be discovered successively. The sun having broken through the thickest cloud, will after that scatter the less, and the day will clear up. There is reason to think God will bring out of particular mistake him that is right in the main; God shall reveal even this unto him (Phil 3:14–16).

V

OUR CONVERSATION
IS IN HEAVEN

Benjamin Whichcote (1651)

*For our conversation is in heaven, from where also we look for
the Savior, the Lord Jesus Christ.*
—Philippians 3:20

...I say universals and generals do not teach anyone; therefore I propose to show the particulars of a heavenly conversation.
Of what matters a heavenly conversation does consist, and I have
chosen to instance six particulars.

First, it requires a just disesteem of the world, a contempt of
it, in comparison and competition.

Secondly, it requires a subduing and a mortifying of fleshly
and inordinate lusts and affections.

Thirdly, it requires patient enduring of evils, which befall us
in our course of life.

Fourthly, it depends upon self-denial, and renouncing of our
own wills, so far as they stand in competition with, or rise up in
opposition against God's will.

Fifthly, it does require sublime thoughts, and noble apprehensions.

Sixthly, it requires purity of mind and sincere intention.

Those eagle-eyed philosophers the Platonists, they were very
sensible, though not acquainted with revelation by scripture, as we
are concerning Adam's apostasy, and how evil broke in, yet these
men were sensible of a decay, that human nature was lapsed, that the
soul of man could not mount up aloft, that deplumed, has lost its
feathers, so that it could not soar aloft;[357] the soul of man grovels

below and does not soar aloft by meditation and contemplation as they imagined it should. They also tell us, that men have become heavy behind, that though they have an inclination in their souls, and a tendency upward, yet they are presently born down by body.[358] Now in this case, those philosophers, though they never had any divine revelation, yet I say in this case, propose for man's recovery, two things.

First, they proposed the study of the mathematics;[359] for in that study, men abstract from matter, for they do only contemplate and speculate upon the ideas, and form of things: thus they propose to take men off from matter, and to subtilize men's parts, and to raise them to more noble and generous apprehensions.

Secondly, they proposed another way, which was more theological and divine, and this they call moral purgation. By it they did understand the freeing the soul of man from all base loves, from all impotent and ungovernable passions: for by affection to these lower things we come to be sunk down, and then we are glued, and tied to them; we are buried, and brought down again from the contemplation of God and heavenly things, and not only so, but our minds are contaminated and defiled by those things.

Thus these noble philosophers proposed, and it is admirable to imagine…where some of these men had some of those notions. For we do imagine that St. John took not any of his forms of words from the Platonists. Now it is marvelous if they, by natural light, should in the use of reason understand the fall and decay of human nature, and speak so excellently for the restoration and recovery of it. Yet we should flatter ourselves, and be sensible of no lameness, who have farther direction. But to speak to those six particulars.

First: Contempt of the world. I mean the vain pomps and glory of the world. I do not mean the world of God's creation, the world in which God has appointed us to live, and to act in, that may be subservient to eternity, but I mean the world in St. John's sense, the wicked world. And in this sense, if any man love the world, the love of the Father is not in him (1 John 2:15). And he tells us what things the world consist of, "the lust of the eyes, and the pride of the life" (1 John 2:16). Now these earthly things cloy and surfeit us; they do not satisfy us, for we soon have enough of them. If a man is hungry, he eats to satisfy nature, and more is a burden. If a man is thirsty, he takes pleasure in drinking, till his thirst is quenched, but if he drinks more, he lays up provision for...many distempers. Sensual delights, through their grossness, do stupify and benumb, for they glutinize and pitch us, they glue us like bird-lime; whereas heavenly joys amplify and enlarge and yet make subtle and spiritualize our faculties. There cannot lodge any generous heaven-born affections in that soul, where the love of the world rules; persons of gross apprehensions are not fit to entertain noble and refined truths. Earthly affections employ themselves in brutish and sensual pleasures. How gross, low, and dull were his apprehensions, who when our Savior represented divine things by a worldly scheme, presently replies, Can a man enter into his mother's womb, and be born a second time (John 3:4)! He whose mind is in heaven, is loose to the world; and in regard of his heart and affection, he is above the world. He is served by it, he does not serve it....This heavenly mindedness depends upon contempt and mean esteem of the things of the world; absolute contempt of the world so far as degenerated and a mean esteem of the world, if it came in competition, etc.

Secondly. It requires and depends upon mortification of the flesh. And pray why do we take so much care of the body, make so much ado for the body, as if we were so much concerned for it, as if our bodies were the more valuable part, or more considerable than the mind? Why are we such slaves to bodily desires? Ask the question; since flesh (as it is) cannot enter into glory, so the apostle says, flesh and blood cannot enter into the kingdom of God (1 Cor 15:50);...flesh and blood as God made Adam in paradise: for Adam in the state of innocence, he needed an advance, a change, that he might be capable of glory, so that it might be said of Adam, as the apostle says of those who shall be alive at the resurrection, They shall be changed (Ps 102:26). Adam, though he had persisted in innocency, should have been changed; for flesh and blood, as he was made at first, could not enter into the kingdom of God. These bodies, as the apostle tells us, are such as God has fitted us with, to converse here. The bodies that here we have, are the bodies that belong to us in the state of humiliation; but it shall be quite another thing, the body that our souls shall be invested with, in the soul's exaltation. It shall be so different from this, that the apostle calls it a spiritual body, which is nonsense to a philosopher, but the word in common construction is well understood (1 Cor 15:44). The apostle uses another word, which signifies they shall quite be changed; the *scheme*, the form, the fashion of these bodies shall be changed. And: The earthly house of this tabernacle shall be dissolved, and we shall have a house, not made with hands eternal in the heavens (2 Cor 5:1). And this I suppose to be an account of what God said to Moses: You can't see my face, and live (Exod 33:20). This is strange, for it is eternal life to know God, and him whom he has sent, and our happiness consists in vision, and if we are not united to God by inflamed affections, we shall never be so happy as we would. But this is spoken in respect to this narrow contracted state; we are not able to bear this now; but in glory we shall see the face of God, that we may live, in glory we shall be ever with the Lord. Or thus, you can't bear so great a light because of the vast disproportion and ineptitude of these gross bodies, why then do we take so great care about them? Why do we dote so much upon them? Now, in a preparation to this state of happiness, we must partake of the virtue and infusion of Christ's death; we must be crucified with Christ, by mortification and dying to sin and to the world (Gal 2:20). Nothing is more distant from the heavenly conversation than to be at the command of the flesh, to be acted, ruled, and governed by it, and to be swallowed up and drowned in its sentiments and pleasures....Now this is a bar, an impediment, to the enjoyment of God; it comes too near the capacity of beasts, of plants and stocks. We are to be discharged of a great deal of that which we call *body*, and then we shall be much more ourselves. Now that we may be capable of entering into heaven, we must be born again by regeneration, and participation of the divine nature—and this superadded to our rational nature. For this we do observe, that there is a descent from above to below, by several degrees, and every higher degree of perfection, as it is preeminent and predominant to that which is below, so it includes the lower degree, and rules over it, and you have four degrees of life.

1. The vegetative life, that is, the life of plants.
2. The sensitive life, and that is the life of beasts, and comprehends and contains the vegetative.
3. The rational life, that is, the life of angels and the spirits and souls of men; now this contains the other two.
4. You have the divine life, which is the life that by regeneration we are born into, and which is the life we shall lead in eternity.

Thirdly. That which a heavenly conversation consists of is patient enduring the evils that befall us in this life. For, suffering of evils may be reckoned upon as that in all probability one time or other will befall all men, even well-doers....It is not desirable for a man to meet with no uncertainties, no difficulties, no losses in the world. It is just as nature is. They that have constant health...whenever they come to be sick, sickness makes a great havoc....It is not always fair weather, but there is an intercourse of storms, which are boisterous and tempestuous. If there are any that have an easy passage through this world, they are those who we commonly call gracious, who are very benevolent, of calm and gentle spirits, and are extremely affable, and courteous, whom none have any suspicion of, as they never stand in any man's way, so that none have occasion to harm them....So St. Paul says: For a just man no one will dare to die, a man that will do right, will do nobody wrong, no man will die for such a one; but for a good man one would venture to die (Rom 6:7)....

The noble philosopher has resolved it into a steady mind, and an intellectual calm, a well-composed mind in outward hurliburlies and confusions, when we can say of a man, his heart is fixed, trusting in the Lord (Ps 112:7). Let the world never be so boisterous, tumultuous, and various, all this affects not a man if he maintains an intellectual calm and a steadiness in his mind. Three things (says the greatest wit that our English nation has bred) make heaven upon earth.

First, for a man to abide in the truth, wherever he is engaged or concerned; for truth will give a good account of itself, but we say of a liar, he had need of a good memory.

Secondly, to dwell in universal love, and hearty good will with all men....

And the third is, to rest satisfied in the issues of providence. Knowing himself to be a creature, a second cause, and under government, and as knowing we have not the government in our hands, we are to be satisfied with what God orders and appoints. That is thus; that which God does, that I do consent to and delight in; that which God permits, I must bear. These three things will make heaven in the world: Always to be in the truth, to dwell in universal love and perfect good will, and to rest in the issues of providence; and if any man has a troublesome life in the world, it is because he fails in these, or some of them....And the scripture admonishes us very much, that we are to make account that troubles and afflictions, one time or other, will befall us, for Through much tribulation we must enter into the kingdom of heaven (Acts 14:22). I confess this is necessary to a state of religion, so a man cannot make it a character; but persons of good conscience in religion may make account that this may befall them. But this they must make account of to abide in the truth, and to refer themselves to what God appoints, or permits in one respect or other. Sickness, losses, disappointments, casualties of this life; God sending of these in one way or other, we shall be tried; for it is to be expected that patience must have exercise here, because there will be no employment for patience hereafter. Now if evils do befall us, then we are to make account that they must produce the peaceable fruits of righteousness; and that they will befall us, we are frequently admonished (Heb 12:11). God does chasten as many as he receives, and we are bastards and not sons, if we have no chastisements (Heb 12:6–8).

Now I do not speak this, as if it were connatural to religion; for a man may decline and avoid a great deal of the troubles of this world, not by the candor of his spirit, but his fair conversation, by his being known to be compassionate and ready to relieve, by having no ill design upon any, but being ready to gratify, and to help, and make an end of all troubles. But, as we must not invite evil (for it is but a matter of temptation and trial to us), so when evil does befall us, we must resolve with patience to bear it. To this purpose, the graces of the divine spirit are given: to calm and quiet, to pacify and compose, and to make us serene and quiet within. In nature...there is still a principle of recovery to calmness and clearness when the heavens are masked with clouds. In the intellectual world of souls and spirits, there is also a principle of restoration and recovery—the reason of our own minds, encouraged by divine assistance, and this must recover us. The pure in heart return to due temper, after discomposure, just as water works all filth to the bottom, and recovers itself to its purity, because it has a principle of purifying itself. So the reason of the mind should be the principle of restoration and recovery, if at any time we are disturbed, discomposed, put into a passion; and *this* should be to us, as the principles that are in nature, for restoration and recovery. For if it were not for this principle, how should we live here? Storms, tempests, mists, and fogs would always prevail. Now in the intellectual world, the reason of our minds encouraged by divine assistance, and under the direction of God, this is the principle of restoration and recovery; and we shall be lost, if we do not make use thereof.

Fourthly, the fourth material of heavenly conversation is resigning our wills to the will of God. For this is most certain, we cannot be citizens of heaven if we are in contention with the Lord of heaven and we are in contention with the Lord of heaven whenever we maintain insubordinate wills; for two contrary wills create disturbance. For this is known in nature: it is not good multiplying persons in government; two contrary wills raise great disturbance. Now we are in contest with God himself whenever we do maintain insubordinate wills; and there will be an unequal contest between man's fallible will and God's irresistible, uncontrollable will. In this competition, God's will carries the cause against man's will because it cannot prevail; and if we are broken of our self-will we fall into discontent. It is necessary that our wills be resigned up, surrendered, and subordinated to God's will. While Adam's will was in a conformity to God, and subject to his will, the approaches of God were born with great satisfaction and content; but the case was quite otherwise, after he had followed his own will in opposition to God's and varied from the divine appointments; then he fears and runs away, and hides himself. Can anything be quiet or enjoy itself while it is in an unnatural, violent state? Can there be peace while the inferior will contradicts the superior, while irregular will is not subject to the infallible, while the arbitrary lusts of sinning contest with the unchangeable rules of righteousness? And here a man may ask Jezebel's question, what peace while such principles of iniquity, of exorbitancy? What peace, while men are lawless and take upon them to do what they wish? If we acknowledge that there is a God, it is implied that we ought to be subject to him....It cannot be that we should have our wills, unless our wills are subject to God's will, for it is practical atheism for any creature to maintain self-will, for he that maintains self-will, that is not subject to reason, he practically denies that there is a God. It cannot be that we should have our wills, unless our will is subject to God's will.

Our blessed Savior, by his life and practice, while he was on earth, restored this notion to the world, that finite and fallible should be regulated by infinite and infallible; for this is the law, upon which all order depends and stands, that will finite and fallible be determined by will infinite and infallible. There is nothing of God with us, nothing of heaven, nothing of happiness; yes, no peace, no quiet, no order, no composure, as to God, if it is not entire self-resignation. For can we contest with the Almighty? Can we resist a will to which all things are subject? If we would have a quiet settled being in the world, it is necessary our wills be changed to the will of God, our wills submitted to the divine will. We fall off from God by pursuing our own wills in opposition to God's will. Our Savior declared the truth of a creature-state. Now the truth of a creature-state is this: that finite and fallible be regulated by infinite and infallible; we fell off from God and threw ourselves out of paradise by pursuing our own wills. Thus we must gain the heavenly paradise by following the head of the recovery, in all ways of submission, self-surrender, self-denial, and entire obedience to God, in opposition to the head of apostasy, whose sin was an usurpation on God.

The head of apostasy and the head of recovery are the two opposites that are in the world; and they went contrary ways one to the other. The first Adam was infamous for disloyalty in setting up his own will, and adhering to his own sense, in a contradiction to the will of God, in violation of God's prohibition. Now the second Adam was as eminent for obedience, and conformity to the uncreated will. For survey the whole life of our blessed Savior, from his nativity to his death—it was a line of subjection, no desire of anything out of the way of God's will and pleasure (Heb 10:7). For it is said of him, that he put himself into the form of a servant (Phil

2:7). What is a servant? A servant as a servant has no will of his own; but he must be subject to another's will. And then the philosopher tells us, a servant is an animated or a rational instrument.[360] Now an instrument is only assumed and determined by the agent. A servant is but in the place of an instrumental cause, and cannot choose, and determine himself; this is the privilege of the principal agent. The virtue of an instrument lies in the use of it.

Now in respect of God, our Savior was an instrument. So our Savior, expressing his natural sense, desires to have the cup pass away from him, but then he does subjoin, not my will but yours be done (Luke 22:42).

Submission to God's will is our Christianity; it is Christ formed in us, to this effect and purpose, by entire self-surrender and resignation, and ceasing to do our own wills we are said in this respect to be planted into the likeness of his death, unless self-will be subdued in us, we are perfect opposites to heaven; for believe it, heaven is a place of the highest perfect observance of God, and full compliance with his will, a place where God only rules; it is God all in all (Rom 6:5). We are not in heaven by self-will, but by self-denial. It is a place of disobedience and confusion, where neither reason nor law takes place but where lust takes place, and that is this wicked world; but heaven is an absolute monarchy, a place where God only rules.

This is the reason why here below, we interfere, contradict, exasperate one another, because we are not all united in the same end. Observe these things, if you will return to the truth of a creature-state, if you will write after the copy of the restorer and recoverer of human nature: (1) To do nothing in contradistinction from God, nothing at all; for in this sense, God must be all in all. (2) Nor in contradiction to God, not at all; for how should dry stubble be able to stand before a consuming fire? Who will venture to rise up in opposition to almighty power? (3) To do nothing in an independence upon God, by arbitrariness, and self-will. (4) We are in this said not to own either his being, or power, for if we do, we are intoxicated, we live in a lie.

Fifthly, heavenly conversation depends upon sublime cogitations and raised apprehensions of God, and the things of another life—worthy thoughts and apprehensions of God.

VI

Aphorisms

Benjamin Whichcote (1651)

Enmity with Righteousness, is Enmity with God.

Those who are united by Religion, should be united by Charity.

He that lives out of Love, is ever contriving Offense, or Defense.

God has set up Two Lights, to enlighten us in our way: The light of Reason, which is the Light of his Creation; and the Light of Scripture, Which is after-Revelation from him. Let us make use of these two Lights, and Suffer neither to be put out.

The Good nature of a Heathen is more Godlike than the furious Zeal of a Christian.

The Proud man has no God: The Unpeaceful man has no Neighbor: The Distrustful man has no Friend: The Discontented man has not himself.

We are made one for another,
and each is to be a Supply to his
Neighbor.

Religion does not destroy Nature
but is built upon it.[361]

Natural Desires are within
bounds, but unnatural Lust is infinite.

In the First man, God married
Material and Intellectual Nature: In
the Second man, the Divine, and
Human Nature.

Power is not a Terror when in
Reconciliation, or acting in a way of
Righteousness.[362]

VII

THE LIGHT OF REASON IS
CALM AND PEACEABLE

Nathaniel Culverwell (1657)

The light of reason is "a calm and friendly light"; it is a candle, not a comet—a quiet and peaceable light. And though this "candle of the Lord" may be too hot for some, yet the lamp is maintained only with soft and peaceable oil. There is no jarring in pure intellectuals; if men were tuned and regulated by reason more, there would be more concord and harmony in the world. As man himself is a sociable creature, so his reason also is a sociable light. This candle would shine more clearly and equally, if the winds of passion were not injurious to it. It were a commendable piece of stoicism, if men could always hush and still those waves that dash and beat against reason. If they could scatter all those clouds that soil and discolor the face and brightness of it, would there be such fractions and commotions in the state, such schisms and ruptures in the church, such hot and fiery prosecutions of some trifling opinions? If the soft and sober voice of reason were more attended to, reason would make some differences kiss and be friends; it would sheath up many a sword, it would quench many a flame, it would bind up many a wound. This "candle of the Lord" would scatter many a dark suspicion, many a sullen jealousy. Men may fall out in the dark sometimes, they cannot tell for what. If the "candle of the Lord" were only among them, they would criticize one another for nothing then but their former breaches. "Knowledge establishes the soul," it calms and composes it; whereas passion, as the grand Stoic Zeno paints it, is "an abounding and over-boiling impetus, a preternatural agitation of soul"; "a commotion of the mind opposed to Right Reason, and contrary to nature," as the orator styles it.[363] The soul is tossed with passion, but it anchors upon reason.

This gentleness and quietness of reason does never commend itself more than in its agreeing and complying with faith, in not opposing those high and transcendent mysteries that are above its own reach and capacity. No, it had always so much humility and modesty waiting and attending upon it that it would always submit and subordinate itself to all such divine revelations as were above its own sphere, though it could not grasp them, though it could not pierce into them, it would bow its head, and adore them. One light does not oppose another—"the lights of faith and reason" may both shine both together, though with far different brightness; "the candle of the Lord" is not impatient of a superior light, it would both "bear an equal and a superior."

The light of the sun, that indeed is "monarchical light," a supreme and sovereign light, that with its golden scepter rules all created sparkles and makes them subject and obedient to the Lord and rule of all light. Created intellectuals depend upon the brightness of God's beams, and are subordinate to them. Angelical starlight is but "an aristocratic light"; it borrows and derives its glory from a more vast and majestic light. As they differ from one another in glory, so all of them infinitely differ from the sun in glory. Yet it is far above the "democratic light," that light which appears to the sons of men. It is above their lamps and torches, poor and contemptible lights, if left to themselves, for do only imagine such a thing as this, that this external and corporeal world should be adjudged never to see the sun or a star again. If God should shut all the windows of heaven and spread out nothing but clouds and curtains, and allow it nothing but the light of a candle, how would the world look like a Cyclops with its eye put out? It is now only an obscure prison, with a few grates to look out at; but what would it be then but a nethermost dungeon, a capacious grave? Yet this were a more grateful shade, a pleasanter and more comely darkness, than for a soul to be condemned to the solitary light of its own lamp, so as not to have any supernatural irradiations from its God. Reason does not refuse any auxiliary beams—it joys in the company of its fellow-lamp, it delights in the presence of an intellectual sun, which will so far favor it, as that it will advance it and nourish it and educate it. It will increase it and inflame it and will by no means put it out. A candle neither can nor will put out the sun, and an intellectual sun can but will not put out the lamp. The light of reason does no more prejudice the light of faith, than the light of a candle does extinguish the light of a star.

The same eye of a soul may look sometimes upon a lamp, and sometimes upon a star; one while upon a first principle, another while upon a revealed truth, as hereafter it shall always look upon the sun, and see God face to face. Grace does not come to pluck up nature as a weed, to root out the essences of men, but it comes to graft spirituals upon morals, that so by their mutual supplies and intercourse they may produce most noble and generous fruit. Can you tell me why the shell and the kernel may not dwell together? Why the bodies of nature may not be quickened by the soul of grace? Did you never observe an eye using a prospective-glass for the discovering and amplifying and approximating of some remote and yet desirable object? And did you perceive any opposition between the eye and the glass? Was there not rather a loving correspondence and communion between them? Why should there be any greater strife between faith and reason, seeing they are brothers? Do they not both spring from the same father of lights; and can the fountain of love and unity send forth any irreconcilable streams? Do you think that God ever intended to divide a rational being, to tear and rend a soul in pieces, to scatter principles of discord and confusion in it? If God is pleased to open some other passage in the soul and to give it another eye, does that prejudice the former?

Man, you know, is ordained to a choicer end, to a nobler happiness, than for the present he can attain, and therefore he cannot expect that God should now communicate himself in such bright and open discoveries, in such glorious manifestations of himself, as he means to give hereafter. But he must be content for the present to look upon those infinite treasures of reserved love in a darker and more shadowy way of faith, and not of vision. Nature and reason are not sufficiently proportioned to such blessed objects, for there are such weights of glory in them as do "weigh down the human mind"; there are such depths...such oceans of all perfections in a Deity, as do infinitely exceed all intellectual capacity but its own. The most that man's reason can do is to fill the understanding to the brim, but faith throws the soul into the ocean, and lets it roll and bathe itself in the vastness and fullness of a Deity. Could the sons of men have extracted all the spirits of reason, and made them meet and jump in one head? No. Should angels and men have united and concentrated all their reason, yet they would never have been able to spy out such profound and mysterious excellencies as faith beholds in one twinkling of her eye. Evangelical beauties shine through a veil that is upon their face; you may see the precious objects of faith, like so many pearls and diamonds, sparkling and glittering in the dark. Revealed truths shine with their own beams; they do not borrow their primitive and original luster from this "candle of the Lord," but from the purer light, with which God has clothed and dressed them as with a garment. God crowns his own revelations with his own beams. "The candle of the Lord" does not discover them; it does not oppose them; it cannot eclipse them. They are no sparks of reason's striking, but they are flaming darts of heaven's shooting, that both open and enamor the soul. They are stars of heaven's lighting; men behold them at a great distance twinkling in the dark. Whatsoever comes in God's name does "either find or make a way."

Whatever God reveals in his word is "above the ordinary providence of the world," is not in the road of nature; and, therefore, for the welcoming and entertaining of it, as a noble author of our own does very well observe, "a kind of supernatural and wonderful sense is developed."[364] There is an opening of a new window in the soul, an intellectual eye looks out at the window, and is much pleased and affected with the orientation of that light that comes springing and rushing in upon it. As there is a "law written," so there is a "gospel written" too; the one is written by the pen of nature, the other by the finger of the Spirit—for "grace begins where nature ends"; and this second edition, set out by grace, is "enlarged and improved," yet so as it does not at all contradict the first edition that was set out by nature. For this is the voice of nature itself, that whatever God reveals, must be true, and this common principle is the bottom and foundation of all faith to build upon.

The soul desires no greater satisfaction than that "God himself has spoken"; for if God himself says it, who can question it, who dares contradict it? Reason will not, reason cannot, for it most immovably acknowledges a Deity, and the unquestionable truth of a Deity. In all believing there is an assent, a yielding to him that speaks by virtue of his own authority, though he does not prove it, though he does not evince it. Now men themselves look upon it as a contempt and injury not to have their words taken, and reason itself dictates this much, that we are to believe such a one whom we have no reason to distrust, for without some faith there would be no commerce nor trafficking in the world—there is no trading without some trusting. A general and total incredulity would threaten present and fatal dissolution to human society. Matters of fact are as certain in being and reality as demonstrations, yet in appearance most of them can never be proved or evinced any other way than by mere testimony. Much historical knowledge, many a truth has been lost and buried in unbelief, whereas many a falsity, in the meantime, has proved more fortunate and triumphant, and has passed currently through the world under the specious disguise of probability. Yet because no created being is infallible because the sons of men are so easily deceived themselves and are so apt and likely to deceive and impose upon others, it will be very lawful to move slowly and timorously, warily and vigilantly, in our assents to them, for a sudden and precocious faith here is neither commendable nor durable. But God being truth itself—eternal, immutable truth, his word being "the vehicle of truth," and all revelations flowing from him shining with the prints and signatures of certainty, his naked word is a demonstration. He that will not believe a God is worse than a devil, is the blackest infidel that ever existed.

This sin is so unnatural that none but an atheist can be guilty of it, for he that acknowledges a Deity and knows what he acknowledges, surely will not offer to make his God a liar. That which might otherwise seem to some to be against reason, yet if it bring the seal of God in its forehead, by this you may know that it is not against reason. Abraham's slaying of his son may seem a most horrid and unnatural act against the "law written," against the "candle of the Lord," yet being commanded and authorized by God himself, the candle dares not oppose the sun. That pattern of faith, the father of the faithful, does not dispute and make syllogisms against it. He does not plead that it is against common notions, that it is against demonstrations, for he had said false if he had said so; but he dutifully obeys the God of nature, that high and supreme Lawgiver, who by this call and voice of his did plainly and audibly proclaim that for Abraham to kill his son in these circumstances was not against the law of nature (Gen 22:1–14).

So that all the stress and difficulty will be to know whether God reveals such a thing or not, for here reason [corrupt reason I mean] is wont to slip and evade, and when it cannot frame a conceit adequate to some transcendent and superlative mysteries, it would then cloud them and eclipse them, that it may quench and avoid the dazzling brightness of them. It would fain make them stoop and condescend to its own capacity, and therefore it puts some inferior notion upon them. When it cannot grasp what God says, it then presently questions whether God says so or not, whether that is the mind of his word.

Hence many may err very deeply and dangerously, who yet will acknowledge the scriptures; they will own and honor them as the word of God, for they are not yet arrived to that full perfection of error, as those lumps and dunghills of all sects [I mean that young and upstart generation of gross antiscripturists, that have a powderplot against the gospel, that would very compendiously behead all Christian religion at one blow, a device which old and ordinary heretics were never acquainted withal].³⁶⁵ Though they have not come to such a height as this, yet, either by their flat and frigid explaining, they endeavor to dispirit and weaken the word of God. Or else, in a more violent and injurious manner, they do even ravish it, and deflower the virginity of it, or else, in a more subtle and serpentine manner, they seek to bend the rule, and expound it to their purposes and advantages: The letter of the word, the "sheath of the word," that does not wound them, that does not strike them; and as for the edge, they think they can draw that as they please, they can blunt it as they wish, they can order it as they will.

But the law of sound reason and nature opposes such unworthy dealings as these are, for men look upon it very heinously to have their words misinterpreted, to have violence done to their meaning. Can you think that the Majesty of heaven will allow or endure that a creature should study or busy itself in perverting his words, in corrupting his meaning, in blending it and mixing it with the crude imaginations of its own brain?

That Spirit which breathed out the word at first, and which convinces and satisfies the soul that it is the word of God,…is the interpreter of it, and he is the commentator upon it. The text is his and the gloss is his, and whoever shall call this a private spirit must be a bold blasphemer.…But they who know what the Spirit of God is will easily grant that the Spirit of God unsheathes his own sword, that he polishes evangelical pearls, that he anoints and consecrates the eye of the soul for the welcoming and entertaining of such precious objects. It is true indeed that some explications are so impertinent and distorted as that a profane and carnal eye may presently discern that there was either some violence or deceit used in them, as who cannot tell when any author is extremely vexed and wronged? But if there is such obscurity as may give just occasion of doubting and diffidence, who then can be fitter to clear and unfold it than the author himself? No, who can explain his mind certainly but he himself?…When God scatters any twilight, any darkness there, is it not by a more plentiful shedding abroad of his own beams? Such a knot as the created understanding cannot untie the edge of, the Spirit presently cuts asunder. Nor yet is Providence lacking in external means which, by the goodness and power of God, were annexed as "seals of the world"—miracles I mean—which are, upon this account, very suitably and proportionately subservient to faith, through being above natural power, as revealed truths are above natural understanding. The one is above the hand of nature as the other is above the head of nature. But miracles, though they are very potent, yet they are not always prevalent, for there were many spectators of Christ's miracles, which yet, like so many pharaohs, were hardened by them, and some of them that beheld them were no more moved by them than some of them who only hear of them, and will not at all attend to them. Thus only the seal of the Spirit can make a firm impression upon the soul, who writes his own word upon the soul with a conquering triumphant sunbeam, that is impatient either of cloud or shadow. Be open, therefore, you everlasting doors, and stand wide open, you intellectual gates, that the Spirit of grace and glory, with the goodly train of his revealed truths, may enter in!

There is foundation for all this in a principle of nature, for we must still put you in mind of the concord that is between faith and reason. Now this is the voice of reason that God can, and that none but God can, assure you of his own mind, for if he should reveal his mind by a creature, there will still be some tremblings and waverings in the soul, unless he satisfies a soul that such a creature communicates his mind truly and really as it is, so that ultimately the certainty is resolved into the voice of God and not into the courtesy of a creature. This Holy Spirit of God creates in the soul a grave answerable to these transcendent objects; you cannot but know the name of it—it is called faith, "a supernatural form of faith," as Mirandola the Younger styles it, which closes and complies with every word that drops from the voice or pen of a Deity, and which facilitates the soul to assent to revealed truths, so as that, with a heavenly inclination, with a delightful propensity, it moves to them as to a center.[366]

Reason cannot more delight in a common notion or a demonstration, than faith does in revealed truth. As the unity of a Godhead is demonstrable and clear to the eye of reason, so the trinity of persons, that is, three glorious revelations in one God, is as certain to an eye of faith. It is as certain to this eye of faith that Christ is truly God, as it was visible to an eye, both of sense and reason, that he is truly man. Faith spies out the resurrection of the body, as reason sees the immortality of the soul. I know that there are some authors of great worth and learning, that endeavor to maintain this opinion, that revealed truths, though they could not be found by reason, yet when they are once revealed, reason can then evince them and demonstrate them. But I much rather incline to the determinations of Aquinas, and multitudes of others that are of the same judgment, that human reason, when it has stretched itself to the uttermost, is not at all proportioned to them but, at the best, can give only some faint illustrations...of them.[367] They were never against reason; they will always be above reason. It will be employment enough, and it will be a noble employment too, for reason to redeem and vindicate them from those thorns and difficulties with which some subtle ones have vexed them and encompassed them. It will be honor enough for reason to show that faith does not oppose reason, and this it may show for else, "those that are within" the enclosure of the church will never rest satisfied, nor "those that are without," Pagans, Muslims, Jews, ever be convinced.

God, indeed, may work upon them by immediate revelation, but man can only prevail upon them by reason; yet it is not to be expected, nor is it required, that every weak and newborn Christian that gives real assent and cordial entertainment to these mysterious truths, should be able to deliver them from those seeming contradictions which some cunning adversaries may cast upon them. There are some things demonstrable which to many seem impossible, so how much more easily may there be some matters of faith which everyone cannot free from all difficulties? It is sufficient therefore for such that they so far understand them, as to be sure that they are not against reason, and that mainly because they are sure God has revealed them. And others that are of more advanced and elevated intellectuals may give such explications of them as may disentangle them from all repugnancy, though they cannot display them in their full glory.

Nor must the multitude or strength and wit of opposers frighten men out of their faith and religion. Though the major part of the world do disesteem and look upon them as mere contradictions, yet this, being the censure of most unequal and incompetent judges, is not at all prejudicial to their worth and excellency; for to most of the world they were never revealed so much as in an external manner, and to all others that refuse and reject them, they were never powerfully revealed by the irradiations of the Holy Ghost. So that one affirmative here is to be preferred before a whole heap of negatives—the judgment of one wise, enlightened, spiritualized Christian is more to be attended to than the votes and suffrages of a thousand gainsayers, because this is undeniable, that God may give to one that eye, that light, that discerning power, which he denies to many others. It is, therefore, a piece of excessive vanity and arrogance in Socinus, to limit and measure all reason by his own.[368]

Nor does this put any uncertainty in reason, but only diversity in the improving of it. One lamp differs from another in glory. And withal it lays down a higher and nobler principle than reason, for in things merely natural, every rational being is there a com-

petent judge in those things that are within the sphere and compass of reason, the reason of all men agrees and conspires, so as
that which implies an express and palpable contradiction cannot
be owned by any. But in things above nature and reason, a paucity
here is a better argument than a plurality, because Providence
opens his cabinets only for his jewels. God shows these mysterious
secrets only to a few friends—his Spirit whispers to a few, shines
upon a few, so that if any tell us that evangelical mysteries imply a
contradiction because they cannot apprehend them, it is no more
than for a blind man confidently to determine that it involves a
contradiction to say there is a sun, because he cannot see it.

Why should you not as well think that a greater part of the
world lies in error as that it lies in wickedness? Is it not defective
in the choicest intellectuals, as well as in the noblest practiced
men?

Or can any persuade himself that a most eminent and refined
part of a mankind, and [that which is very considerable] a virgin
company which kept itself untouched from the pollutions of
Antichrist, upon mature deliberation, for long continuance, upon
many debates, examinations, discussions, constant prayers to God
for the discovery of his mind, should all this while embrace mere
contradictions for the highest points of their religion? Or can any
conceive that these evangelical mysteries were invented and contrived and maintained by men? Could the head of a creature
invent them? Could the arm of a creature uphold them? Have they
not a divine superscription upon them? Have they not a heavenly
original? Or can you imagine that Providence would have so
blessed and prospered a contradiction, as always to pluck it out of
the paws of devouring adversaries? When the whole Christian
world was ready to be swallowed up with Arianism, dared any to
say that God then prepared an ark only for the preserving of a contradiction? Providence does not countenance contradictions so as
to let them ride in triumph over truth.

The most that any opposer can say, if he will speak truth, is
no more than this, that they seem to him to imply a contradiction;
which may very easily be so, if he wants a higher principle of faith,
suitable and answerable to these matters of faith. Both of them, the
principle and object, I mean, being supernatural, neither of them

contranatural; for there is a double modesty in reason very remarkable—as it does not "assert many things," so it does not "deny many things"; as it takes very few things for certain, so it concludes very few for impossible.

No, reason, though she will not put out her eye, for that is unnatural, yet she will close her eye sometimes that faith may aim the better, and that is commendable. And faith makes reason abundant compensation for this, for as a learned author of our own, and a great patron both of faith and reason, does notably express it, "Faith is a supply of reason in things intelligible, as the imagination is of light in things visible." The imagination, with her witty and laborious pencil, draws and represents the shapes, proportions, and distances of persons and places, taking them only by the help of some imperfect description, and it is reluctant to stay here till it is better satisfied with the very sight of the things themselves. Thus faith takes things upon a heavenly representation and description—on a word, upon a promise. It sees a heavenly Canaan in the map, before an intellectual eye can look upon it in a way of clear and open vision; for men are not here capable of a present heaven, and happiness of a complete and beatifical vision, and therefore they are not capable of such mysteries in their full splendor and brightness; for they, if thus unfolded, would make it (a present heaven). However, they now flourish only in the lattices, as Christ himself, the Head of these mysteries; they do "tabernacle among us," they put a veil upon their face, out of pure favor and indulgence to an intellectual eye, lest it should be too much overcome with their glory. The veils of the law were veils of obscurity, but the veils of the gospel are only to allay the brightness of it. It is honor enough for a Christian if he can but touch the hem of evangelical mysteries, for he will never see a full commentary upon the gospel till he can behold the naked face of God.

Yet the knowledge which he has of him here, "an imperfect knowledge of things most illustrious," is most pleasant and delicious. It is better to know a little of God and Christ than to see all the creatures in their full beauty and perfection. The gleaning of spirituals is better than the vintage of naturals and morals. The least spangle of spiritual happiness is better than a globe of temporal. This sets a gloss and luster upon the Christian religion, and highly commends the purity and perfection of it above all other whatsoever, in that it has "the deep things of God."

...The very principles of Christian religion are attractive and magnetic, they enamor and command, they overpower the understanding, and make it glad to look upon such mysterious truths as are reflected in a glass, because it is unable to behold them "face to face" (1 Cor 13:12).

This speaks the great preeminence of Mount Zion above Mount Sinai. In the law you have the "candle of the Lord" shining; in the gospel you have "the dayspring from on high," the sun arising (Luke 1:78). Nature and reason triumph in the law, grace and faith flower out in the gospel.

By virtue of this wise and free dispensation, weak ones chiefly receive the gospel, for they are as well able to believe as any others; no, they are more apt to believe than others. If it had gone only by the advancement of intellectuals, by the heightenings and clarifyings of reason, who then would have been saved but the grandees of the world? The scribes, the Pharisees, the philosophers, the disputers? But God has framed a way that confounds those heads of the world, and drops happiness into the mouths of babes. There are some understandings that neither spin nor toil, and yet Solomon in all his wisdom and glory was not clothed like one of these. For this way of faith is a more brief and compendious way: the way through reason is long, through faith short. Very few understandings, much less all, can demonstrate all that is demonstrable; but if men have a power of believing, they may presently assent to all that is true and certain. That which reason would have been sweating for, this many a year, faith sups up the quintessence of in a moment. All men in the world have not equal abilities, opportunities, advantages of improving their reason, even in things natural and moral, so that reason itself tells us, that these are in some measure necessitated to believe others. How many are there that cannot measure the just magnitude of a star, yet if they will believe an astronomer they may know it presently, and if they are sure that this mathematician has skill enough and will speak nothing but truth, they cannot then have the least shadow of reason to disbelieve him?

It is thus in spirituals. Such is the weakness of human understanding in the present state, as that it is necessitated to believing here; yet such is its happiness, that it has one to instruct it who can neither deceive nor be deceived. God has chosen this way of faith that he may stain the pride and glory of man, that he may pose his intellectuals, that God may maintain in man great apprehensions of himself, of his own incomprehensibleness, of his own truth, of his own revelations, as that he may keep a creature in a posture of dependency so as to give up his understanding, so as to be disposed and regulated by him. And if the cherubim are ambitious of stooping, if angelical understanding does so earnestly stoop down and look into it, I think then the sons of men might fall down at the beautiful feet of evangelical mysteries, with that humble acknowledgment: Of this mystery I am unworthy to loose the shoelace. Only let my faith triumph here for it shall not triumph hereafter; let it shine in time, for it must vanish in eternity.

You see then that reason is no enemy to faith, for all that has been said of faith has been fetched out of reason. You see there are mutual embraces between the law and the gospel. Nature and grace may meet together, reason and faith have kissed each other.

VIII

THE EXCELLENCY AND NOBLENESS OF TRUE RELIGION, CHAPTER 2

John Smith (1660)

1. ...A good man that is actuated by religion lives above the world and all mundane delights and excellencies. The soul is a more vigorous and puissant thing when it is once restored to the possession of its own being....It will break forth with the greatest vehemence, and ascend upward toward immortality. And when it converses more intimately with religion, it can scarce look back upon its own converses (though in a lawful way) with earthly things without being touched with a holy shamefacedness and a modest blushing, and, as Porphyry speaks of Plotinus...it seems to be ashamed that it should be in the body.[369]

It is only true religion that teaches and enables men to die to this world and to all earthly things, and to rise above that vaporous sphere of sensual and earthly pleasures, which darken the mind and hinder it from enjoying the brightness of divine light; the proper notion of religion is still upward to its first original. Whereas, on the contrary, the souls of wicked men,...as Plato somewhere speaks, being moistened with the exudations of their sensual parts, become heavy and sink down into earthly things, and couch as near as may be to the center.[370] Wicked men bury their souls in their bodies; all their projects and designs are bounded within the compass of this earth, which they tread upon. The fleshly mind never minds anything but flesh, and never rises above the outward matter, but always creeps up and down like shadows upon the surface of the earth; and if it begins at any time to make any faint essays upward, it presently finds itself laden with a weight of sensuality which draws it down again....

2. A good man, one that is actuated by religion, lives in converse with his own reason; he lives at the height of his own being....He knows how to converse with himself and to truly love and value himself. He measures himself not, like the Epicure, by his inferior and earthly part, but by an immortal essence and that of him which is from above; and so does...climb up to the height of that immortal principle which is within him. The Stoics thought no man a fit auditor of their ethics till he were dispossessed of that opinion, that man was nothing but a weaving together of the soul and body, as professing to teach men how to live only according to *logos*, as they speak. Perhaps their divinity was in some things too rigid; but I am sure a good man acts in the best of this their doctrine in the best sense, and knows better how to reverence himself, without any self-flattery or admiration, than ever any Stoic did. He principally looks upon himself as being what he is rather by his soul than by his body; he values himself by his soul, that being which hath the greatest affinity with God, and so does not seek himself in the fading vanities of this life, nor in those poor and low delights of his senses, as wicked men do....And when the soul thus retires into itself and views its own worth and excellency, it presently finds a chaste and virgin love stirred up within itself toward itself, and is from within the more excited and obliged,...as Simplicius speaks, to mind the preserving of its own dignity and glory.[371]

To conclude this particular, a good man endeavors to walk by eternal and unchangeable rules of reason. Reason in a good man fits in the throne and governs all the powers of his soul in a sweet harmony and agreement with itself, whereas wicked men live only a life of opinion, being led up and down by the foolish fires of their own sensual apprehensions. In wicked men there is a democracy of wild lusts and passions, which violently hurry the soul up and down with restless motions.

All sin and wickedness is...a sedition stirred up in the soul by the sensitive powers against reason. It was one of the great evils that Solomon saw under the sun, servants on horseback, and princes going as servants upon the ground. We may find the moral of it in all wicked men, whose souls are only as servants to wait upon their senses (Eccl 10:7). In all such men the whole course of nature is turned upside down, and the cardinal points of motion in this little world are changed to contrary positions. But the motions of a good man are methodical, regular, and concentrical to reason. It's a fond imagination that religion should extinguish reason, when religion makes it more illustrious and rigorous; and they that live most in the exercise of religion, shall find their reason most enlarged.

I might add that reason in relation to the capacitating of man for converse with God was thought by some to be the formal difference of man. Plutarch, after a long debate whether brutes had not reason in them as well as man, concludes it negatively upon this ground, because they had no knowledge and sense of the deity....In Cicero's account this capableness of religion seemed to be nothing different from rationality, and therefore he doubts not to give this for the most proper characterism of reason, that it is the church of God and man.[372] And so with them (not to name others of the same apprehensions) a rational animal and an animal capable of religion seemed to be of the like importance; reason, as enabling and fitting man to converse with God by knowing him and loving him, being a character most unquestionably differencing man from brute creatures.

3. A good man, one that is informed by true religion, lives above himself, and is raised to an intimate converse with the Divinity. He moves in a larger sphere than his own being, and cannot be content to enjoy himself, except he may enjoy God too, and himself in God....

IX

THE EXCELLENCY AND NOBLENESS OF TRUE RELIGION, CHAPTER 8

John Smith (1660)

...God made the universe and all the creatures contained within it as so many prisms in which he might reflect his own glory. He has copied forth himself in the creation, and in this outward world we may read the lovely characters of the divine goodness, power, and wisdom. In some creatures there are darker representations of God, there are the prints and footsteps of God, but in others there are clearer and fuller representations of the Divinity, the face and the image of God....But how to find God here and feelingly to converse with him, and being affected with the sense of the divine glory shining out upon the creation, how to pass out of the sensible world into the intellectual, is not so effectually taught by that philosophy which professed it most, as by true religion. That which knits and unites God and the soul together can best teach it how to ascend and descend upon those golden links that unite, as it were, the world to God. That divine wisdom that contrived and beautified this glorious structure can best explain her own art and carry up the soul back again in these reflected beams to him who is the fountain of them. Though good men, all of them, are not acquainted with all those philosophical notions touching the relation between created and the uncreated being, yet may they easily find every creature pointing out to that Being whose image and superscription it bears and climb up from those darker resemblances of the divine wisdom and goodness shining out in different degrees upon several creatures...as the ancients speak, till they sweetly rest in the bosom of the Divinity. And while they are thus conversing with this lower world, and are viewing the invisible things of God in the things that are made, in this visible and outward creation, they find God many times secretly flowing into their souls, and leading them silently out of the court of the temple into the Holy Place. But it is otherwise with wicked men—they dwell perpetually upon the dark side of the creatures, and converse with these things only in a gross, sensual, earthly, and unspiritual manner; they are so encompassed with the thick and foggy mist of their own corruptions that they cannot see God there where he is most visible: the Light shines in darkness, but darkness comprehends it not. Their souls are so deeply sunk into that house of clay which they carry about with them, that were there nothing of *body* or bulky *matter* before them, they could find nothing to exercise themselves about.

But religion, where it is in truth and in power, renews the very spirit of our minds, and, in a manner, spiritualizes this outward creation to us; and, in a more excellent way, performs that which the Peripatetics are inclined to affirm of their active intellect, in purging bodily and material things from the...dregs of matter, and separating them from those circumstantiating and straightening conditions of time and place and the like, and teaches the soul to look at those perfections which it finds here below, not so much as the perfections of this or that body, as they adorn this or that particular being, but as they are so many rays issuing forth from that first and essential perfection, in which they all meet and embrace one another in the closest friendship.[373]

Every particular good is a blossom of the first goodness, every created excellency is a beam descending from the Father of lights; and should we separate all these particularities from God, all affection spent upon them would be unchaste, and their embraces adulterous. We should love all things in God, and God in all things, because he is all in all, the beginning and original of being, the perfect idea of the goodness, and the end of their motion. It is nothing but a thick mist of pride and self-love that hinders men's eyes from beholding that sun, which both enlightens them and all other things, but when true religion begins once to dawn upon men's souls, and with its shining light chases away their black night of ignorance, then they behold themselves and all things else enlightened (though in a different way) by one and the same sun, and all the powers of their souls fall down before God and ascribe all glory to him.

Now it is that a good man is no more solicitous whether this or that good thing be mine, or whether my perfections exceed the measure of this or that particular creature; for whatsoever good he beholds anywhere, he enjoys and delights in it as much as if it were his own, and whatever he beholds in himself, he looks not upon it as his property, but as a common good; for all these beams come from one and the same fountain and ocean of light in whom he loves them all with a universal love. When his affections run along the stream of any created excellencies, whether his own or anyone else's, yet do not stay here, but run on till they fall into the ocean, they do not settle into a fond love and admiration either of himself or any other excellencies, but he owns them as so many pure...emanations from God, and in a particular being loves the universal goodness...

Thus may a good man walk up and down the world as in a garden of spices, and suck divine sweetness out of every flower. There is a twofold meaning in every creature, as the Jews speak of their Law, a literal, and a mystical, and the one is but the ground of the other....So a good man says of everything that his senses offer to him, it speaks to his lower part, but it points out something above to his mind and spirit. It is the drowsy and muddy spirit of superstition which, being lulled asleep in the lap of worldly delights, is fain to set some idol at its elbow, something that may jog it and put it in mind of God. Whereas true religion never finds itself out of the infinite sphere of the Divinity, and wherever it finds beauty, harmony, goodness, love, ingenuity, wisdom, holiness, justice, and the like, it is ready to say, here and there is God. Wherever any such perfections shine out, a holy mind climbs up by these sunbeams, and raises itself up to God.

And seeing God has never thrown the world from himself, but runs through all created essence, containing the archetypal ideas of all things in himself, and from there deriving and imparting several prints of beauty and excellency all the world over. A soul that is truly...Godlike, a mind that is enlightened from the same fountain, and has its inward senses affected with the sweet relishes of divine goodness, cannot but everywhere behold itself in the midst of that glorious unbounded being who is indivisibly everywhere. A good man finds every place he treads upon holy ground, to him the world is God's temple; he is ready to say with Jacob: How dreadful (awesome) is this place! This is none other but the House of God (Gen 28:17).

To conclude, it was a degenerous and unworthy spirit in that philosophy which first separated and made such distances between metaphysical truths and the truths of nature, whereas the first and most ancient wisdom among the heathens was indeed a philosophical divinity, or a divine philosophy, which continued for diverse ages. However, as men grew worse, their queasy stomachs began to loathe it; which made the truly wise Socrates complain of the Sophisters of that age which began now to corrupt and debase it, whereas before this the spirit of philosophy was more generous and divine, and did more purify and ennoble the souls of men, commending intellectual things to them, and taking them off from settling upon sensible and material things here below, still exciting them to endeavor after the nearest resemblance of God the supreme goodness and loveliness, and an intimate conjunction with him; which, according to the strain of the philosophy, was the true happiness of immortal souls.

X

THE TRUE WAY OR METHOD OF ATTAINING TO DIVINE KNOWLEDGE

John Smith (1660)

It has been long since well observed, that every art and science has some certain principles upon which the whole frame and body of it must depend, and he that will fully acquaint himself with those mysteries must come furnished with some presuppositions that I may speak in the language of the Stoics. Were I indeed to define divinity, I should rather call it a divine life than a divine science; it being something rather to be understood by a spiritual sensation, than by any verbal description, as all things of sense and life are best known by sentient and vital faculties....As the Greek philosopher has well observed: Everything is best known by that which bears a just resemblance and analogy with it, and therefore the scripture is inclined to set forth a good life as the...fundamental principle of divine science. Wisdom has built her a house, and hewn out her seven pillars: But the fear of the Lord is...the beginning of wisdom, the foundation of the whole fabric (Prov 24:3).

We shall therefore, as a preface...speak something of this true method of knowing, which is not so much by notions as actions, as religion itself consists not so much in words as things....He that is most practical in divine things, has the purest and sincerest knowledge of them, and not he that is most dogmatical. Divinity indeed is a true efflux from the eternal light, which, like the sunbeams, does not only enlighten, but heat and enliven; and therefore our Savior has in his Beatitudes connected purity of heart with the beatifical vision. And as the eye cannot behold the sun, unless it is sunlike, and has the form and resemblance of the sun drawn in it,[374] so neither can the soul of man behold God...unless it is Godlike, has God formed in it, and is made a partaker of the divine nature. And the Apostle St. Paul, when he would lay open the right way of attaining to divine truth, he said that knowledge puffs up, but it is Love that edifies (1 Cor 13). The knowledge of divinity that appears in systems and models is but a poor pale light, but the powerful energy of divine knowledge displays itself in purified souls. Here we shall find...as the ancient philosophy speaks, the land of truth.

To seek our divinity merely in books and writings is to seek the living among the dead (Luke 24:4–6);[375] we do but in vain seek God many times in these, where his truth too often is not so much enshrined as entombed: no...seek for God within your own soul, he is best discerned...as Plotinus phrased it, by an intellectual touch of him:[376] we must see with our eyes, and hear with our ears, and our hands must handle the word of life, that I may express it in St. John's words....[377] The soul itself has its sense, as well as the body, and therefore David, when he would teach us how to know what the divine goodness is, calls not for speculation but sensation—taste and see how good the Lord is (Ps 34:8). That is not the best and truest knowledge of God which is drawn out by the labor and sweat of the brain, but that which is kindled within us by a heavenly warmth in our hearts. As in the natural body it is the heart that sends up good blood and warm spirits into the head, whereby it is best enabled to its several functions, so that which enables us to know and understand correctly the things of God must be a living principle of holiness within us. When the tree of knowledge is not planted by the tree of life, and does not suck sap from it, it may be as well fruitful with evil as with good, and bring forth bitter fruit as well as sweet. If we would indeed have our knowledge thrive and flourish, we must water the tender plants of it with holiness....It is but a thin, airy knowledge that is received by mere speculation, which is ushered in by syllogisms and demonstrations; but that which springs forth from true goodness,...as Origen speaks, brings such a divine light into the soul, as is more clear and convincing than any demonstration.[378] The reason why, notwithstanding all our acute reasons and subtle disputes, truth prevails no more in the world is we so often disjoin truth and true goodness, which in themselves can never be disunited—they grow both from the same root and live in one another. We may, like those in Plato's deep pit with their faces bent downward, converse with sounds and shadows, but not with the life and substance of truth, while our souls remain defiled with any vice or lusts. This is the black lethe-lake which drench the souls of men. He that wants true virtue in heaven's logic is blind and cannot see afar off. Those filthy mists that arise from impure and terrene minds, like an atmosphere, perpetually encompass them, so that they cannot see that sun of divine truth that shines about them, but never shines into any unpurged souls; the darkness does not comprehend it, the foolish man does not understand. All the light and knowledge that may seem sometimes to rise up in unhallowed minds is but like those...flames that arise up from our culinary fire, that are soon quenched in their own smoke, or like those foolish fires that fetch their birth from terrene exudations, that merely hop up and down, and flit to and fro upon the surface of this earth where they were first brought forth, and serve not so much to enlighten as to delude us, nor to direct the wandering traveler into his way but to lead him farther out of it. While we lodge any filthy vice in us, this will be perpetually twisting up itself into the thread of our finest-spun speculations; it will be continually climbing up into...the hegemonical powers of the soul, into the bed of reason, and defile it. Like the wanton ivy twisting itself about the oak, it will twine about our judgments and understandings, till it has sucked out the life and spirit of them. I cannot think such black oblivion should possess the minds of some as to make them question that truth which to good men shines as bright as the sun at noonday, had they not foully defiled their own souls with some hellish vice or another, however fairly it may be they may hide it....

Such as men themselves are, such will God himself seem to be. It is the maxim of most wicked men that the Deity is some way or other like themselves; their souls do more then whisper it, though their lips speak it not, and though their tongues are silent, yet their lives cry it upon the housetops, and in the public streets. That idea which men generally have of God is nothing else but the picture of their own complexion. That archetypal notion of God which has the supremacy in their minds is none else but such a one as has been shaped according to some pattern of themselves, though they may so clothe and disguise this idol of their own, when they carry it about in a pompous procession to expose it to the view of the world, so that it may seem very beautiful, and indeed anything else rather than what it is....Men's corrupt hearts will not suffer their notions and conceptions of divine things to be cast into that form that a higher reason, which may sometime work within them, would put them into.

I would not be thought all this while to banish the belief of all innate notions of divine truth, but these are too often smothered, or tainted with a deep dye of men's filthy lusts. It is but...light buried and stifled in some dark body, from where all those colored, or rather discolored, notions and apprehensions of divine things are begotten. Though these common notions may be very busy sometimes in the vegetation of divine knowledge, yet the corrupt vices of men may so clog, disturb, and overrule them (as the Naturalists say this unruly and masterless matter does the natural forms in the formation of living creatures), that they may produce nothing but monsters miserably distorted and misshapen. This kind of science, as Plotinus speaks, accompanying too familiarly with matter, and receiving and imbibing it into itself, changes its shape by this incestuous mixture....[379] Sin and lust are always of a hungry nature, and suck up all those vital affections of men's souls which should feed and nourish their understandings.

What are all our most sublime speculations of the Deity that are not impregnated with true goodness but insipid things that have no taste nor life in them, that swell like empty froth in the souls of men? They do not feed men's souls, but only puff them up and fill them with pride, arrogance, and contempt and tyranny toward those that cannot well know their subtle curiosities, as those philosophers that Cicero complains of in his times...which made their knowledge only a matter of ostentation, to venditate and set off themselves, but never caring to square and govern their lives by it. Such as these do but spiderlike take a great deal of pains to spin a worthless web out of their own bowels, which will not keep them warm. These indeed are those silly souls that are ever learning, but never come to the knowledge of the truth. There are hidden mysteries in divine truth, wrapped up one within another, which cannot be discerned but only by divine seers.

We must not think we have then attained the right knowledge of truth, when we have broken through the outward shell of words and phrases that house it, or when by logical analysis we have found out the dependencies and coherencies of them, one with another; or when, like stout champions of it, having well guarded it with the invincible strength of our demonstration, we dare stand out in the face of the world, and challenge the field of all those that would pretend to be our rivals.

We have many grave and reverend idolaters that worship truth only in the image of their own wits, that could never adore it so much as they may seem to do, were it anything else but such a form of belief as their own wandering speculations...were it not that they find their own image and superscription upon it.

There is a knowing of the truth as it is in Jesus, as it is in a Christlike nature, as it is in that sweet, mild, humble, and loving spirit of Jesus, which spread itself like a morning sun upon the souls of good men, full of light and life. It profits little to know Christ himself after the flesh, but he gives his spirit to good men, who search the deep things of God. There is an inward beauty, life, and loveliness in divine truth, which cannot be known but only when it is digested into life and practice. The Greek Philosopher could tell [that]...without virtue and real goodness God is but a name, a dry and empty notion.[380] The profane sort of men, like those old Gentile Greeks, may make many ruptures in the walls of God's Temple, and break into the holy ground, but yet may find God no more there than they did.

Divine truth is better understood as it unfolds itself in the purity of men's hearts and lives, then in all those subtle niceties into which curious wits may lay it forth. And therefore our Savior, who is the great Master of it, would not, while he was here on earth, draw it up into any system or body, nor would his disciples after him. He would not lay it out to us in any canons or articles of belief, not being indeed so careful to stock and enrich the world with opinions and notions as with true piety and a Godlike pattern of purity, as the best way to thrive in all spiritual understanding. His main scope was to promote a holy life as the best and most compendious way to a right belief. He hangs all true acquaintance with divinity upon the doing God's will, if any man will do his (God's) will, he shall know of the doctrine, whether it is of God. This is that alone which will make us, as St. Peter tells us, that we shall not be barren nor unfruitful in the knowledge of our Lord and Savior (2 Pet 1:8). There is an inward sweetness and deliciousness in divine truth, which no sensual mind can taste or relish. Corrupt passions and terrene affections are apt of their own nature to disturb all serene thoughts, to precipitate our judgments, and warp our understandings. It was a good maxim of the old Jewish writers...the Holy Spirit dwells not in terrene and earthly passions. Divinity is not so well perceived by a subtle wit...as by a purified sense, as Plotinus phrases it.[381]

Neither was the ancient philosophy unacquainted with the way and method of attaining to the knowledge of divine things, and therefore Aristotle himself thought a young man unfit to meddle with the grave precepts of morality, till the heat and violent precipitancy of his youthful affections was cooled and moderated.[382] And it is observed of Pythagoras, that he had several ways to try the capacity of his scholars, and to prove the sedateness and moral temper of their minds, before he would entrust them with the more sublime mysteries of his philosophy. The Platonists were in this so wary and solicitous that they thought the minds of men could never be purged enough from those earthly dregs of sense and passion, in which they were so much steeped, before they could be capable of their divine metaphysics. And therefore they so much solicit...as they are wont to phrase it, a separation from the body, in all those that would...as Socrates speaks...sincerely understand divine truth, for that was the scope of their philosophy.[383] This was also intimated by them in their defining philosophy to be...a meditation of death,[384] aiming in this way at only a moral way of dying, by loosening the soul from the body and this sensitive life, which they thought was necessary for a right contemplation of intelligible things. Therefore, besides those purifications by which the souls of men were to be separated from sensuality and purged from fleshly filth, they devised a further way of separation more accommodated to the condition of philosophers, which was their mathematical contemplations, whereby the souls of men might farther shake off their dependency upon sense, and learn to go, as it were, alone, without the crutch of any sensible or material things to support them, and so be a little inured, being once got up above the body, to converse freely with immaterial natures, without looking down again and falling back into sense....[385]

And thus we should pass from the topic of our discourse, upon which we have dwelt too long already, but that before we quite let it go, I hope we may fairly make this use of it farther (besides what we have openly driven at all this while), which is, to learn not to devote or give up ourselves to any private opinions of dictates or men in matters of religion, nor too zealously to propugne the dogma of any sect. As we should not like rigid censurers arraign and condemn the creeds of other men with which we do not comply before a full and mature understanding of them, ripened not only by the natural sagacity of our own reasons, but by the benign influence of holy and mortified affection. Neither should we over-hastily...subscribe to the symbols and articles of other men. They are not always the best men that blot the most paper; truth is not, I fear, so voluminous, nor swells into such a mighty bulk as our books do. Those minds are not always the most chaste that are most parturient with the learned discourses, which too often bear upon them a foul stain of their unlawful propagation. A bitter juice of the corrupt affections may sometimes be strained into the ink of our greatest clerks; their doctrines may taste too sour of the cask they come through. We are not always happy in meeting with that wholesome food (as some are inclined to call the doctrinal part of religion) which has been dressed out by the cleanest hands. Some men have too bad hearts to have good heads; they cannot be good at theory who have been so bad at the practice, as we may justly fear too many of those from whom we are apt to take the articles of our belief have been. While we plead so much our right to the patrimony of our fathers, we may take too fast a possession of their errors as well as of their sober opinions. There are...innate prejudices, and deceitful hypotheses, that many times wander up and down in the minds of good men, that may fly out from them with their graver determinations. We can never be well assured what our traditional divinity is, nor can we securely enough addict ourselves to any sect of men. That which was the philosopher's motto...we may a little enlarge, and so fit it for an ingenuous pursuer after divine Truth: He that will find truth, must seek it with a free judgment, and a sanctified mind. He that thus seeks, shall find, he shall live in truth, and truth shall live in him. Truth shall be like a stream of living waters issuing out of his own soul, and he shall drink of the waters of his own cistern, and be satisfied. He shall every morning find this heavenly manna lying upon the top of his own soul, and be fed with it to eternal life; and he will find satisfaction within, feeling himself in conjunction with truth, though all the world should dispute against him....

XI

CHARITIE AND HUMILITIE

Henry More (1647)

Farre have I clambred in my mind
But nought so great as love I find:
Deep-searching wit, mount-moving might
Are nought compar'd to that good spright
Light of delight and soul of blisse!
Sure source of lasting happinesse!
Higher then Heaven! lower than hell!
What is thy tent? where maist thou dwell?
  My mansion hight humilitie,
Heavens vastest capabilitie.
The further it doth downward tend
The higher up it doth ascend;
If it go down to utmost nought
It shall return with that it sought.
  Lord stretch thy tent in my strait breast,
Enlarge it downward, that sure rest
May there be pight; for that pure fire
Wherewith thou wontest to inspire
All self-dead souls. My life is gone,
Sad solitude's my irksome wonne.
Cut off from men and all this world
In Lethes lonesome ditch I'm hurld.
Nor might nor sight doth ought me move,
Nor do I care to be above.
O feeble rayes of mentall light!
That best be seen in this dark night,
What are you? what is any strength

If it be not laid in one length
With pride or love? I nought desire
But a new life or quite t'expire.
Could I demolish with mine eye
Strong towers, stop the fleet stars in skie,
Bring down to earth the pale-fac'd Moon,
Or turn black midnight to bright Noon:
Though all things were put in my hand,
As parch'd as dry as th'Libyan sand
Would be my life if Charity
Were wanting. But Humility
Is more then my poore soul durst crave
That lies intombd in lowly grave.
But if't were lawfull up to send
My voice to Heaven, this should it rend.
   Lord thrust me deeper into dust
That thou maist raise me with the just.

XII

IN THE DIVINE DIALOGUES THE SONG CONCERNING DIVINE PROVIDENCE, DIALOG. 2, SECT. 28

Henry More (1647)

Where's now the objects of thy fears:
Needless signs and fruitless tears?
They be all gone like idle dream
Suggested from the Body's steam.
O Cave of horrour, black as pitch!
Dark Den of Spectres that bewitch
The weakned phansy[386] sore affright
With the grim shades of grisely Night.
What's Plague and Prison? Loss of friends?
War, Dearth and Death, that all things ends?
Mear Bug-bears for the childish mind,
Pure Panick terrours of the blind.
　　　Collect thy Soul into one sphear
Of light, and 'bove the Earth it rear.
Those wild scattered thoughts that erst
Lay loosely in the World disperst
Call in: thy Spirit thus knit in one
Fair lucid orb; those fears be gone
Like vain impostures of the Night
That fly before the Morning bright,
Then with pure Eyes thou shalt behold
How the first Goodness doth infold
All things in loving tender arms:

That deemed mischiefs are no harms
But sovereign salves; and skilful cures
Of greater woes the World endures;
That man's stout Soul may win a state
Far rais'd above the reach of fate.
    Power, Wisdom, Goodness sure did frame
This Universe, and still guide the same.
But thoughts from passions sprung, deceive
Vain Mortals. No man can contrive
A better course than what's been run
Since the first circuit of the Sun.
    He that beholds all from on high
Knows better what to do than I,
I'm not my own, should I repine
If he dispose of what's not mine.
Purge but thy Soul of blind self-will,
Thou streight shalt see God doth no ill.
The World he fills with the bright rayes
Of his free Goodness. He displays
Himself throughout. Like common air,
That Spirit of life through all doth fare,
Suck'd in by them as vital breath,
That willingly embrace not death.
But those that with that living Law
Be unacquainted, cares do gnaw;
Mistrust of God's good Providence
Doth daily vex their wearied sense.

XIII

AN EXPLANATION OF
THE DIVINE MYSTERY
OF GODLINESS
BOOK VIII

Henry More (1660)

1. ...The promise of the spirit may seem so sufficient of itself to some...that they professedly take up here, and exclude, or at least neglect, all that advantage that was obtained from the history of Christ, and in this way antiquate the Christian religion. These are those great Spiritualists that talk so much of the Light within them, and the Power within them; and boast that they want nothing without to be their guide and support, but that they can go themselves without any external help.[387] For keeping to the Light within them, the power of God and the Spirit of God will assist them, and will lead them into all truth. And truly I cannot but say amen to what they declare. For I know assuredly that it is most true, if they would leave off their canting language, and say in downright terms, that keeping sincerely to the dictates of reason and conscience, and the perpetually denying themselves in such things as they know or suspect to be evil [with devout addresses to the throne of grace for the assistance and illumination of the Holy Spirit, to discover and overcome all error, falseness, pride and hypocrisy that may lurk in their hearts]; I say, I am well assured that this dispensation, faithfully kept to, will in due time lead to all saving truth; and that such a one at the last cannot fail to become a Christian in the soundest and the fullest sense, such as firmly adhered to Christ in the first and purest ages of the church. But if they will call any hot, wild imagination or forcible and unaccountable suggestion, the Light within them, and follow

that, this is not to keep to reason and conscience, but to be delivered up to a reprobate sense, and to expose a man's self to all the temptations that either the devil or a man's own lust or sordid melancholy can entangle him in.

2. Therefore by the Light within them they must understand an accountable and rational conscience within them, unless they are perfect fanatics or madmen, or, what is worse, mere impostors and cheats, who would pretend to a conscience, but yet irrational and unaccountable to anyone, and thus have the liberty of doing what they please, being given up at length to nothing but fury and lust.

And then lastly, this conscience within them is not a thing so absolutely within them, that it can take no information from what is without. For it is manifest that this lamp of God that burns in us, is fed and nourished from external objects. For the invisible things of him from the creation of the world are clearly seen, being understood by things that are made; for by these from without are we advertised of his eternal power and Godhead (Rom 1:20). And as we are thus taught by the outward book of nature concerning the existence of God and his general providence in the world as to the necessities of life both of men and beasts; so may we also by external writings or records be more fully informed of a more special providence of his to the sons of men, concerning the state in the other world, and of that eternal life manifested by Christ. But I grant that it is still this Light within us, that judges and concludes after the perusal of either the volumes of nature or divine revelation.

3. But as he that gives his mind to mathematics, architecture, animal husbandry, gardening, and the like, if he out of a foolish conceit of light and reason being only within one, and not without (as certainly neither ink nor paper, nor both put together, are any more partakers of the light of reason than of sense and life), he would make no use of the writings of Euclid, suppose for mathematics, nor any other author that has writ of such matters, and so of the rest of the faculties I named, nor converse with any man by word of mouth, nor cast his eyes upon what they have done, but only think with himself and sit still by the light of his own lamp within doors; he will be a very sorry mathematician,

architect, husbandman or gardener: so certainly for moral and divine truth, he that will be so taught by himself, that he will not use outward advantages, such as the Holy Scriptures especially afford, will be found at last to have been the scholar of a very foolish and imperfect master.

4. Besides that, these men contradict themselves in their own practices. For they vilify that by which they have been taught, and retain the very phrases of what they have learned out of scripture, and know not how to speak without scripture-terms, nor can make any show without scriptural allusions; and that grand document of keeping to the Light within us they borrow out of St. John's Gospel: and yet they are so frantic and peevish that they would fling away the staff without which they are not able to make one step in religion. Moreover if this Light within us is so precisely within us, that it wants no information from without us, why do they themselves scribble such abundance of pamphlets, make catechisms, set out prophecies? Why do they exhort, rebuke, no reproach and rail against men to convert them, if what is without cannot reach that which is within? Or why do they meet together to hear someone of their assembly (after he has fallen down as in a trance, and got up again) dictate oracles out of his disturbed breast? For his words which they hear are without, and beat upon the ear; they are not the Light within. Therefore it is plain, that the Light within may be informed by something which is without, whether by voice or writings: And if so, there is an obligation upon this Light within to be so considerate, as to seek the most punctual information it can from what is most likely to inform it from without.

5. And therefore they are with all diligence to examine the most venerable records of religion, and especially of that religion under which they were not only born, but which is absolutely of itself the most renowned religion that ever was in the world. Which (religion) therefore none but such as are utterly averse from all religion, as being wholly given up to lust and profanity, can without examination dare to relinquish; and if they will examine it, I mean the Christian religion (as it refers to the person of Christ, that died between two thieves at Jerusalem, but rose again the third day, that ascended visibly into heaven, and shall again return in a visible manner to judge the quick and the dead), I appeal to this Light

within them, to their reason and conscience, and that of the most cunning impostors among them all, or of whoever will join with them, if the evidence for this religion from prophecy, history, and from the nature of the religion itself, is not such, as that nothing but ignorance of its true meaning and of its right design can hinder it from being acknowledged as a most certain truth by any, but those that are afraid that any religion that leads to holiness, or promises anything after this life, should be found true.

6. As for that objection taken from the mighty power of the Spirit of God, as if that were so sufficient of itself, that belief in it and assistance from it would anticipate the mention and use of any other power whatsoever that may seem to confer to the end of the gospel, the sanctification of our souls; I answer to this, that they who do after this manner argue, do err not knowing the scriptures. For this power of the Spirit communicable to believers is not an absolute and omnipotent power, not to be resisted, not to be frustrated, if there are not due means and wise accommodations concurring with its workings or attempts to work. But I may in some manner illustrate its condition from what is observable in the spirit of nature, the principle of all natural generations, growths, and perfections; in which there is a kind of hypothetical omnipotency as to the work of nature; that is, that this spirit will not fail to assist and complete, provided that such and such circumstances in corporeal agents are not lacking. So is it also in this divine Spirit, or the Holy Ghost, as it is communicable to us; it will certainly assist and finish its work, if there is no impediment on our side, which it behooves us to remove out of the way, nor anything lacking which we can apply ourselves to for the advance of our faith and perfecting of the holy life; such as meditating on the scriptures, conferring with holy men, experienced Christians, and using with devotion and reverence all the ordinances of Christ....I shall now proceed to the four last powers of the gospel, which are mainly instrumental to the work of the Spirit upon the hearts of all true believers.

7. And the first of these is the example of our ever-blessed Savior, who has given us no other precepts than what himself was the most exact pattern of; and himself such a pattern of life, that is, of faith in God, of humility, love, and purity, that we cannot doubt in following his footsteps that we are in a wrong way, he

being by voices from heaven and by his miracles upon earth proved and declared to be the only begotten Son of God. Therefore the nearer we keep to his path, the surer we are that we walk upon sound ground. Besides that, he is our Lord and Sovereign, and therefore natural ingenuity will urge us forward to compose our lives so as is most agreeable to his fashion. And he does expressly require this as a testimony of our love and loyalty to him: If you love me, keep my commandments, of which a principal one is That as I have loved you, you love also one another (John 14:15). So he gives his disciples an example of being humble to one another, in that he washed their feet. If I then, your Lord and Master, have washed your feet, you ought also to wash one another's feet. For I have given you an example, that you should do as I have done to you (John 13:14–15). And in Matthew 2, Take my yoke upon you, and learn of me, for I am meek and lowly in heart; and you shall find rest unto your souls (Matt 11:29).

8. ...The whole history of Christ, all his actions and ways of living, tend to the most effectual recommending of the divine life unto us. We shall only take the opportunity here to wipe off such stains as the soul and unsound breath of some blasphemous mouths have of late endeavored to stain this bright mirror of divine perfection, which will be not only a piece of indispensable duty and loyalty to the person of our Savior, but also the better encouragement to his sincere followers....

XIV

AN EXPLANATION OF THE DIVINE MYSTERY OF GODLINESS BOOK X

Henry More (1660)

1. It is clear…that liberty of religion is the common and natural right of all nations and persons, that is to say, that they have a power, as they are rational men, and believe that there is a God and a life to come, to examine what is the best way to serve him for their future advantage, and not to be tied up to that religion [which] is first proposed to them. Indeed they have a right to suspect, especially if they do not like it, that there is some better, and therefore that they may confer with those of other religions, send for them out of one nation into another, entertain them when they arrive, hear them diligently, and, if they are convinced, openly profess it. Or if they come of their own accord, they are to be entertained with the same security that an agent of state is, and may freely converse with them of the nation that have a mind to hear them. For this is a piece of their right of liberty, to speak as well as the others to hear. These transactions would breed no disturbance at all, if this right of liberty of religion was universally understood and acknowledged by all the nations of the world, as certainly it is their right.

2. …It seems plainly to follow, that any nation or people that does heartily acknowledge the reasonableness of this right…may send from those of the religion themselves into their neighboring nations to communicate their religion to them, and to try if they can convince them of that which they are persuaded is true, and to show

them the errors of their own; but at seasonable times, and without reproach or tumult, or any way confronting them in the exercise of their religion (a thing very barbarous and insufferable at home, much more abroad in countries where they are strangers)....

And if these agents for religion, neither injuring nor defrauding anyone of their civil rights, shall be evilly treated by those they offer to instruct, or if they abuse them by imprisonment or any other hard dealing, or finally put them to death, that state or kingdom to which they belong may require their blood at their hands, as having grossly and barbarously transgressed against the law of nations, and the common right of all mankind that have not forfeited it some way or other....[They should be] firmly resolved, if it should come to a war, and they are conquerors of their ill neighbors, to use no other means to turn their new subjects from their old religion, but by peaceably and patiently showing them its vanity, and the excellency and solidity of their own; which cannot by any means be called the propagation of religion by the sword, when there shall not be so much force put upon them to change their former religion, if they were found conscientious, as to compel them to be present at the solemnities of the new. Only they shall swear fealty to their conquerors, and be well indoctrinated in that common right of mankind, that no man is to be persecuted for religion, if he has not forfeited that right by taking upon him the liberty of persecuting others. And therefore they may enjoy their religion if they can still like it, upon equal terms with the conquerors, as to their private capacities. If the Spaniard had made himself master of the Indies upon these conditions, and had abstained from his execrable cruelties, he might have justified himself to all the world.[388] For this had not been to propagate religion by the sword, but to maintain a man's natural right.

3. This theory I think is very sound at the bottom, and is very clearly what ought to be, but [is] hugely unpracticable by reason of the general perverseness and corruption of men. Yet I thought it worthwhile to expose it to view, its acknowledgment being the greatest advantage to Christian religion that can possibly be conceived, there being nothing so effectual for the easy fall of Islam and paganism into the profession of Christ as this principle we have explained—our religion being not only solid in itself, but incomparably more demonstrable to all rational spirits than

any religion ever extant in the world. Besides, though its use will not extend so far at first, yet it may be something serviceable to these parts of the world whose eyes are more open to truth than others are. And verily in my judgment, this principle I do thus recommend, as it seems to me to deserve the reception of all men as true, so of all Christians especially, not only upon point of policy, but as more suitable to that spirit they are of, abhorring from force and cruelty; who are therefore to permit full liberty of conscience to all those who do not forfeit it by mixing with their religion such principles as are contrary to good manners and civil right, or repugnant to this very principle of liberty we speak of.

4. Therefore those that under pretense of religion would corrupt the people with such doctrines as plainly countenance vice and tend to the rooting out of the sense of true honor and virtue out of a nation, have lost this common right we contend for, as being infectors and poisoners of the people among whom they live; and therefore the public magistrate of whatever nation or religion has a power to restrain them, their doctrine being so dangerous to the welfare of a state, and contrary to the light of nature and suffrage of the wisest men in all places of the world and in all ages. No religion fraught with such rotten ware as this is to be received in any coast where they would put in, but to be kept out by strangers and suppressed at home.

5. Again, those also would forfeit this right of liberty, whose religion should contain anything in it that would weaken the state which received it. As if there were some such absurd superstition, as upon pretense of a high esteem of virginity…whereby the country would be depopulated, and the inhabitant made unserviceable for its defense; there is no question but the magistrate might inhibit such a religion as this.

6. As [however] he might [inhibit] in the last place all such as have intermixed with them that wolfish and ferine humor of persecuting others for their religion, that would live quietly by them, and would not force anyone to their own faith, nor disturb the public exercise of religion in others. For these have no right to be suffered further than at the discretion of the magistrate;[389] nor can more reasonably plead for liberty than the wolf and fox crave leave to have their kennels or holes in the midst of a sheepfold, or

the owl or night-raven to put their note in the midst of a choir of nightingales.

7. But you'll say, all religions and sects are such foxes and wolves, and therefore there is no liberty of religion at all to be given. Those that are so, I confess, are at the mercy of the magistrate, as having forfeited their right. Which forfeiture he may exact more or less severely accordingly as he has more or less security than these crafty and wild creatures may do no mischief. But I do not believe that all men that do profess religion are of this partial nature; no, on the contrary, I do truly believe that they that are the most truly religious, are the most abhorrent from persecution for conscience's sake. Therefore as many as are ready to profess, upon oath if it is required, that it is their judgment (and their practice does not contradict it) that no man is to be denied in his civil rights, his liberty, estate or life, for the cause of such a religion whose principles teach not to deny others, and do avow that theirs is such, and that they will be as faithful to the prince or state in which they live as those of his own religion; these in no way forfeited their right of liberty, neither this way nor any other, by intermingling practices or principles against the light of nature and laudable morality; it is the highest piece of injustice that can be committed to abridge them of the safe profession thereof.

XV

A DISCOURSE OF THE FREEDOM OF THE WILL

Peter Sterry (1675)

The Preface to the Reader.
Christian and candid reader,
I entreat some few things of you, for your own sake and for mine:
   1. Study the love of God, the nature of God, as he is love, the work of God, as it is a work of love. Moses in his dying song begins with God, and the perfection of his work: He is the Rock, his work is perfect (Deut 32:4). St. Paul, descended from the Paradise in the third heavens, brings this with him down unto the world, as the sacred mystery, and rich ground of all truth, from which all the beauties and sweetness of Paradise, of all the heavens spring: That love is the bond of perfection. It is love then, which runs through the whole work of God, which frames, informs, unites all into one masterpiece of divine love.

   If God is love, the attributes of God are the attributes of this love—the purity, simplicity, the sovereignty, the wisdom, the almightiness, the unchangeableness, the infiniteness, the eternity of divine love. If God is love, his work is the work of love, of a love unmixed, unconfined, supreme, infinite in wisdom and power, not limited in its workings by any preexistent matter, but bringing forth freely and entirely from itself its whole work both matter and form, according to its own inclination and complacency in itself.

   Campanella teaches us that all second causes are so many modifications of the first cause, so many forms and shapes in which the first cause appears and acts. All the works of God, are the divine love, in so many modes and dresses. There is diversity of manifestations, there are diversities of operations, which compose the whole frame and business of this creation, which are as diverse persons acting diverse parts upon this stage. But there is one Spirit, one Lord, one God, one love, which works in all.

It is the divine love, with its unsearchable riches, which is the fullness that fills all persons, and all parts upon the stage of time or eternity. If any man does not know the way to the sea, let him follow a river in the course of its stream, says the Comedian.[390]

Dear Reader, if you would be led to that sea, which is as the gathering together, and confluence of all the waters of life, of all truths, goodness, joys, beauties, and blessedness, follow the stream of the divine love, as it holds on its course, from its head in eternity through every work of God, through every creature. So shall you be not only happy in your end, but in your way, while this stream of love shall not only be your guide by the side, but shall carry you along in its soft and delicious bosom, bearing you up in the bright arms of its divine power, sporting with you all along, washing you white as snow in its own pure floods, and bathing your whole spirit and person in heavenly inexpressible sweetness.

This is my first request to you:

2. Study and practice that great command of love, as the lesson of your whole life, with which alone you are to entertain yourself, and all the heavenly company, both here and in eternity. This is the first and great command: That you love God with your whole self (Mark 12:30); and then, That you love your neighbor as yourself (Mark 12:31), which is a second law, a second love, as the first. Indeed it is so like, that it is one with it. Be yourself in your whole person, the sacrifice of a whole burnt-offering, ascending in a sacred flame of heavenly love to God, the only and eternal beauty. As the zeal of the House of God, which is love flaming, ate up David and Christ (Ps 69:9; John 2:17), so let this heavenly love of the divine beauty, which is the beauty itself, descending in a pure and sweet flame upon you, by consuming you, convert you into one spiritual flame with itself. Now live nowhere, but where you love, in your Beloved. Let your Beloved alone now live in you; when you have thus lost yourself by a heavenly love in your Beloved, in your God; when you have thus by the sacred and sweet mystery of this love found your Beloved, your God, in the palace of yourself: Then love your neighbor as yourself. Love your

neighbor in your Jesus, your God. Love your Jesus, your God, in your neighbor. Let his neighborhood of divine love be as large as the God of love himself is. Let every other person and spirit, which lives and moves and has its being in God, within the encompassing, upon the ground and root of the Divine Being, be your neighbor, your brother, another self, as yourself to yourself—the object to you of a heavenly and incorruptible love.

Upon this commandment, says Jesus Christ, hang all the Law and the Prophets. This love is the center and the circle of all the works of God, of all motions and rests, of all mysteries in nature and grace, in time and eternity. Plato says "that three sorts of persons are led to God, the musician by harmony, the philosopher by the beam of truth, the lover by the light of beauty."[391] All these conductors to the Supreme Being meet in this love, of which we speak; the first and only true beauty, being the first birth, the first effulgency, the essential Image of the Supreme Goodness, is also the first, the Supreme, the only Truth, the Original, the measure, the end of all truth, which by its amiable attractive light, conducts all understandings in the search of truth, and gives them rest only in its transparent and blissful bosom. This also is the first, the only, the universal harmony, the music of all things in heaven and on earth; the music, in which all things of earth and of heaven meet to make one melodious concert.

While the holy Lover then pursues the tracts of this beauty, through all the works and ways of God, he is encompassed with the light of divine truth shining through him, and round about him. He is carried on in the spirit by the force of the divine harmony; he carries along this harmony of things, charming all things round about him, as he passes on. So he sees the God of gods at last on Mount Zion, the perfection of beauty, harmony, truth, and goodness, which all center in the divine love, the divine unity, the band of perfection.

3. Let no differences of principles or practices divide you in your affections from any person. He who seems to me as a Samaritan to a Jew, most worthy of contempt and hatred, most apt to wound or kill me, may hide under the shape of a Samaritan a generous, affectionate neighbor, brother, and friend. When I lie wounded and dying, neglected by those who are nearest to me,

most esteemed by me, this person may pour wine and oil into my wounds, with tender and constant care, at his own expense, and bring me back to life and joy. How evident has it been in the history of all times, that in parties most remote one from the other, most opposed one to the other, persons have been found of equal excellencies, in all kinds, of equal integrity to truth and goodness. Our most orthodox divines, who have been heated and heightened with the greatest zeal of opposition to the pope, as the Antichrist, yet have believed a pope to have ascended from the papal chair to a throne in heaven.[392] Had my education, my acquaintance, the several circumstances and concurrences been the same to me, as to this person from whom I now most of all dissent, that which is now his sense and state might have been mine. Have the same just, equal, tender respects and thoughts with the same allowances of another, which you require from him to yourself. It is a rule in philosophy, that there is the same reason of contraries.[393] Two opposed parties or persons, by reason of the opposition, for the most part looking through the same disturbed and colored medium, behold one another under the same uncomely form, in the same displeasing colors. Has there not been frequent experience of those, who by being of differing parties, alienated, exasperated, having their fancies filled with strange images of each other, when they have been brought together by some intervening providence, have discovered such agreeable beauties of morality and humanity, such a harmonious agreement in essentials, in radical principles of divine truth, of the true and everlasting good, that they have conversed with highest delight, and have departed with a higher esteem of each other, their souls inseparably united with angelical kisses and embraces? Some entertaining strangers have entertained angels (Heb 13:2). Do you so believe that in every encounter you may meet under the disguise of an enemy, a friend, a brother, who, when his helmet shall be taken off, may disclose a beautiful, and a well known face, which shall charm all your opposition into love and delight at the sight of it.

But now, Reader, I fall at your feet, I take hold of your knees, by all things moving and obliging I beseech you, if there are any bowels, or comforts of love, any peace, pleasantness, strength, prosperity in union, any good in unity, that you would take deeply into your heart, and treasure up safely there, and frequently with fixed, studious eyes, contemplate this (as I humbly conceive it) most sure and reconciling truth, which I shall now, as I am able, represent to you.

Often, yes for the most part, two opposed parties have something on each side, excellently good, something exorbitantly evil, although perhaps in unequal degrees. Both mutually set after an immovable manner before their eyes—their own good, the evil on the other part. Thus they blind their minds to all sense or belief of any good there. Thus they lift up themselves above all sense of their own evil. So they heighten themselves by self-justifications, by mutual condemnations, to an extinguishing of every beam of good, to an increase of their evils, to a blackness of darkness, until by these mutual mistakes they have drawn on upon themselves mutual and absolute ruin. How much better were it to obey that precept of the Holy Ghost, which offers itself to us, like an olive-branch in the mouth of this sacred dove: Every man should look not to his own things, but to the things of another.

Oh, that now I had a hundred mouths, a hundred tongues, a voice like thunder, like the voice of God that rends the rocks, to cry to all sorts of persons and spirits in this land, in all the Christian world through the whole Creation: Let all that differ in principles, professions, or opinions, and forms, see that good which is in each other, and the evil in themselves. Join in this, to extirpate the evil, the common evil, your common enemy, and so quench that fire which burns upon your estates, your houses, your relations, your bodies, your souls, even to the nethermost hell. Unite the good which is in you, so shall the good on one side make up that which is imperfect and defective in the good on the other side, to a perfection of good in both. So shall the good on one side be as a proper antidote to extinguish the evil on the other side. Thus while the evil is the privation, the loss of yourselves, and the good of your true selves (as Horace calls Virgil, *Dimidium anima mea*), you will meet like two halves of each other, filling up the circle of each other's being, beauties, joys, and be now completed in one. How inexpressible would the fruits of this union be? How would it heighten you in all the beauties and blessedness of truth and goodness, in which your immortality and conformity to God are placed? Yes, how would this union strengthen those outward interests, and sweeten those natural enjoyments, for whose sake, now like adders, you stop your ears to the wisest charmer and the most potent charms, that would draw you home into the bosom of each other, for whose sake now you cast down to the ground all ingenuity and integrity. You make your way over their sweetest beauties and most tender bowels, to the heart-blood of one another, until you have drowned in blood those very darling interests and enjoyments, together with your own lives and persons, your native country, the Christian world, the face of the whole earth? But ah, when will poor mankind on earth be wise, to understand its own good, or be good, that it may make me wise? Blessed is he that comes in the name of the Lord (Ps 118:26; Mark 11:9). We wait for your salvation, your Jesus, O God! To him shall the gathering of the people be, the true Shiloh, for whom this glory is reserved.

It seems indeed, according to my humble sense, necessary to divide those principles and practices, which divide mankind into three heads:

1. Some seem to be of a nature perfectly indifferent, neither good nor evil, but according to the intention and spirit which act them.
2. Some differ in the degrees, mixtures, or varieties of good and evil.
3. Others differ in the whole kind of good and evil.

In this last state of things, it is the part of every child of light to maintain the divine love in his spirit, like the sun in the firmament, encompassing the whole earth, from one end to the other, shining upon all, both good and bad, upon dry and sandy deserts, the habitation of wild beasts, and venomous serpents, as well as cultivated gardens, flourishing with wholesome herbs, pleasant flowers, and all sorts of fruits. Thus God himself is propounded to us for a pattern by the Son of God.

Distinguish between good and evil. Love takes pleasure in the good. Hate the evil. Advance the good. Oppose the evil upon all occasions, with all your forces. But everywhere distinguish carefully, with all tenderness of spirit, between the person, and the evil of the person. Be wise as serpents, but innocent as doves (Matt

10:16), according to the counsel and command of Jesus Christ, who is the Supreme Wisdom and Love both in one. Discern the evil with a quick and curious eye, guard yourselves with all your might from it, maintain an aversion, an enmity to it, eternally irreconcilable. Thus be a serpent to the evil, but at the same time be a dove to the person, without gall, without anything to offend, moaning over it, groaning for it, as your mate, till it is recovered from the evil, which captivates it into a fellowship with you, in the purity and love of the divine nature.

Have always most tender feelings for, and a most sensible sympathy, with all men in their greatest deformities and defilements, as your brethren tied to you by a double consanguinity.

1. All men are made of the same blood in Adam.
2. All men are redeemed by the same blood of the Lord Jesus, who has given himself a ransom for all, to be testified in the proper times.

This person also now most of all lost in the depth of all evils, may have his proper time yet to come—a time for the taking off the disguise of these filthy rags from him, for the discovery of the glory, as of a Son of God in him. As his time comes later, so it may come with a fuller glory. As Zipporah said to Moses, whether bitterly, or in the sweet sense of a sacred mystery, pointing to the Messiah, You are a husband to me in blood (Exod 4:26). So look you on every man as a brother to you, in both these bloods, of which one was once pure and precious, as that of the sacred Image of God in Paradise. The other is eternally pure and precious, as the blood of God himself.

Forgiving one another freely for Christ's sake is the language of St. Paul (2 Cor 2:10). Look upon every person through this twofold glass, the blood, and the beauties of Christ. Christ has died for all. The natural being of every person has his root in the grave of Christ, and is watered by his blood. Christ lives in all; his resurrection is the life of the whole Creation. He is the wisdom, the power, the righteousness of God in every work of nature, as well as of grace. He is the root, out of which every natural, as well as every spiritual plant springs, which brings himself forth through every natural existence, and out of it, as the flower, the brightness of the glory of God. He is the root and truth of all things; all things are by him, and for him, to the praise and glory of God in him. His name is excellent through all the earth. Read then this name of excellency, of glory, the name of Christ in every part and point of the earth, the darkest, the lowest, the least; forgive the spots upon this name in every person, for the namesake engraved upon it.

Receive one another into the glory of God, as is the rule of St. Paul (Rom 15:7). Divines distinguish between the person…and the evil. The person, the nature, springs forth from God, and so is good, and has a divinity and glory in it—a divine root, a divine image. It stands in the glory of God, as a flower in the garden, a beam in the sun; it is maintained by a continual emanation from the bosom of the supreme glory. Thus you are to receive every person, clouded with the greatest evils, as he is the work of nature, and of God, into the glory of God. Thus every other person is to be your neighbor, your brother in the glory of God, and the object of a divine love.

No evil is the nature or choice of any person, but the mishap, and the disease. Truth is the only object of every understanding, the only white at which it aims. Like the marigold, it opens itself only to this sun, or that which shines upon it in the glorious form of the sun, and so descends in seeming beams of this divine beauty into its bosom. Good is the only object of the will. As the needle touched by the loadstone is governed in its motion and rest by the North Pole, so is the will moved and attracted by that alone which touches it with a sense of good. It rests in no bosom, but that which courts and woos it under the divine form of good, with the seeming charms of this its only Beloved and Bridegroom.

St. Paul says: Sin deceived me, and slew me (Rom 7:11). No person is willingly deceived in his belief of truth, or disappointed in his expectation of good. Every evil is a degree of death—a disease, and in the end, death. When it appears like itself, all things fly from it, as from death. But as Cupid, in the form of the young and flourishing Prince Ascanius, by treacherous embraces and kisses, breathed a fatal poison into the veins of the Carthaginian queen,[394] so does sin and evil, by the hellish enchantments of the Prince of Darkness, form itself into the most alluring resemblance of the heavenly image, composed of truth and goodness, meeting in one immortal form. It adorns itself all over with the most curious and sparkling counterfeits of all its most amiable, most divine sweetness and beauties. Thus it insinuates itself into the eyes and hearts of the sons of God, and fills them with its false sweetness, enflames them with a false love, as the poison and fire from hell. Yet still, in the midst of these enchantments and deaths, as the Athenians in the midst of their atheism and idolatry had an altar inscribed to the unknown God (Acts 17:23), the understanding and the will, according to their own proper natures, stand in every natural spirit as altars in a temple, shining and burning, with continual fires by night and by day, aspiring to the highest and clearest heavens, through all opposed clouds of darkness, while this inscription in clear characters appears engraved round these altars: To the unknown Good, the unknown God, to the unknown truth, the unknown Jesus.

If any person, then, is fallen into any evil, let those that are spiritual restore him with a spiritual skill, with a spirit of meekness and divine love. Apply reproofs and chastisements to evil persons in their seasons, as a brother gives an antidote to a beloved brother that by a mistake has been poisoned, or as one hand applies medicine to the other hand, or to the eye, when it suffers by any wound or distemper....

If I am lifted up to heaven by manifold excellencies, together with Corazin and Bethsaida, from where I look down upon another far beneath me, laying like Sodom and Gomorrah (Gen 13:10) in a loathed and hated deep of darkness, defilements, disgraces, let me then think that this Sodom may have a better spirit, a better ground of good at the bottom of its spirit than myself. Let me think that if the seed of love and light which has been sown in me had been sown with the same advantage there, it would have far excelled me in its fruits. Yes, let me think that it may not only have a better ground, but a divine seed, hidden deep in that ground beneath all this soil and dung, beneath all this darkness, deformity, and deadness of its winter season, which may rise up in its proper spring into pleasant flowers and fruits, as the garden of God. Thus let me think, and let these thoughts instruct me to love every other person, removed to the greatest distance from me, cast down to the greatest depth beneath me, as my neighbor, my brother, myself.

XVI

THE PRINCIPLES OF THE MOST ANCIENT AND MODERN PHILOSOPHY, CHAPTER 5

Anne Conway (1690)

1. ...By the Son of God, the first begotten of all creatures, whom we Christians do call by the name of Jesus Christ, according to the scriptures, as is above declared, not only is meant his divinity, but also his humanity, in eternal union with the divinity; that is, as his heavenly humanity was united with the divinity before the world was, and so by consequence before he came in the flesh. Of whom the ancient Cabbalists have delivered many things concerning the Son of God, how he was created, and of his existence in the order of nature, before all creatures; also that all receive benediction and sanctification in him, and by him, whom also in their writings they call the Heavenly Adam, Adam Kadmon, or first man, the great priest, husband, or spouse of the church, as Philo Judaeus calls the first begotten Son of God.[395]

2. This Son of God, the first begotten of all creatures, to wit, this heavenly Adam, and great priest, as the Jewish doctors call him, is properly a medium between God and the creatures. And that there is such a middle being, is as demonstrable as that there is a God; where is meant such a being, which in its own nature is indeed less than God, and yet greater and more excellent than all other creatures; where also for his excellency he is properly called this Son of God...who is called by the Jews, Adam Kadmon....

3. In order to this demonstration we must first consider the nature or being of God, the Chief Being; and then the nature and

essence of creatures, which are to be compared one with another, from where this middle nature will immediately discover itself to us. The nature and essence of God, as is shown in the preceding chapters, is altogether unchangeable, which not only the Holy scriptures, but also the strength of reason which God has imbued our minds with, sufficiently declares; for if there should be any mutability in God, it tends some higher degree or measure of goodness, and then he would not be the Chief Good, which is contradictory; for if any thing advances to a greater degree of goodness, this wholly comes to pass by reason of some greater being, of whose virtue and influence it does participate: but there is no greater being, than God, and so by consequence he is no way meliorated, nor can become better than he is, much less decrease, which would argue an imperfection; therefore it is manifest that God, or the Chief Being, is altogether unchangeable. Now seeing the nature of creatures is really distinct from the nature of God, so that there are some attributes of God, which are incommunicable to creatures, among which is reckoned immutability. Hence it necessarily follows that creatures are changeable, or else they would be God himself. Moreover also daily experience teaches us that creatures are changeable, and do continually vary from one state unto another. But there is a twofold mutability, the one which has a power in it of changing itself either unto good or evil; and this is common to all creatures, but not to the first begotten of all creatures; the other is only a power to proceed from goodness to goodness. Here is therefore a threefold class or rank of beings: the first whereof is that which is wholly unchangeable; the second changeable only to good, so that that which in its own nature is good, may become yet better; the third is that which though it was in its own nature indeed good yet could be indifferently changed, as well into good, as from good into evil. The first and last of these are extremes; and the second is a natural medium between them, by which the extremes are united, and this medium participates of both extremes, and therefore is the most convenient and proper medium; for it participates of the one extreme, mutability, to wit, from good to a greater degree or measure of goodness, and of the other extreme, that is altogether unchangeable from good into evil; and such a medium was necessarily required in the very nature of things; for otherwise there would remain a chasm or gap, and one extreme would be united with another, without a medium, which is impossible, and repugnant to the nature of things, as appears in the whole course of the universe. By the immutability of the Messiah, here we must understand that which is moral, not that which is natural. There are some who object, Christ was tempted in vain, if he was naturally unchangeable....There are also more arguments, merely philosophical; of which in *Philosophia Kabbalistica*...are urged to prove that from the first beginning, there flowed forth only one thing begun and perfected, which is also confirmed by the authority of ancient and modern philosophers, together with an answer to the objections made on the contrary.[396]

4. This middle being is not to be understood in so gross a manner, as if it stood in a middle place, between two extremes, as the trunk of the body is between the head and feet; but is a medium in respect of its nature, as silver is between tin and gold, or water between air and earth, which are but gross comparisons in regard of the thing itself; neither can anyone suppose the Son to be such a medium between God and the creatures, as though God was not immediately present in all his creatures, and immediately filled all things; for he immediately operates in all things in a proper sense. But this is to be understood of that union and communion which creatures have with God; so that although God immediately operates in all things, yet he uses this medium as an instrument, by which he cooperates in his creatures; because it is, in regard of its nature, more near unto them; and yet because he is more excellent than all other productions, which we call creatures, and that too is his own nature. Therefore it is, he is deservedly called the first begotten of all creatures, and the Son of God, rather than a creature of God; and his production is rather a generation, or emanation from God, than creation, if the Word is taken in a strict sense; although, according to the larger sense and use of this word, he may be said to be created or formed, as the scripture somewhere speaks of him. But if the thing itself is duly understood, it is needless to contend about words. Yet nevertheless a man's son is rather said to be begotten of him, than made or created by him. Of a

house, or a ship, built or made by a man, we do not say it is his son, but his work; because his son is the living image and similitude of himself, which cannot be said of a house or a ship. So this first production of God…to without, is more fitly and properly termed his Son than a creature; because this is the living image of himself, and is greater, and more excellent than all creatures. Now it follows that the Son himself must be immediately present in all these, that he may bless and benefit them. And seeing he is that true medium, between God and the creatures, he must need exist within them, that so by his operation he may stir them up to a union with him. And seeing he is the most excellent production of God…and the most perfect and express image of him, he must need be like God in all his attributes, which without contradiction may be said to be communicated to him; and so by consequence he must necessarily be omnipresent. Besides, if he were not present in all creatures, there would wholly remain a chasm, or wide gap between God and the creatures where he was not, which is absurd.

5. Moreover, as he is partaker of the immutability of God, and the mutability of creatures, and so a medium between that, which is altogether unchangeable, and that which is altogether changeable, as partaking of both; so also he may be said to be a partaker of eternity (which is proper to God) and time, (which is proper to creatures); and although it is said in the preceding chapters that nothing interceded between eternity and time, or between the creatures, and the will of God which created them. Time and creatures are there to be taken in a larger sense, with respect to all the productions of God, made *ad extra*. So that this middle being is as well there comprehended as the rest. Neither can we conceive this middle being to be before creatures in time, but only in the order of nature; so that indeed nothing of time strictly taken happened between the creatures, and the all-creating power and will of God that created them.

6. But if by time, according to the common understanding of the word, we understand a succedaneous increase or decrease of things, according to which they grow and increase into a certain pitch or period, and then again fail from it, until they die or are changed into another state or condition of life; in this sense it may be positively affirmed, that neither this middle being, nor any

creature perfectly united with the same, is subject to time, or the laws thereof; for the laws of time reach but until a certain period or age; and when that period is completed, then those things which are subject to time decay and are consumed, and so die and are changed into quite another species of things, according to that old saying of the Poet:

Thus spiteful age, and time that eats up things,
All things consumes, and to destruction brings.[397]

And for this reason time is divided into four parts, according to the age of a man living in this world, which is infancy, youth, manhood, and old age, even until death; so that all things which are bounded with time are subject to death and corruption, or are changed into another *species* of things, as we see water changed into stones, stones into earth, and earth into trees, and trees into animals or living creatures. But in this most excellent middle being is neither decay nor corruption; nor to speak properly has death any place in him. He is a most powerful and effectual balsam, which can preserve all things from death and corruption, which are joined to him or united with him; so that here all things are perpetually new, springing up fresh and green; here is perpetual youth without old age; and here is the perfection of old age, to wit, great increase of wisdom and experience without any imperfection of age. But when Christ came in the flesh, and in that body which he bare [sic] with flesh from heaven (for every created spirit has a certain vehicle, either terrestrial, aerial, or ethereal, as this was), he took upon him something of our nature, and by consequence the nature of all things (because the nature of man has in it the nature of all creatures, therefore also he is called the microcosm), which nature having assumed in flesh and blood, he sanctified, that by that he might sanctify all things, and so was as that little leaven that changed the whole lump (Gal 5:9). He descended then within time, and for a certain space or period, of his own accord subjected himself to the laws of time, so as to endure great torments, even death itself; but death did not long detain him, for the third day he rose again, and this was the end of all his sufferings, even of his death and burial, viz., that he might heal, cure, and redeem his creatures from death and corruption, which came upon them by the fall, and so at length therefore put an end to times, and elevate the creatures above time to himself, where he abides, who is the same yesterday, today, tomorrow, and forever, without decay, death, or corruption. In like manner, in his spiritual and internal appearance in man, whereby he aims to save, heal, and redeem the soul, he does as it were, after a certain manner, subject himself to a kind of death and passion; and so for a certain space submits himself to the laws of time, that he might elevate the souls of men above time, and corruptibility to himself, where they receive blessing, and grow from one degree of goodness and virtue unto another, forever.

By the same reason, those who are come into a perfect union with Christ, are mounted up into a region or sphere of perfect tranquility, where nothing is seen or perceived to move or compel; for although there exist the most swift and vehement motions; yet nevertheless because the same do so uniformly, so equally, and harmoniously move without the least contrariety or disorder, they seem altogether to rest, from whose many examples may be given in external things. For indeed there are two kinds of motion, which to our bodily sight seem to want motion, that which is exceedingly quick and speedy, and that which is exceedingly slow; so that the middle sort is only discernable by us. Now under time, and the laws may be comprehended not only the earth, and earthly things, but also the sun, moon, and stars, and all the visible part of the world, together with more that is invisible. So that after a long tract of time, all those things may be plainly changed into quite another species of things, and that by the same order and course of divine operation which God has placed in all creatures, as a law or justice which, in his divine wisdom, he has purposed to reward every creature according to its works....

NOTES

1. Michael L. Morgan, *Platonic Piety: Philosophy and Ritual in Fourth Century Athens* (New Haven, CT: Yale University Press, 1990).

2. "Introduction," p. 6.

3. Jean Daniélou, *Platonisme et thélogie mystique: Essai sur la doctrine spirituelle de saint Grégoire de Nysse* (Paris: Aubier, 1944).

4. Jaroslav Pelikan, *Christianity and Classical Culture: The Metamorphosis of Natural Theology in the Christian Encounter with Hellenism*, Gifford Lectures at Aberdeen (New Haven, CT: Yale University Press, 1993), pp. 40–56, pp. 200–214.

5. Anne Conway, *The Principles of the Most Ancient and Modern Philosophy*, Chapter 5, MS # XVI, p. 188.

6. Henry More, *Charitie and Humilitie*, MS # XI, p. 165.

7. Ralph Cudworth, *A Sermon Preached before the Honorable House of Commons at Westminster*, MS # I, p. 59.

8. Mark 12:29–30 AV; italics added.

9. John Smith, *The Excellency and Nobleness of True Religion*, Chapter 2, MS # VIII, p. 152.

10. Benjamin Whichcote, *Our Conversation Is in Heaven*, MS # V, p. 126.

11. 2 Pet 1:4 NEB.

12. Cudworth, *Sermon*, p. 69.

13. Ibid., p. 79.

14. Henry More, *An Explanation of the Divine Mystery of Godliness*, Book X, MS # XIV, p. 176.

15. Origen cited in Jean Danielou, *Origen* (New York: Sheed and Ward, 1955), pp. 107–8.

16. See, for example, Margaret Miles, *Fullness of Life* (Philadelphia: Westminster, 1981).

17. For helpful texts that explore the impact of Platonism on Christianity, see W. R. Inge *The Platonic Tradition in English Religious Thought* (London: Longmans, Green and Co., 1926); and J. H. Muirhead, *The Platonic Tradition in Anglo-Saxon Philosophy* (New York: MacMillan, 1931). Nicholas Sagovsky offers a constructive portrait of

Plato's contribution to Christianity in *Ecumenism, Christian Origins and the Practice of Communion* (Cambridge: Cambridge University Press, 2000), chap. 2. For a good historical study, see C. Bigg, *The Christian Platonists of Alexandria* (Oxford: Clarendon, 1968).

18. *Plato's Epistles*, trans. G. R. Morrow (Indianapolis: Bobbs-Merrill, 1962), pp. 240–41.

19. Plato, *Euthyphro* 14:e.

20. Phil 4:8 KJ.

21. Taliaferro has offered some arguments that undergird Cambridge Platonism in *Consciousness and the Mind of God* (Cambridge: Cambridge University Press, 1994) and *Evidence and Faith: Philosophy and Religion since the Seventeenth Century* (Cambridge: Cambridge University Press, forthcoming).

22. Anthony Tuckney (1599–1670) was Master of Emmanuel in 1645 and of St John's in 1653. His correspondence with Whichcote between September and December 1651, which prompted the latter's declarations of crucial Cambridge Platonist rational tenets, was instrumental in forming the "benchmark of the theological liberty and philosophical orientation of Cambridge Platonism" (see *The Dictionary of Seventeenth-Century British Philosophy*, vol. 2, ed. Andrew Pyle [Bristol: Thoemmes, 2000]; and Edward Augustus George, *Seventeenth Century Men of Latitude* [New York: Scribner's and Sons, 1908], p. 70).

23. Whichcote's benevolence is also exhibited in the fact that, despite his differences with Tuckney on the role of reason in religion (see the Whichcote/Tuckney correspondence in *Moral and Religious Aphorisms*, republished by Samuel Salter, 1753), he elected Tuckney to the Divinity Chair in the University (*Moral and Religious Aphorisms*, p. xxv).

24. John Marshall, *John Locke: Resistance, Religion and Responsibility* (Cambridge: Cambridge University Press, 1994), pp. 78–79.

25. For example, Whichcote left £1000 to Emmanuel College for the founding of four scholarships and £20 to buy books (Emmanuel College Archives, 14.1).

26. See "Preface," in *Select Sermons* (1698), ed. Shaftsbury, p. ix.

27. Bishop Burnet, *History of His Own Time*, vol. 1 (1753), p. 186.

28. John Tulloch, *Rational Theology in England in the Seventeenth Century*, vol. 2 (Edinburgh: W. Blackwood, 1874), p. 46.

29. Herbert of Cherbury, who has mistakenly been regarded by many as the founder of deism, influenced Whichcote's idea of Christianity's "common notions" (see David Pailin, "Should Herbert of Cherbury Be Regarded as a Deist?" in *Journal of Theological Studies* 51 [2000], pp. 114–49). More generally, the idea was a common Ciceronian

NOTES

one, popular in the Renaissance (see Benjamin Whichcote, *Moral and Religious Aphorisms* [1703], p. 969).

30. Ibid., p. 109.

31. Whichcote, *Discourse VVII: "The Illustrious Manifestations of God, and the Inexcusable Ignorance of Man*, in *Works* (Aberdeen, 1751), p. 167.

32. I have used the Latin here as it conveys more closely the theological implications involved in a term itself disputed in meaning (see the Whichcote/Tuckney correspondence in *Moral and Religious Aphorisms* [1753], ed. Salter).

33. Tuckney rebuked Whichcote for using this phrase in an "over-frequentile" *[sic]* manner. For a fascinating discussion of the origin of this renowned saying, see Robert A. Greene, "Whichcote, the Candle of the Lord, and Synderesis," *Journal of the History of Ideas* 52 (1991), pp. 451–70. See also Tuckney, September 15, 1651, in Whichcote/Tuckney correspondence in *Moral and Religious Aphorisms* (1753), ed. Salter, p. 20.

34. Frederick Beiser regards such arguments as an attack on extreme Calvinism, and even the role of Calvinist theology in Hobbesian atheism (see *The Sovereignty of Reason—A Defense of Rationality in the English Enlightenment* [Princeton, NJ: Princeton University Press, 1996], p. 143).

35. Whichcote, *Discourse LVIII: "The Illustrious Manifestations of God, and the Inexcusable Ignorance of Man*, in *Works* (1751), p. 187.

36. Whichcote, September 8, 1651, in Whichcote/Tuckney correspondence in *Moral and Religious Aphorism* (1753), ed. Salter, p. 15.

37. Henry More's preface to his philosophical volume, in *The Life of Henry More, Part 1*, ed. Sarah Hutton and others (Dordrecht: Kluwer, 2000), p. 10

38. Marjorie Hope Nicolson, "Introduction," in *The Conway Letters—The Correspondence of Anne, Viscountess Conway, Henry More and Their Friends, 1642–1684*, ed. Marjorie Hope Nicolson, rev. ed. by Sarah Hutton (Oxford: Clarendon 1992), p. 40. Masters at Eton at this time included the latitudinarian and eirenicist John Hales (1584–1656).

39. Mede became a fellow in 1613 of Christ's College, Cambridge, through the influence of Lancelot Andrewes. His interests ranged widely, into subjects including mathematics and astronomy. He corresponded with Archbishop Laud and with Continental scholars whom, with Samuel Hartlib's help, he made contact with in the 1630s. An eirenicist, his millennian writings include *Clavis Apocalyptica* (1627).

40. Nicolson, "Introduction," p. 41.

41. Hutton, *The Conway Letters*, More-Conway, July 14, 1671, p. 342.

42. Ibid., letters of summer 1660.

43. Ibid., More-Conway, January 7, 1655/56, p. 128.

44. More's *Conjectura Cabbalistica* (1653), his commentary on the first book of Genesis, was encouraged by Conway, though he never was as unreservedly enthusiastic about the Cabbala as was Conway. Indeed, it has been argued that he did "scarcely more than flirt" with it (see Stuart Brown, "Leibniz and More's Cabbalistic Circle," in *Henry More— Tercentenary Studies*, ed. Sarah Hutton [Dordrecht: Kluwer, 1990], p. 81; for Conway's anti-dualistic reaction to More's philosophy, see Sarah Hutton, "Anne Conway: critique de Henry More," *Archives de Philosophie* 58 [1995], pp. 371–84).

45. More, *The Philosophical Poems of Henry More* (1647), in *The Complete Poems of Henry More*, ed. Rev. Alexander B. Grosart (Edinburgh: T. and A. Constable, 1878), p. 137.

46. More, "Psychathanasia"—The Second Part of "The Song of the Soul," in *The Philosophical Poems of Henry More*, in Grosart, *The Complete Poems of Henry More*, p. 45.

47. A. Jacob, *"Introduction,"* in *Immortality of the Soul* (Dordrecht: Kluwer, 1987), p. x. More has been considered by some to be "the founder of the school [of Cambridge Platonism] and its most eminent member" (see C. A Staudenbaur, "Platonism, Theosophy, and Immaterialism: Recent Views of the Cambridge Platonists," *Journal of the History of Ideas* 35 [1974], pp. 157–69).

48. More, *An Antidote against Atheism* (1655), preface.

49. Hutton, *The Conway Letters*, More-Conway, May 7, 1655, p. 109.

50. More, *Immortality of the Soul* (1662), p. 20. More claims that Descartes' views on the mechanical powers of matter would still "fall short," presumably because they do not allow enough room for the spiritual.

51. More, *Immortality of the Soul* (1662), p. 19.

52. Henry More, "Preface," in *Collection of Several Philosophical Writings of Dr. Henry More* (1662), p. vi.

53. For a good discussion of More and Cartesianism, see A. Rupert Hall, *Henry More, Magic, Religion, and Experiment* (Oxford: Blackwell, 1990).

54. Spirit differed from matter in that it is penetrable and indivisible. In stressing the extension of spirit, More is not expressing a universally Platonic concept, and indeed Ralph Cudworth disagreed fundamentally on

the issue, maintaining that spirit could not be extended, else God would be extended and thus divided. For more on More's views on spirit, see Samuel I. Mintz, *The Hunting of Leviathan* (Cambridge: Cambridge University Press, 1962), chap. 5.

55. More, *Enchiridion Metaphysicum* (1671), p. 351.

56. Sarah Hutton, in Pyle, *Dictionary of Seventeenth-Century British Philosophy*, p. 591. A. Rupert Hall asserts that it was very likely that More and Newton had known each other long before they met in Cambridge in 1662, as the brother of Newton's roommate had been a pupil of More's (*Henry More*, p. 82).

57. Henry More, *The Immortality of the Soul* (1659), p. 55. The works were: *Antidote against Atheism* (1653), *Immortality of the Soul* (1659), *Divine Dialogues* (1668), and *Enchiridion Metaphysicum* (1671). A fascinating story alleges that Hobbes had been heard to exclaim, "That if his own Philosophy was not True, he knew of none that he should sooner like than More's of Cambridge" (see Richard Ward, *The Life of the Learned and Pious Dr. Henry More*, in Hutton and others, *The Life of Henry More*, p. 55). For an interesting, if tenuous, view on the similarity of More's view of the afterlife to Hobbes's regarding its materialism and sensuality, see John Henry, "A Cambridge Platonist's Materialism—Henry More and the Concept of Soul," *Journal of the Warburg and Courtauld Institutes* 49 (1986), pp. 172–95.

58. More, *An Antidote against Atheism* (1655), p. 278. This dictum is derived from King James I.

59. More, *The Immortality of the Soul* (1662), p. 67.

60. Robert Crocker, "Henry More: A Biographical Essay," in Hutton, *Henry More—Tercentenary Studies*, p. 3.

61. More, *The Immortality of the Soul* (1662), p. 18.

62. Ibid., p. 254.

63. Ibid., p. 267.

64. Ward, *The Life of the Learned and Pious Dr. Henry More*, p. 34.

65. It is interesting to consider whether More's thought changed in emphasis at all. A. Rupert Hall argues that More turned more from philosophy to religion in the mid 1650s (see *Henry More*, p. 122). Certainly More became more engrossed in spiritual mysticism rather than natural philosophy, with subjects such as the Cabbala and religious "enthusiasm" occupying his mind more than previously. In particular, Lady Conway's later conversion to Quakerism grieved him. Despite his friendship with certain Quakers, such as George Keith, whom he met in 1674, he declared Quakers to be "deluded souls," "intoxicated with vapours from the lowest part of their body" (*Enthusiasmus Triumphatus*, in *A Collection of Several*

Philosophical Writings of Dr. Henry More [1712]). He criticized their reject-ing, as he saw it, of the historical Christ (see *An Explanation of the Divine Mystery of Godliness* [1660], p. xii). On one occasion, on meeting a Quaker who argued for taking away all external observance and ritual, professing only spirit, More claimed that she was like "one that would flay the skin and haire from off a living creature that nothing but the mere substantiall and vitall parts of the animal might remain, and asked her how well she thought the animal might live" (see Hutton, *The Conway Letters*, More-Conway, September 15, 1670, p. 308).

66. More, "Preface," in A *Collection of Several Philosophical Writings of Dr. Henry More* (1662), p. vi.

67. More, *Divine Dialogues* (1668), p. 404.

68. Jacob, "Introduction," p. xliv. More's work had already been brought to the attention of royalty (see John Worthington, *The Diary and Correspondence of Dr. John Worthington*, ed. James Crossley, vol. 1 [Manchester: Chetham Society, 1847], p. 308).

69. Ward, *The Life of the Learned and Pious Dr. Henry More*, p. 101.

70. Marjorie Hope Nicolson, in Hutton, *The Conway Letters*, p. 473. See also Marjorie Hope Nicolson, "James Marsh and the Vermont Trancendentalists," *Philosophical Review* 34 (1925), pp. 28–50. News of More's thought, along with Anne Conway's, reached the ears of Leibniz through Van Helmont (ibid., p. 455).

71. Ibid., p. 475. See also "The Diary of Samuel Newton, Alderman of Cambridge" (Cambridge: Cambridge Antiquarian Society, 1890).

72. Ward, *The Life of the Learned and Pious Dr. Henry More*, p. 132.

73. Tulloch, *Rational Theology*, p. 193.

74. Thomas Birch, "An Account of the Life and Writings of Ralph Cudworth," in *The Intellectual System of the Universe* (1743), p. vi.

75. Ibid.

76. However, despite similarities in certain areas of their thought, particularly with regard to their eirenicism and the role of self-love and sin, there were also differences in their thought, particularly regarding Cudworth's more positive view of religious "enthusiasm" (see J. A. Passmore, *Ralph Cudworth, an Interpretation* (Cambridge: Cambridge University Press, 1951), pp. 53–55.

77. Tulloch, *Rational Theology*, p. 193. J. A. Passmore maintains that it is "very likely" that Cudworth taught More, despite being the younger of the two (*Ralph Cudworth, an Interpretation*, p. 16).

NOTES

78. Cudworth also held a variety of other clerical positions, such as the rectorships of North Cadbury (1650), Toft, Cambridgeshire (1656), and the prebendary of Gloucester (1678).

79. Tulloch, *Rational Theology*, p. 207.

80. Cudworth sustained personal friendships with men on both sides of the political divide. His own family had had strong relations with the monarchy, and he was a firm supporter of the royalist Richard Holdsworth (master of Emmanuel from 1637 to 1643 and vice-chancellor of Cambridge from 1642 to 1643); later he was a friend of John Thurloe (1616–68, secretary of state to Cromwell) and was consulted by Parliament about appointments to government positions (see G. A. J. Rogers, "The Other-worldly Philosophers and the Real World: The Cambridge Platonists, Theology and Politics," in *The Cambridge Platonists in Philosophical Context—Politics, Metaphysics and Religion*, ed. G. A. J. Rogers, J. M. Vienne and Y. C. Zarka [Dordrecht: Kluwer, 1997]).

81. We shall later hear mention of the cure of Cudworth's son at the hands of the Irish healer Valentine Greatrakes (in Hutton, *The Conway Letters*, More-Conway, April 28, 1666, p. 273).

82. Lady Masham's son, Francis Cudworth Masham, became one of the masters of the High Court of Chancery and the accountant general.

83. See Sarah Hutton, "Between Platonism and Enlightenment: Damaris Cudworth, Lady Masham," *British Journal for the History of Philosophy* 1 (1993), pp. 29–54.

84. Cudworth claimed that after encouragement from More he determined to set about his ethical work, only to hear three months later that More had "begun a discourse on the same subject." An "amazed" Cudworth remarked that it would be "not only superfluous but very absurd for two friends at the same time to write on the same argument" (see Cudworth-Dr. Worthington, January 1664–65, John Worthington, *The Diary and Correspondence of Dr. John Worthington*, ed. James Crossley, vol. 2 [Manchester: Chetham Society, 1855], p. 159). In the end, More's *Enchiridion Ethicum* was published in 1667, while Cudworth's manuscript was never published.

85. *A Treatise concerning Eternal and Immutable Morality* was published in 1731, while his *Treatise of Free Will* did not appear until 1838. Some of Charles II's courtiers "endeavored to destroy the reputation of it" (Birch, "An Account," in *True Intellectual System*, p. xiii). Cudworth was accused of being "tritheistic," that is, claiming that the Son and the Holy Ghost are the same substance with the Father but are not numerically or individually the same (see Tulloch, *Rational Theology*, p. 274).

86. British Library Add MSS 4978–82.

87. See Rosalie Colie, *Light and Enlightenment* (Cambridge: Cambridge University Press, 1957), for the influence of Cudworth's *True Intellectual System* in Holland in the early eighteenth century.

88. Sarah Hutton maintains in "Cudworth, Boethius, and the Scale of Nature" (in Rogers, Vienne, and Zarka, *Cambridge Platonists in Philosophical Context*) that the poetry quoted by Cudworth in *True Intellectual System*, Book I, section IV, was from Boethius's *De Consolatione Philosophiae Bk V,* and thus this is the "starting-point" for "reclaiming" the Platonist label for Cudworth (p. 94). Cudworth's Neoplatonism is affirmed by his adoption of Boethius's hierarchal framework, which links directly with Plotinus's ontological view (p. 98).

89. British Library Add MSS 4985 is a collection of Cudworth's notes and consists of a great many works by humanist authors.

90. Danton B. Sailor, "Newton's Debt to Cudworth," *Journal of the History of Ideas* (1988), pp. 511–17, particularly pp. 511–12. Sailor maintains that Cudworth's influence is particularly evident in Newton's *Theologia gentilis origines philosophicae* (p. 517).

91. Cudworth, *True Intellectual System*, p. 557.

92. "Several ministers, doctors and preachers and some merchants and lawyers were convened to consider with Cromwell and council on 4th December 1655, and two or three days weekly to 18th, proposals made on behalf of Jews by Manesseh Ben Israel" (Worthington, *Diary and Correspondence*, ed. Crossley, 1:78).

93. Millenarianism—or the expectation of Christ's imminent kingdom on earth—was particularly strong at this disordered time. Indeed, it is "difficult to exaggerate the extent and strength of millenarian expectations among ordinary people in the 1640s and early 1650s" (Christopher Hill, *The World Turned Upside Down* [London: Temple Smith, 1972], p. 73).

94. Cudworth himself was never a politically active millenarian, although he maintained a scholarly interest in it, for example, working on the prophetic predictions in the book of Daniel.

95. Richard H. Popkin, *The Third Force in Seventeenth-Century Thought* (Leiden: E. J. Brill, 1992), p. 346.

96. See Colie, *Light and Enlightenment*, for the links and correspondence between the Cambridge Platonists (particularly Cudworth) and the eirenical Dutch Arminians.

97. Cudworth, *Sermon*, March 31, 1647, p. 14.

98. Ibid., p. 61.

99. Ibid., p. 33.

NOTES

100. Sarah Hutton, "Ralph Cudworth," in Pyle, *The Dictionary of Seventeenth-Century British Philosophers*, p. 226.

101. Passmore maintains that Cudworth was indebted to Descartes for his mind-body relation and theory of sensation (see Passmore, *Ralph Cudworth, an Interpretation*, p. 10).

102. Ibid., p. 3. Significantly, however, Cudworth never directly refers to Hobbes by name, unlike his other adversaries, which, as Passmore comments, is in the same tradition of talking about the devil! (ibid., p. 11).

103. Mintz, *The Hunting of Leviathan*, p. 50. Scargill later recanted and was readmitted to the university. Cudworth was also aware of other newly appearing atheistical/deistical views; he knew Adam Boreel, who was also on the committee regarding the readmission of the Jews. Boreel had written an answer to the "three imposters" theory of Moses, Christ, and Mohammed as frauds that Henry Oldenburg had reported from Oxford in 1656, and through More, who had a copy, Cudworth would have read Boreel's refutation (see Richard H. Popkin, *Third Force*, p. 343).

104. Mintz, *The Hunting of Leviathan*, p. 54.

105. It is important to note that "self-determination" and other "self" constructs were first used in English by Cudworth (see Roland Hall, "New Worlds and Antedatings from Cudworth's *Treatise on Freewill*," in *Notes and Queries* 205, pp 427–32; "Treatise on Freewill," in *Treatise concerning True and Immutable Morality* [1731], ed. Sarah Hutton [Cambridge: Cambridge University Press, 1996], p. 157).

106. Quoted in Stephen Darwall, *The British Moralists and the Eternal "Ought," 1640–1740* (Cambridge: Cambridge University Press, 1995), p. 140.

107. Humans can "actively change themselves and determine themselves contingently or fortuitously, when they are not necessarily determined by causes antecedent" ("Treatise on Freewill," p. 164). See Darwall, *British Moralists*, chap. 5, for Cudworth's practical/ethical idealism. Darwall states that, for Cudworth, things don't spring only from intellectual forms in the mind, which are also printed on the soul, but from a more inward, vital principle, or an *inward determination in the soul* (p. 127).

108. "Treatise on Freewill," in *Treatise concerning True and Immutable Morality*, p. 196.

109. Cudworth, *True Intellectual System*, p. 53.

110. Ibid., p. 682.

111. Derived from the Stoic *pneuma* and Platonic *anima mundi*.

112. Cudworth, *True Intellectual System*, p. 147.

113. For more on "plastic nature," see William B. Hunter, "The Seventeenth-Century Doctrine of Plastic Nature," *Harvard Theological Review* 43 (1950), pp. 196–213. It was a widespread doctrine in its seventeenth-century heyday and "commanded the allegiance of nearly every important thinker in England" (ibid., p. 202). By the time of Newton, Leibniz, and Locke, the theory was considered outmoded.

114. Cudworth, *True Intellectual System*, p. 150.

115. Ibid., p. 147. All this work on plastic nature may seem at best quaint—the equivalent of early scientific speculation over ether. Still, the Cambridge Platonist demonstrated a keen commitment to a theory of nature in which the spiritual life can flourish. They therefore did not seek a spirituality that was isolated from contemporary science. On that front we commend their goal.

116. Cudworth, *A Treatise concerning True and Immutable Morality*, p. 16. In the same way Cudworth stated that God's will is ruled by God's justice, and not God's justice ruled by God's will (*True Intellectual System*, p. 897).

117. More precisely, it is not because God matches some external standard that God can be said to be morally good, but because God's actual will is itself a standard of perfect mind (see Darwall, *British Moralists*, p. 128).

118. Cudworth, *Treatise concerning True and Immutable Morality*, p. 18.

119. Cudworth, *True Intellectual System*, pp. 146, 196.

120. Ibid., p. 698.

121. Ibid., p. 25.

122. Cudworth, "A Treatise of Freewill," in *Treatise concerning True and Immutable Morality*, pp. 177, 180.

123. Ibid., p. 185.

124. John Locke, *Some Thoughts concerning Education*, ed. John and Jean Yolton (Oxford: Oxford University Press, 1989), p. 248.

125. For Locke and Cudworth, see Passmore, *Ralph Cudworth, an Interpretation*, pp. 91–95.

126. John Locke, *The Reasonableness of Christianity, as Delivered in the Scriptures* (Bristol: Thoemmes, 1997), p. 143.

127. Ibid., p. 188.

128. See particularly Cudworth, *Sermon*, pp. 14 and 28.

129. Robert A. Greene and Hugh MacCallum, "Introduction," in *An Elegant and Learned Discourse of the Light of Nature* (Toronto: University of Toronto Press, 1971), p. x.

NOTES

130. The master of Emmanuel, William Dillingham (1617–89), remarked that Culverwell was treated kindly by his colleagues in Emmanuel, "especially while he lay under the discipline of so sad a providence" (see Greene and MacCallum, "Introduction," p. xii).

131. Seven discourses were published alongside the main *Discourse* in 1652, although they were written beforehand, in 1645–46 (Greene and MacCallum, "Introduction," p. xiii). Significantly, the scientist Robert Boyle may have been behind the publishing of "Spiritual Opticks" (1668) and the fourth edition of the *Discourse* (1669) (see Greene and MacCallum, "Introduction," p. xxi).

132. Francisco Suarez (1548–1614) was a Spanish Jesuit. The role of both Aquinas and Suarez can be seen particularly in Culverwell's espousal of the role of final causes in Creation and in the precedence of the divine intellect in the establishment of natural law, respectively.

133. Greene and MacCallum, "Introduction," p. xlviii. From a different angle, Patrides maintained that Culverwell was too much of a Calvinist to ever be able to penetrate to the center of Cambridge Platonism (C. A. Patrides, *The Cambridge Platonists* [Cambridge, Mass: Harvard University Press, 1970], p. xxvi).

134. D. W. Dockrill, "The Fathers and the Theology of the Cambridge Platonists," in *Studia Patristica* 17 (part 1, 1982), pp. 427–33. Culverwell is also included in E. T. Campagnac, *The Cambridge Platonists* (Oxford: Clarendon, 1901).

135. Nathaniel Culverwell, *An Elegant and Learned Discourse of the Light of Nature* (1652), p. 89.

136. Ibid., p. 90.

137. Ibid., p. 158.

138. Ibid., 91.

139. Ibid., p. 152. Culverwell criticized Plato's belief in connate ideas by maintaining that he had "plac't all his security in some uncertaine airy and imaginary Castles of his own containing and building and fortifying" (ibid.).

140. Ibid., p. 54. Culverwell is, however, very wary about Herbert of Cherbury's idea of "common notions" in religion, claiming its inferiority to Reason itself: "Reason cannot more delight in a common notion or demonstration than Faith does in revealed truth" (ibid., p. 175).

141. Ibid., p. 68.

142. Ibid.

143. Ibid., p. 160.

144. See Knud Haakonssen, "Moral Philosophy and Natural Law: From the Cambridge Platonists to the Scottish Enlightenment," *Political Science* 40, no. 1 (July 1988).

145. Darwall, *British Moralists*, p. 26. As Darwall comments, herein lies Culverwell's dissimilarity to John Locke, as Locke *does not* believe in the Thomist guaranteeing of rational motives of the law of nature inevitably leading us to the good. Instead, we can have conclusive rational motives for doing what an obligating law commanded by God demands *independent* of it (ibid., p. 47). Another related difference lies in the Lockean espousal of reward and punishment as guaranteeing what is in the agent's rational interest, whereas Culverwell maintains that rational motives of obedience to God do not depend on such sanctions (ibid., p. 38).

146. Culverwell, *An Elegant and Learned Discourse*, p. 207.

147. Ibid., p. 50.

148. Ibid., p. 96.

149. Ibid., pp. 93, 178.

150. Ibid., p. 6.

151. Culverwell remarks on the contemporary religious radicalism exemplified in the errors of the antinomians—"wild Seraphick set on fire of hell" (ibid., p. 130) and, specifically, the Seekers, "this wanton and lascivious Sect, that will espouse themselves to no one opinion, that they may the more securely go on whoring all the more" (ibid., p. 149).

152. Ibid., p. 198.

153. See Greene, "Whichcote, the Candle of the Lord, and Synderesis," *Journal of the History of Ideas* 52 (1991), p. 640; and Culverwell, *An Elegant and Learned Discourse*, p. 113.

154. Culverwell, *An Elegant and Learned Discourse*, pp. 122, 70.

155. Ibid., p. 86.

156. Ibid., p. 154.

157. Ibid., p. 168.

158. Ibid., pp. 2, 3.

159. Culverwell's Calvinism is also apparent in his distaste of "outward performances" in worship, his dislike of the Arminians' views on grace, and the "glorious" grace involved in election (ibid., pp. 28–30, 38–39, 138). The language of Puritan devotion is very much evident in his writings; for example, "The Gospel's like a sweet and precious honeycombe" (ibid., p. 40).

160. Ibid., p. 104. This note of Calvinist caution is similar to Peter Sterry's, "[Reason is] but a candle...not the sun itself" (Peter Sterry, *The Spirit's Conviction of Sinne*, sermon before the House of Commons, November 26, 1645, p. 10). Culverwell highlights the boundaries of the

NOTES

candle of the Lord, with regard to divine revelation, claiming that God had decreed that: "hither shalt thou shine, and no further" (Culverwell, *An Elegant and Learned Discourse*, p. 122).

161. Culverwell, *An Elegant and Learned Discourse*, p. 5.
162. Ibid., p. 169.
163. Ibid., p. 4.
164. Ibid., p. 1.
165. Ibid., p. 6.
166. Ibid., p. 70.
167. Ibid., p. 143.
168. Ibid., pp. 189, 53.
169. Ibid., "Mount Ebal," p. 94.
170. Ibid., "The Schisme," p. 19.
171. Ibid., p. 19.
172. Ibid., p. 166.
173. Matthew Arnold maintained that the *Select Discourses* are "much the most considerable work left to us by this Cambridge school" and that, as well as their undoubted religious worth, they should also have a place in English literary history ("Introduction," in *Select Discourses— "The Natural Truth of Christianity—Selections from the Select Discourses of John Smith*," ed. W. M. Metcalfe [London: Alexander Gardiner, 1882], p. xi; see also Tulloch, *Rational Theology*, p. 122).
174. John Worthington, "To the Reader," in *Select Discourses* (1660), p. vi.
175. Smith was buried in Queen's College chapel.
176. Simon Patrick, sermon preached at the funeral of John Smith, in *Select Discourses* (1660), p. 511.
177. Ibid., pp. 537, 515.
178. Ibid., p. 506.
179. Worthington is also widely known for his fascinating *Diary and Correspondence*, which included correspondence with More and Cudworth as well as Samuel Hartlib, among others.
180. W. E. Hough, "The Religious Philosophy of John Smith," *The Baptist Quarterly* 3 (1927), p. 357.
181. Ibid.
182. Smith's library suggests a "comprehensive" reading of Descartes, and various phrases in the *Select Discourses*, such as the "machina" of the body, "mechanicks," and so forth, further suggest Descartes' influence (see J. E. Saveson, "Descartes' Influence on John Smith, Cambridge Platonist," *Journal of the History of Ideas* 20 [1959], p.

258; and J. E. Saveson, "Differing Reactions to Descartes among the Cambridge Platonists," *Journal of the History of Ideas* 21 [1960], p. 560).

183. Saveson, "Differing Reactions to Descartes among the Cambridge Platonists," p. 567.

184. Smith, *Select Discourses*, p. 9.

185. Ibid., pp. 15–16.

186. Ibid., p. 16.

187. Saveson, "Differing Reactions to Descartes among the Cambridge Platonists," p. 564. Such differences between the Cambridge Platonists arise from the fact that their separate systems are based on different parts of Neoplatonic philosophy (p. 567).

188. George, *Seventeenth Century Men of Latitude*, p. 96.

189. Smith, *Select Discourses*, p. 20.

190. Ibid., p. 157.

191. Ibid., p. 148.

192. Ibid., p. 20.

193. Ibid., p. 3.

194. Ibid., p. 16.

195. Ibid.

196. Ibid., p. 13.

197. Ibid., p. 6.

198. Ibid., p. 382.

199. Ibid., pp. 126–27. Smith maintains that the "smothering" of the candle of the Lord is in no way advantageous to religion (p. 448).

200. Ibid., p. 388.

201. Ibid., p. 3.

202. Ibid., pp. 359–61.

203. Smith claims that the good Christian should try to do good, show mercy and compassion, advance justice and righteousness, and be full of charity and good works (ibid., p. 157).

204. Ibid., p. 2.

205. Ibid., p. 372.

206. Ibid., p. 2. Smith takes this image from Plotinus, *Enneads* 1:6. Again we can see the Cambridge Platonists' deification idea.

207. "Hell is rather a nature than a Place: and Heaven cannot be so fully defined by anything *without* us, as by something that is *within* us" (ibid., p. 447). Smith here echoes Whichcote who maintained that both heaven and hell have their foundation with our own consciences (see Whichcote, *Moral and Religious Aphorisms* [1703], p. 35).

208. Smith, *Select Discourses*, p. 28.

209. Ibid., p. 330.

NOTES

210. Many studies of Cambridge Platonism have omitted Sterry; those who *do* include Sterry under the banner of Cambridge Platonism include F. J. Powicke (London, 1926) and, more recently, Sarah Hutton *(A Treatise concerning Eternal and Immutable Morality)*, p. x. C. A. Patrides *does not* include Sterry in his Cambridge Platonist anthology because of his "denial of free will" *(The Cambridge Platonists*, p. xxvi). Others, such as De Pauley (London: SPCK, 1937) and Tulloch (Edinburgh: Blackwood, 1872) also omit Sterry. However, it seems only right to include Sterry within Cambridge Platonism as his ideas of free will lie close to Cudworth's "self-determination," and his ideas on love and toleration, unity of the will and understanding, and general Platonic world view surely place him under the umbrella of Cambridge Platonism. Sterry's work has been greatly neglected since its original publication, although extracts were printed in the 1785 *Prayers Selected from Thomas a Kempis, Everard, Law, and (Chiefly) Peter Sterry* and one of his sermons appeared in *Fourteen Sermons* (1831). More recently, Vivian de Sola Pinto, in *Peter Sterry—Platonist and Puritan* (Cambridge: Cambridge University Press, 1934), included extracts from Sterry's writings. N. I. Matar ed., *Peter Sterry—Select Writings* (New York: Peter Lang, 1994) has published a collection of work from Sterry's personal manuscripts of letters and sermon notes, available in Emmanuel College, Cambridge (MS 289–95).

211. Peter Sterry, *The Appearance of God to Man in the Gospel and the Gospel Change...* (1710) (publisher to reader).

212. Ibid. Sadly, the funeral sermon is not extant.

213. MS Percy 7, Queen's University Belfast, *The Diary of Samuel Rogers*, entries for December 17, 1634, and May 17, 1636, directly allude to Sterry as part of the fasting, devotional group meeting in Emmanuel.

214. Ibid., April 6, 1636.

215. Perhaps one of the reasons Sterry left Emmanuel was that by about 1635, Emmanuel was "not a happy place," and there were several rows in the college as to whether masters could retain their livings, as well as conflicts over leases (see Francis Ames-Lewis, ed., *Sir Thomas Gresham and Gresham College—Studies in the Intellectual History of London in the Sixteenth and Seventeenth Centuries* [Aldershot/Brookfield: Ashgate, 1999], p. 123). In addition, it seemed that the college's Puritanism was under threat—although only a slight one—of Laudianism at around this time: Samuel Rogers railed against the "cursed formalists, who (seem to) be making a fuss for people to wear vestments in chapel" (Queen's University Belfast, *The Diary of Samuel Rogers*, April 6, 1636). There was also evidence of crucifixes in some chambers and two fellows, Nicholas Hall and Thomas Holbech, bowed at the name of Jesus and upon entering and

leaving the chapel (Sarah Bendell, Christopher Brooke, Patrick Collinson, *A History of Emmanuel College, Cambridge* (Woodbridge: Boydell Press, 1999), pp. 206–7.

216. For more on this Puritan network, see Ann Hughes, *Politics, Society and Civil War in Warwickshire, 1620–1660* (Cambridge: Cambridge University Press, 1987).

217. Baker MSS vi 84, as quoted by Vivian De Sola Pinto, "Introduction," in *Speculum Religionis*, ed. F. C. Burkitt (Oxford: Oxford University Press, 1929), p. 165. John Sadler was Sterry's contemporary at Emmanuel in the 1630s and was later master of Magdalene.

218. Therefore, it is clear that, contrary to the entry on Peter Sterry in *The Dictionary of Seventeenth-Century British Philosophy* (ed. Pyle, p. 769), Sterry was chaplain to Lord Brooke *before* and not *after* 1643. Among much other evidence, Lord Brooke's death in 1643 confirms this point (*The Diary of Thomas Dugard*, British Library Add MSS 23146, entry for July 19, 1638).

219. Seven pounds was paid, through Sterry, to a Dr. Rutterford (an intermediary between the opposition and the Scots) and a Dr. Frost (himself a Scot) (John Halford, "John Halford's Accounts," MS CR 1886 Warwick County Record Office).

220. Robert Greville, Lord Brooke, "Postscript," in *The Nature of Truth* (1642).

221. W. R. Sorley, *A History of English Philosophy* (Cambridge: Cambridge University Press, 1920), p. 42.

222. Sterry's marriage with the like-minded Frances was extremely happy. On one occasion in 1662 he wrote to her: "How difficult is it for me to break (off) Conversation with you, and leave your Company, who are as an Orbe of Heaven, in which my Sun, my Jesus fixeth His Throne" (MS 289, Emmanuel College Library, pp. 4–9).

223. For more on the manuscripts, see P. J. Croft and Nabil Matar, *The Peter Sterry MSS at Emmanuel College, Transactions of the Cambridge Bibliographical Society* 8 (1981).

224. "To Frances," MS 289, Emmanuel College Library, pp. 65–67.

225. "To Peter," MS 290, Emmanuel College Library, p. 13.

226. His sermon was *The Spirit's Conviction of Sinne*, preached November 26, 1645.

227. Blair Worden, "Toleration and the Cromwellian Protectorate," in *Studies in Church History*, vol. 21, *Persecution and Toleration*, ed. W. J. Sheils (Oxford, 1984), p. 208.

NOTES

228. Blair Worden, "Providence and Politics in Cromwellian England," *Past and Present* 109 (1985), p. 57. Sterry was not unusual here; indeed, Providentialism was "ubiquitous" in the seventeenth century (p. 55).

229. Peter Sterry, *The Commings Forth of Christ in the Power of His Death* (sermon before Parliament, November 1, 1649).

230. Matar, *Peter Sterry—Select Writings*, p. 4.

231. Sterry was one of the Cambridge Platonists who sat on the committee in 1655 considering the proposals made by the self-appointed ambassador for the Jews, Menasseh ben Israel, to readmit the Jews to England. The millenarian interest in such a proposal is clear (for Sterry's millenarianism, see particularly *The Clouds in which Christ Comes* (sermon before the Commons, October 27, 1647), *The Commings Forth of Christ in the Power of His Death* (sermon before Parliament, November 1, 1649), and *England's Deliverance from the Northern Presbytery, Compared with Its Deliverance from the Roman Papacy* (sermon to Parliament, 1652).

232. By the 1640s and 1650s the work of the Saxon mystic Jacob Boehme (1575–1624) was published in England, Holland, Germany, and elsewhere. Boehme's work grew in popularity during the mid-seventeenth century, with men such as Sir Henry Vane Jr. and John Milton reading him with interest. N. I. Matar claims that Sterry's political millenarianism of the years from 1649 to 1652 had given way, by 1654, to an internalized eschatology (N. I. Matar, "Peter Sterry and Morgan Llwyd," *The Journal of the United Reformed Church History Society* 2, no. 8 [October 1981], p. 277).

233. Viscount Lisle (1619–98), later Earl of Leicester, was a member of the Council of State during the Commonwealth and sat in Cromwell's House of Lords, although he exercised little political influence (*Dictionary of National Biography*, ed. Sidney Lee, vol. 52, p. 225). Contrary to the *Dictionary of Seventeenth-Century British Philosophy* (ed. Pyle, p. 769), Sterry retired to *West* Sheen, not *East* Sheen.

234. Sterry applied for a license to preach on May 10, 1672, sadly only two weeks before his death.

235. Sterry, *The Spirit's Conviction of Sinne*, p. 27.

236. Ibid.

237. Sterry, *The Teachings of Christ in the Soule of Man*, (sermon before the House of Peers, March 29, 1648), p. 24.

238. Such a joining together of the will/understanding and the heart is evident in Sterry's quoting of Iamblichus: "The first use of our Reason is not the Seeing, but Feeling of God" (MS 295, Emmanuel College Library, p. 36). For more on passional reason, see William J.

Wainwright, *Reason and the Heart—A Proglegomenon to a Critique of Passional Reason* (Ithaca, NY: Cornell University Press, 1995).

239. Peter Sterry, "Preface," in *Discourse of the Freedom of the Will* (1675).

240. Ibid.

241. Sterry, *A Discourse of the Freedom of the Will*, p. 138.

242. Ibid., p. 16.

243. Ibid., p. 186.

244. Ibid., p. 16.

245. Privation is the "principle and form of all evil" (Sterry, *A Discourse of the Freedom of the Will* [1675], p. 144; Sterry, *The Rise, Race, and Royalty of the Kingdom of God in the Soul of Man* [1683], p. 279).

246. MS 291 Emmanuel College Library, p. 9. This is in contrast to the senses of the body, which converse only with "particular things in a divided state."

247. Sterry remarks that Christ alone is the "true Mercury, the Mediatour, and same through all Duration, States and formes of things" (MS 289, Emmanuel College Library, p. 154).

248. Ibid., p. 174.

249. Ibid., pp. 61–63.

250. Sterry, *Appearance*, p. 388.

251. Sterry, *The Rise, Race, and Royalty of the Kingdom of God in the Soul of Man* (1683). Also see D. P. Walker, *The Decline of Hell—Seventeenth Century Discussions of Eternal Torment* (London: Routledge and Kegan Paul, 1964).

252. Sterry, *Discourse of the Freedom of the Will* (1675), p. 190. Frederick Beiser in his excellent book *The Sovereignty of Reason* (Princeton, NJ: Princeton University Press, 1996) argues persuasively that the Cambridge Platonists viewed the fear of a wrathful God as a "root cause of atheism," as atheism in contrast brought with it a kind of deliverance (p. 142).

253. Sterry, *"Preface,"* in *A Discourse of the Freedom of the Will*.

254. Ibid.

255. Powicke, *The Cambridge Platonists*, p. 187.

256. Sterry, "Preface," in *A Discourse of the Freedom of the Will*.

257. In his love for his fellow humans and desire for unity and friendship, Sterry passes beyond being concerned *only* for the salvation of souls into a concern for society at large.

258. Sterry, *The Spirit's Conviction of Sinne*, p. 15.

259. Sterry, *A Discourse of the Freedom of the Will* (1675), p. 70.

NOTES

260. Hutton, *The Conway Letters*, Conway-More, May 24, 1664, p. 224.

261. He was granted an earldom in 1679, the year of Anne's death, and subsequently was made secretary of state in 1682.

262. Hutton, *The Conway Letters*, Conway-More, November 28, 1660, p. 181.

263. Ibid., More-Conway, April 28, 1666, p. 273. Greatrakes's appearance in Ragley in 1666 occasioned the presence of the Cambridge Platonists More, Whichcote, and Cudworth, all eager to see the Irish healer. Cudworth consequently professed public gratitude for the curing of his son.

264. Sarah Hutton, "Medicine and Henry More's Circle," in *Religio Medici: Medicine and Religion in Seventeenth-Century England*, ed. Andrew Cunningham and Ole Peter Grell (Hampshire: Scholar Press, 1996).

265. Hutton, *The Conway Letters*, More-Mrs Elizabeth Foxcroft, June 10, 1669, p. 297.

266. Ibid., Conway-More, May 24, 1664, p. 224.

267. More invited Van Helmont to dine in his rooms in Christ's in October 1670. He held a high opinion of the Dutchman, claiming to Conway that he "has a hearte so good, so kind, so officious, so plaine and simple, and so desirous of the public good" (Hutton, *The Conway Letters*, More-Conway, March 14, 1670/71, p. 329).

268. Richard Ward, *The Life of the Learned and Pious Dr. Henry More*, p. 124.

269. Ibid., p. 669.

270. The Lurianic Cabbala was based on the Cabbalistic writings of Isaac Luria (1534–72) and his disciples.

271. See Allison Coudert and Taylor Corse, "Introduction to Anne Conway," in *The Principles of the Most Ancient and Modern Philosophy* (Cambridge: Cambridge University Press, 1996). Coudert stresses the impact of the Lurianic Cabbala on Conway overmuch when she claims that *The Principles* "show the impact of Helmont's thought at every turn" (see Allison Coudert, "A Cambridge Platonist's Kabbalist Nightmare," *Journal of the History of Ideas* 36 [1975], pp. 633–51).

272. See Henry More, "What Is Plato, But Moses Atticus?" in *Conjectura Cabbalistica* (1713), preface. Despite this surface similarity regarding the *prisca theologia* and the Cabbala, in fact More's views were very different. His philosophical "Cabbala" was of his own creation and was vastly different from the esoteric Jewish mysticism that caught the imagination of his friend, the viscountess. Indeed, Stuart Brown claims that "More did scarcely more than flirt with the cabbala" and was probably

"appalled" at Conway's zeal in pursuing it (see "Leibniz and More's Cabbalistic Circle," in Hutton, *Henry More—Tercentenary Studies*, p. 81).

273. See *The Encyclopedia of Religion*, ed. Mircea Eliade, vol. 12 (New York: Macmillan, 1987), pp. 130–31.

274. Hutton, *The Conway Letters*, Conway-More, November 29, 1675, p. 407.

275. Ibid., p. 409. Conway remarked that Van Helmont "is growne a very religious Churchman; he goes every Sunday to the Quakers meetings."

276. The Quakers were persecuted greatly at this time. The Anglican Conventicle Acts of 1664 and 1670 meant that there were huge numbers of arrests, and many died in prison. Lord Conway paid fees to release Quakers from prison, for his wife's sake, though he found them "a senseless, wilful, ridiculous generation of people" (Hutton, *The Conway Letters*, Lord Conway-Anne Conway, October 30, 1678, p. 444).

277. Hutton, *The Conway Letters*, Conway-More, February 4, 1675/76, pp. 421–22.

278. There *are* additional similarities between Cambridge Platonism's contemplative idea of "Christ within" and the Quaker idea of the "inner light," although it is going too far to say, with Marjorie Hope Nicolson, that Henry More and the Quakers were "integral parts of the same movement" (Nicolson, in Hutton, *The Conway Letters*, p. 379).

279. Ward, *The Life of the Learned and Pious Dr. Henry More*, p. 120. For More's attempts at "setting her right," see, e.g., Hutton, *The Conway Letters*, More-Conway, December 29, 1675, and January 10, 1676. Lord Conway was also extremely concerned at his wife's conversion and had little liking for the Quakers, claiming that those around his wife were "an unpleasing sort of people, silent, sullen, and of a removed conversation" (Hutton, *The Conway Letters*, Lord Conway-Sir George Rawdon, December 28, 1677, p. 439).

280. One such man was the Quaker George Keith, about whom More commented: "Setting aside his Schismaticallnesse, which I roundly told him of, and the ridiculous rusticity of that sect, I found him a man very considerably learned, of good witt, and quick apprehension, and which is the best of all, heartily breathing after the attainment of the new life of a Christian" (Hutton, *The Conway Letters*, More-Conway, August 11, 1674, p. 391).

281. Ibid., p. 122.

282. Ibid., Lord Conway-Sir George Rawdon, December 28, 1677, p. 439.

NOTES

283. Carolyn Merchant, "The Vitalism of Anne Conway: Its Impact on Leibniz's Concept of the Monad," *Journal of the History of Philosophy* 17 (1979), p. 258.

284. Hutton, "Anne Conway—critique de Henry More," p. 384.

285. Contrary to Descartes' mechanism, Conway believed nature to be a "living body which has life and perception" (*Principles*, p. 64). She attacks Hobbes and Spinoza on pages 64–65. As well as a close affinity with More's work, one can also see particular similarities between Conway's thought and Peter Sterry's. Both emphasize universal salvation, stress the love rather than tyranny of God, and highlight the importance of Christ as mediator. Sterry bravely defended the Quaker James Naylor before Parliament in 1656 and leaned toward monism. Certain phrases are also strikingly similar; for example, Conway warns people against conceiving God "as an Idol of their own Imagination" (*Principles*, p. 21), and Sterry claims: "All images here...set up as the true and proper Appearance of God to the Spirit of Man are Idols" (*Appearance*, p. 185). Such similarities occur both as a result of, and even as a reaction to, More's work. We also find the influence of other Christian platonist texts, such as Ficino and Origen, and other works, such as the *Theologia Germanica*, Boehme's writings, and the Cabbala. However, there is no evidence of a direct influence of Peter Sterry himself on Conway, though it is very possible that, encouraged by More, she may have read some of Sterry's work.

286. Conway, *Principles* (1996), pp. 37, 38.

287. Universal salvation (an ancient heresy found in Origen among others) is also in Peter Sterry (*Rise, Race, and Royalty of the Kingdom of God in the Soul of Man*, p. 36). A hint of this "laying down" the horrors and eternity of hell is also present in Whichcote, who stressed that hell (as heaven) was more a nature than a place, and a "guilty conscience" already knows hell (*Works*, p. 243).

288. Conway, *Principles* (1996), p. 37.

289. Hutton, "Anne Conway—critique de Henry More," p. 384.

290. Conway, *Principles* (1996), p. 56.

291. Jacob, *Immortality of the Soul*, p. 199; Conway, *Principles* (1996), p. 57.

292. Conway, *Principles* (1996), p. 58.

293. Ibid.

294. Ibid., pp. 39, 20. Note that the term *monad* was adopted by Leibniz later on.

295. Ibid., p. 40.

296. Ibid.

297. Ibid., p. 29.

298. Ibid., p. 20.

299. Ibid., p. 35.

300. Ibid., pp. 24–26.

301. For example, Marjorie Nicolson claims that Conway had a great influence on Leibniz (in Hutton, *The Conway Letters*, p. 456).

302. See Merchant, "The Vitalism of Anne Conway," p. 255.

303. Carolyn Merchant, *The Death of Nature—Women, Ecology, and the Scientific Revolution* (San Francisco: Harper & Row, 1980), chap. 11, p. 254. Merchant explains that Conway's significance was unknown, largely because the academic Heinrich Ritter, writing a couple of centuries later, assumed that Van Helmont, instead of Conway, was the author rather than the editor of the *Principles* (p. 267).

304. Quoted in Merchant, *The Death of Nature*, p. 257.

305. See Merchant, "The Vitalism of Anne Conway," p. 255.

306. Hutton, *The Conway Letters*, Charles Coke-Lord Conway, February 23, 1679, p. 451.

307. Ibid.

308. Ibid. (quoted from Ward, *The Life of the Learned and Pious Dr. Henry More*).

309. George, *Seventeenth Century Men of Latitude*.

310. The Cambridge Platonists retained a tolerant stance apart from the conflicts of their own day. Peter Sterry was the most partisan of the group through aligning himself with Cromwell, although he professed toleration, even when it made him unpopular with Parliament, as seen in his defense of the Quaker James Naylor (*The Way of God with His People in These Nations* (1656).

311. In 1572, Queen Elizabeth was excommunicated from the Roman Catholic Church by the pope.

312. John Spurr, *English Puritanism 1603–1689* (New York: St. Martin's Press, 1998), p. 89. Thomas Cartwright's sermons in 1570 and the vicious anti-episcopal "Martin Marprelate" tracts in 1588 are examples of radical Puritanism in Elizabethan England.

313. The King James version of 1611.

314. Nicholas Tyacke, *Anti-Calvinists and the Rise of English Arminianism 1590–1640* (Oxford: Oxford University Press, 1987), p. 106. Arminianism was based on the theology of the Dutchman Jacobus Arminius (1560–1609). As far as the Calvinists were concerned, the emphasis of the Arminians on good works would have seemed ominously similar to that of the Roman Catholics.

NOTES

315. Robert Greville, Lord Brooke, the Parliamentarian leader, claimed that the clergy wasted much time in debating matters that were "indifferent" and scoffed: "Cassocks, Gowns, Tippets....Weighty matters indeed, for Grave, Learned, Reverend Divines to spend their time and thoughts upon" (*A Discourse concerning the Nature of That Episcopacy Which Is Exercised in England* [1642], p. 15).

316. The negotiations came to nothing, and Charles married French Catholic Princess Henrietta Maria instead.

317. Montagu was the author of the Arminian tract *A New Gag for an Old Goose* (1624). William Laud (1573–1645) was created Archbishop of Canterbury in 1633.

318. Robert Greville, Lord Brooke, *A Discourse concerning the Nature of That Episcopacy Which Is Exercised in England*, p. 16.

319. Laudianism, named after Archbishop Laud, was the type of High Church Arminianism promoted by Charles I and deeply distasteful to Calvinists.

320. Tom Webster, *Godly Clergy in Early Stuart England—The Caroline Puritan Movement, 1620–1643* (Cambridge: Cambridge University Press, 1997), p. 97.

321. Ibid., p. 8.

322. The accounts of Warwick Castle 1640–41 show that money was paid out to the "Scots Lords," and that they stayed in Warwick Castle (John Halford, "John Halford's Accounts," MS CR 1886 Warwick County Record Office).

323. There is some scholarly debate today on the extent of Puritan damage to religious images. As for Cambridge, colleges such as Peterhouse and St. John's had also admitted many Laudian High Church conventions (such as vestments, candles, and bowing) into their worship (see John Twigg, *The University of Cambridge and the English Revolution 1625–1688* [Cambridge: Cambridge University Press, 1990], p. 89). This suggests that when the Cambridge Platonists were in Emmanuel College, it maintained its Puritan reputation and was far from being the "bastion of Laudianism" that the rest of the university was reputed to be.

324. Although the Westminster Assembly contained both Presbyterians and Independents (such as the Cambridge Platonist Peter Sterry), it was the ideas of the former group that held sway, although the "Directions" produced were of such a mild Presbyterianism as to annoy the Scots, who believed that the church should be more separate from the state. Presbyterians and Independents were subtly different: Independents did not believe in the need for the rigid structure of elders and so forth in decision-making but instead claimed more power for the congregation as

a whole. Robert Greville, Lord Brooke—an Independent—was typical of his group when he claimed that "in the election of officers, in decision of Controversies, in cases of Conscience, in Excommunication, the *whole* Church disposes everything, not the Bishops, not the Presbyters alone" (*Discourse concerning the Nature of That Episcopacy Which Is Exercised in England*, p. 85). Politically, the Independents were keener on social reforms and religious liberty, and they were prepared to fight the king until he was defeated; the Presbyterians preferred the idea of a settlement with Charles and were more suspicious of the radicals in the New Model Army.

325. By 1646 there existed only a "patchwork" Presbyterian church in England (see Spurr, *English Puritanism*). It was true that the creation of a new Presbyterian national church would have been contrary to the wishes of a large section of the population.

326. Hill, *The World Turned Upside Down*, p. 47. Royalists and Parliamentarians were scattered about the country, although the main concentrations of Royalists could be found in the north and west, while the Parliamentarian strongholds were mainly in the south and east.

327. Charles Carlton, "The Impact of the Fighting," in *The Impact of the English Civil War*, ed. J. S. Morrill (London: Collins and Brown, 1991), p. 20.

328. This was for a variety of reasons, including Laudianism, refusal to accept the Solemn League and Covenant, or other scandals (see Spurr, *English Puritanism*).

329. The forces sent to Ireland to quell the rebellious populace and prevent the people from supporting Charles Stuart were led by Oliver Cromwell and caused great carnage and destruction: three thousand Irish were killed at Drogheda, while another two thousand died at Wexford.

330. Charles Stuart (1630–85) had been proclaimed King Charles II in Edinburgh in 1649, although he was not to regain his father's English throne until 1660.

331. Burnet, *History of His Own Time*, p. 92.

332. The other four monarchies had been Babylon, Persia, Greece, and Rome.

333. See Sterry, *Way of God*.

334. Whichcote, Cudworth, and Sterry served on the committee.

335. This was over 350 years after their expulsion from England.

336. The ejectors consisted of thirty-eight local boards, while the thirty-eight triers included Baptists and Presbyterians as well as Independents. Peter Sterry acted as a trier.

NOTES

337. Wilbur Cortez Abbott, ed., *The Writings and Speeches of Oliver Cromwell*, vol. 4 (Cambridge, Mass: Harvard University Press, 1947), p. 473.

338. Paul Seaward, *The Restoration* (Hampshire: Macmillan, 1991), p. 41.

339. Ibid.

340. John Gascoigne, *Cambridge in the Age of the Enlightenment* (Cambridge: Cambridge University Press, 1989), p. 30.

341. Seaward, *Restoration*, p. 57.

342. Ibid., p. 62.

343. Ibid., p. 68.

344. Evelyn Underhill, *The Mystics of the Church* (Southampton: Camelot Press, 1975; originally published 1925), p. 222.

345. Walter Wakefield, "Anglican Spirituality," in *Christian Spirituality; Post-Reformation and Modern*, ed. L. Dupre and D. E. Saliers (New York: Crossroad, 1989), p. 270, vol. 18, *World Spirituality: An Encyclopedic History of the Religious Quest*.

346. Ibid., p. 271. For further support, see E. G. Rupp, "A Devotion of Rapture," in *Reformations, Conformity and Dissent*, ed. R. B. Knox (London: Epworth, 1976).

347. Plutarch (AD 45–125), biographer and moralist, wrote *Parallel Lives*, which was extremely popular in early modern England.

348. This word was used by the Hebrews to uncover fleeing enemy Ephrainites, who had difficulty pronouncing the "sh."

349. Aristotle, *Magna Moralia* 2.15.7.4.

350. Athanasius, *De Incarnatione*.

351. Plato, *Euthyphro* 10a.

352. Cf. Smith, *Select Discourses*, in which the infant Christ is formed in the soul ("Of the True Way or Method of Attaining to Divine Knowledge," section 3).

353. The Danaides were the fifty daughters of Danaeus. At their father's command, they murdered their husbands and were thus condemned to Hades, eternally pouring water into a perforated vessel.

354. See Seneca Minor, *Investigations of Nature (Quaestiones Naturales)* 2.31.1.

355. Augustine, *On the Psalms*, commentary on Psalm 32.

356. "Enthusiasm," or spiritual fervor, was increasingly found in the multitude of Protestant sects and was most evident in the contemporary "Quakings" of the Society of Friends, or Quakers. Peter Sterry sympathized in that "God sends forth this spirit after a new manner into human hearts, that they boyl and run over. They are no more in their own

power, they can no longer contain themselves" (*Way of God*, p. 27). However, generally the Cambridge Platonists were wary of irrational "enthusiasm," as we see here, although Henry More believed that a praiseworthy "enthusiasm" was also found in the ancient Platonists ("Preface," in *An Antidote against Atheism*).

357. Plato, *Phaedrus*, 248b, d.

358. Ibid., 248a.

359. Plato, *Republic*, 524e-26b.

360. Servant as instrument, see Aristotle, *The Politics*, 1253 b. 35.

361. Aquinas, *Summa Theologica* I: quaest. i, art. viii, ad. 2.

362. Aquinas discusses meekness as the mitigating power of anger and clemency as moderating punishment (*Summa Theologica* II:II: quaest. 157.

363. Quoted by Cicero in *Tusculan Disputations* IV, VI.

364. This refers to Robert Greville, Lord Brooke, Parliamentarian and Platonist, who was patron to fellow Cambridge Platonist Peter Sterry (Brooke, *The Nature of Truth*).

365. Here Culverwell would be thinking particularly of Thomas Hobbes (1588–1679), whose *Leviathan* (1651) attacked Orthodox Christianity.

366. Pico della Mirandola describes the ascent to unity, truth, and goodness by the unifying light and love of God (*Of Being and Unity*, chap. X, 79–81).

367. Aquinas, *Summa Theologica* I:II, quaest. 68, art. 2.

368. Letus Socinus (1526–62) and his nephew Faustus Socinus (1539–1604) questioned the divinity of Christ and, through applying human reason, rejected all mysteries in religion.

369. Porphyry, *Life of Plotinus I*.

370. Plato, *Phaedrus*, 248d.

371. Simplicius was a fifth-century commentator and Neoplatonist.

372. Cicero believed that the existence of the moral obligation is co-eternal with that of the divine mind, and that the divine mind cannot live in a state devoid of reason (*De Legibus*, Book II:4).

373. The Peripatetics drew on Aristotle's notion of the active intellect (*De Anima*, Book 3).

374. Plotinus, *Ennead*, 1.1.6.

375. A reference to the angels at the empty tomb.

376. Plotinus, *Ennead*, 5.3.17.

377. 1 John 1:1.

378. Origen discourses on the divine light in *Commentary on the Gospel of John*, Book X, 25.

NOTES

379. Plotinus, *Ennead*, 4.4.42–43.

380. Ibid., 2.9.15.

381. Plotinus believed there was need for the eye to become "sun-like to see the sun" (ibid., 1.6.9).

382. Aristotle, *Nicomachean Ethics* I, 3.

383. E.g., Plotinus, *Ennead*, 2.9.7; Iamblichus, *Theurgia* or *The Egyptian Mysteries*, chap. XII.

384. Plato, *Phaedrus*, 250c, 5–6; and Philo, *Quaestiones in Genesis (Exodus)*.

385. Reminiscent of Plato, *Phaedrus*, 247c.

386. Phansy = imagination.

387. More is referring here to the Society of Friends (or Quakers), whom he elsewhere attacked for placing too great an emphasis on spiritual enthusiasm and for placing an allegorical rather than historical emphasis on Christ ("Enthusiasmus Triumphatus," in *A Collection of Several Philosophical Writings of Dr. Henry More* [1712], pp. 17–18).

388. The Spanish began to occupy the West Indies in the 1490s. However, it was rumored that atrocities were committed against the native population, such as those described by Bartolome de Las Casas in 1518.

389. The role of the godly magistrate is described in the Westminster Confession (1646): "God...has ordained Civil magistrates to be under him over the people, for his own glory and the public good; and to this end, has armed them with the power of the sword, for the defense and encouragement of them that are good, and for the punishment of evildoers" (23:1).

390. It is probable that the reference here is to the fourth century BC writer of Greek comedies, Aristophanes.

391. See Plato, *Symposium*, 210e–12a.

392. Sterry is most likely writing here of Pope Gregory I (540–604).

393. Aristotle, *Physics*, 188b, 21–26.

394. Vergil, *Aeneid*, Book I.

395. The term *Adam Kadmon* is a Cabbalistic one, which Conway here seems to conflate with Philo's doctrine of the "logos" (e.g., *De Hominis Opificio* VI).

396. The esoteric Jewish mystical philosophy of the Lurianic Cabbala was based on the writings of Isaac Luria (1534–72) and influenced Conway through Francis Mercury Van Helmont.

397. Ovid, *Metamorphoses*, Book XV, 234. *"Tempus edax rerum, tuque,/invidiosa vetustas, omnia destruitis."*

BIBLIOGRAPHY

Primary Literature
A Selection of Some Major Cambridge Platonist Texts

Whichcote, Benjamin

Religious Aphorisms Collected from the Manuscript Papers...with additions by Samuel Salter (London, 1793).
Works (Aberdeen, 1751).

Sterry, Peter

Discourse of the Freedom of the Will (London, 1675).
The Rise, Race, and Royalty of the Kingdom of God in the Soul of Man (London, 1683).
The Appearance of God to Man in the Gospel and the Gospel Change (London, 1710).
The Spirit's Conviction of Sinne—A Sermon before the Honourable House of Commons (November 26, 1645).
The Teachings of Christ in the Soule—A Sermon before the House of Peers in Covent-Garden Church (March 29, 1648).

More, Henry

A Platonicall Song of the Soul (Cambridge, 1642).
Philosophical Poems (Cambridge, 1647).
An Antidote against Atheism, or An Appeal to the Natural Faculties of the Minde of Man, Whether or Not There Be a God (London, 1652).
Enthusiasmus Triumphatus (London, 1656).

BIBLIOGRAPHY

The Immortality of the Soul, So Farre Forth as It Is Demonstrable from the Knowledge of Nature and the Light of Reason (London, 1659); also ed. A. Jacob (Dordrecht: Kluwer, 1987).

An Explanation of the Grand Mystery of Godliness, or A True and Faithful Representation of the Everlasting Gospel of our Lord and Saviour Jesus Christ (London, 1660).

Enchiridion Ethicum (London, 1667); also trans. *Handbook of Ethics* (London, 1690).

Divine Dialogues (London, 1668).

Enchiridion Metaphysicum (London, 1671); trans. *Handbook of Metaphysics* (London, 1690).

(Many of the above are included in *Opera Omnia*, 3 vols. [London 1675–79].)

Cudworth, Ralph

A Sermon Preached before the Honourable House of Commons (Cambridge, 1647).

The True Intellectual System of the Universe: The First Part; Wherein All the Reason and Philosophy of Atheism Is Confuted; and Its Impossibility Demonstrated (London, 1678; reprinted with intro. G. A. J. Rogers, Bristol: Thoemmes, 1995).

A Treatise concerning Eternal and Immutable Morality (London, 1731). A new edition by Sarah Hutton also includes *Treatise of Freewill* (Cambridge: Cambridge University Press, 1996).

Smith, John

Select Discourses (London, 1660; reprint, New York: Scholars' Facsimilies and Reprints, 1978).

Culverwell, Nathaniel

An Elegant and Learned Discourse of the Light of Nature (London, 1652; Toronto: University of Toronto Press, 1971).

Conway, Anne

The Principles of the Most Ancient and Modern Philosophy (London, 1690; Cambridge: Cambridge University Press, 1996).

Additional Manuscript Sources Consulted in the Preparation of This Volume

Dugard, Thomas. *The Diary of Thomas Dugard* (British Library, Add MSS 23146).

Halford, John. *Accounts for Midsummer 1640–42* (Warwickshire County Record Office MS CR 1886).

Rogers, Samuel. *The Diary of Samuel Rogers* (MS Percy 7, Queen's University, Belfast).

Sterry, Peter. Various manuscripts (MS 289–95, Emmanuel College Library, Cambridge).

Relevant Contemporary Works

Baillie, Robert. Letters and journals (1775).

Burnet, Bishop. *History of His Own Time*, vol. 1 (1753).

Conway, Anne. Ed. Marjorie Hope Nicolson, rev. ed. Sarah Hutton, *The Correspondence of Anne, Viscountess Conway, Henry More, and Their friends, 1642–1684* (Oxford: Oxford University Press, 1992).

Greville, Robert, Lord Brooke. *The Nature of Truth* (London, 1640).

———. *A Discourse concerning the Nature of That Episcopacy Which Is Exercised in England* ((1642).

———. *A Speech at the Elections of Captains at Warwick Castle* (Thomasin Tracts, E90[27]).

Mede, Joseph. *Clavis Apocalyptica* (London, 1642).

P(atrick), S(imon). *A Brief Account of the New Sect of Latitude-Men* (London, 1662).

Rust, George. *A Letter of Resolution concerning Origen* (1661), ed. Marjorie Hope Nicolson (New York: Facsimilie Press Society, Columbia University Press, 1933).

Tuckney, Anthony. *None but Christ* (London, 1654).

Ward, Richard, ed. *The Life of the Learned and Pious Dr. Henry More* ([London, 1710]; Sarah Hutton et al., eds. [Dordrecht: Kluwer, 2000]).

White, Jeremiah. *The Restoration of All Things* (London, 1712).

Worthington, John. *The Diary and Correspondence of Dr. John Worthington*, ed. James Crossley, vols. 1 and 2 (Manchester: Chetham Society, 1847 and 1855).

Secondary Literature

The Cambridge Platonists

Armstrong, Robert L. "Cambridge Platonists and Locke on Innate Ideas," *Journal of the History of Ideas* 30 (1969), pp. 187–201.

Austen, Eugene M. *The Ethics of the Cambridge Platonists* (Philadelphia, 1935).

Beiser, Frederick C. *The Sovereignty of Reason—The Defense of Rationality in the Early English Enlightenment* (Princeton, NJ: Princeton University Press, 1986).

Burnham, Frederick B. "The More-Vaughan Controversy: The Revolt against Philosophical Enthusiasm," *Journal of the History of Ideas* 35 (1974), pp. 33–48.

Campagnac, E. T. *The Cambridge Platonists* (Oxford: Oxford University Press, 1901).

Cassirer, Ernst. *The Platonic Renaissance in England* (Edinburgh: Nelson, 1953).

Coudert, Allison. "A Cambridge Platonist's Kabbalist Nightmare," *Journal of the History of Ideas* 36 (1975), pp. 633–51.

Cragg, Gerald R. *The Cambridge Platonists* (Oxford: Oxford University Press, 1968).

Darwall, Stephen. *The British Moralists and the Internal "Ought"* (Cambridge: Cambridge University Press, 1995).

De Pauley, W. C. *The Candle of the Lord—Studies in the Cambridge Platonists* (London: SPCK, 1937).

De Sola Pinto, Vivian. *Peter Sterry—Platonist and Puritan* (Cambridge: Cambridge University Press, 1934).

Dockrill, D. W. "The Fathers and the Theology of the Cambridge Platonists," *Studia Patristica* 17 (1982), pp. 427–33.

Greene, Robert A. "Henry More and Robert Boyle on the Spirit of Nature," *Journal of the History of Ideas* 23 (1962), pp. 451–70.

———. "Whichcote, Wilkins, 'Ingenuity' and the Reasonableness of Christianity," *Journal of the History of Ideas* 42 (1987), pp. 227–51.

———. "Whichcote, the Candle of the Lord, and Synderesis," *Journal of the History of Ideas* 52 (1991), pp. 617–44.

Hall, A. Rupert. *Henry More—Magic, Religion, and Experiment* (Oxford: Oxford University Press, 1990).

Hedley, Douglas. *Coleridge, Philosophy, and Religion* (Cambridge: Cambridge University Press, 2000).

Henry, John. "A Cambridge Platonist's Materialism—Henry More and the Concept of Soul," *Journal of the Warburg and Courtauld Institutes* 49 (1986), pp. 172–95.

Hough, W. E. "The Religious Philosophy of John Smith," *The Baptist Quarterly* 3 (1927), pp. 357–61.

Hutton, Sarah. *Henry More—Tercentenary Studies* (Dordrecht: Kluwer, 1990).

———. "Anne Conway: critique de Henry More," *Archives de Philosophie* 58 (1995), pp. 371–84.

———. "Between Platonism and Enlightenment: Damaris Cudworth, Lady Masham," *British Journal for the History of Philosophy* 1 (1993).

Lichtenstein, Aharon. *Henry More—The Rational Theology of a Cambridge Platonist* (Cambridge, MA: Harvard University Press, 1962).

Matar, N. I., ed. *Peter Sterry, Select Writings* (New York: Peter Lang, 1994).

Merchant, Carolyn. "The Vitalism of Anne Conway: Its Impact on Leibniz's Concept of the Monad," *Journal of the History of Philosophy* 17 (1979), pp. 255–68.

Nicolson, Marjorie Hope. "George Keith and the Cambridge Platonists," *The Philosophical Review* 39 (1930), pp. 36–55.

Passmore, J. A. *Ralph Cudworth—An Interpretation* (Cambridge: Cambridge University Press, 1951).

Patrides, C. A, ed. *The Cambridge Platonists* (London: Edward Arnold, 1969).

Pawson, G. P. H. *The Cambridge Platonists and Their Place in Religious Thought* (London: SPCK, 1930).

Power, J. E. "More and Newton on Absolute Space," *Journal of the History of Ideas* 31 (1970), pp. 289–96.

Powicke, F. J. *The Cambridge Platonists* (London: J. M. Dent, 1926).

Roberts, James Deotis. *From Puritanism to Platonism in Seventeenth-Century England* (The Hague: Martinus Nijhoff, 1968).

Rogers, G. A. J., J. M. Vienne, and Y. C. Zarka, eds. *The Cambridge Platonists in Philosophical Context* (Dordrecht: Kluwer, 1997).

Sailor, Danton B. "Newton's Debt to Cudworth," *Journal of the History of Ideas* 49 (1988), pp. 511–17.

Saveson, J. E. "Differing Reactions to Descartes among the Cambridge Platonists," *Journal of the History of Ideas* 31 (1960), pp. 560–67.

———. "Descartes' Influence on John Smith, Cambridge Platonist," *Journal of the History of Ideas* 20 (1959), pp. 258–62.

Schneewind, J. B. *The Invention of Autonomy—A History of Modern Moral Philosophy* (Cambridge: Cambridge University Press, 1998).

Tulloch, John. *Rational Theology in England in the Seventeenth Century* (Edinburgh: W. Blackwood, 1874).

Webster, C. "Henry More and Descartes: Some New Sources," *British Journal for the History of Science* 4 (1969), pp. 359–76.

General Seventeenth-Century Background

Aylmer, G. E. *The Interregnum—The Quest for Settlement, 1646–1660* (Hamden, CT: Archon Books, 1972).

Bendell, Sarah, Christopher Brooke, and Patrick Collinson. *A History of Emmanuel College* (Woodbridge: Boydell Press, 1999).

Bush, Sargent Jr., and Carl J. Ramassen, eds. *The Library of Emmanuel College (1584–1637)* (Cambridge: Cambridge University Press, 1987).

Capp, B. S. *The Fifth Monarchy Men* (London: Faber, 1972).

Colie, Rosalie. *Light and Enlightenment* (Cambridge: Cambridge University Press, 1957).

Collinson, Patrick. *Godly People—Essays on English Protestantism and Puritanism* (London: Hambledon Press, 1983).

Coward, Barry. *The Stuart Age* (London: Longman, 1980).

Cragg, Gerald R. *Reason and Authority in the Eighteenth Century* (Cambridge: Cambridge University Press, 1964).

Grell, Ole Peter, and Andrew Cunningham. *Religio Medici— Medicine and Religion in Seventeenth-Century England* (Aldershot: Scholar Press, 1996).

Haller, William. *The Rise of Puritanism* (New York: Columbia University Press, 1938).

Harrison, Peter. *"Religion" and the Religions in the English Enlightenment* (Cambridge: Cambridge University Press, 1990).

Hill, Christopher. *The World Turned Upside Down* (London: Temple Smith, 1972).

Hughes, Ann. *Politics, Society, and Civil War in Warwickshire, 1620–1660* (Cambridge: Cambridge University Press, 1987).

Hunter, William B. "The Seventeenth-Century Doctrine of Plastic Nature," *Harvard Theological Review* 43 (1950), pp. 198–213.

Inge, W. R. *The Platonic Tradition in English Religious Thought* (New York: Longmans Green and Co, 1926).

Jones, Rufus. *Spiritual Reformers in the Sixteenth and Seventeenth Centuries* (London: Macmillan, 1914).

Knight, Janice. *Orthodoxies in Massachusetts* (Cambridge, MA: Harvard University Press, 1994).

Lamont, William. *Puritanism and Historical Controversy* (Montreal/Kingston: McGill Queen's University Press, 1996).

Lennon, Thomas M., John M. Nicholas, and John W. Davis, eds. *Problems of Cartesianism* (Kingston: McGill Queen's University Press, 1982).

BIBLIOGRAPHY

Manning, Brian. *Politics, Religion, and the English Civil War* (London: Edward Arnold, 1973).

McAdoo, H. R. *The Spirit of Anglicanism* (New York: Scribner, 1965).

Merchant, Carolyn. *The Death of Nature—Women, Ecology and the Scientific Revolution* (San Francisco: Harper & Row, 1980).

Miller, Perry. *The New England Mind* (New York: Macmillan, 1939).

Mitchell, W. Fraser. *English Pulpit Oratory from Andrewes to Tillotson* (London: SPCK, 1932).

Morgan, Edmund S., ed. *Puritan Political Ideas* (Indianapolis, IN: Bobbs-Merrill, 1965).

Morrill, J. S. *The Impact of the Civil War* (London: Collins and Brown, 1991).

Nuttall, Geoffrey F. *The Holy Spirit in Puritan Faith and Experience* (Oxford: Blackwell, 1946).

Pailin, David A. "Should Herbert of Cherbury Be Regarded as a Deist?" *Journal of Theological Studies* 51 (2000), pp. 114–49.

Pyle, Andrew, ed. *The Dictionary of Seventeenth-Century British Philosophers* (Bristol: Thoemmes, 2000).

Seaward, Paul. *The Restoration* (Hampshire: Macmillan, 1991).

Spurr, John. "Rational Religion in Restoration England," *Journal of the History of Ideas* 49 (1988), pp. 564–83.

———. *English Puritanism 1603–1689* (New York: St Martin's Press, 1998).

Twigg, John. *The University of Cambridge and the English Revolution, 1625–1688* (Cambridge: Cambridge University Press, 1990).

Tyacke, Nicholas. *Anti-Calvinists and the Rise of English Arminianism 1590–1640* (Oxford: Oxford University Press, 1987).

Venn, John, and J. Venn. *Alumni Cantabrigienses* (Cambridge: Cambridge University Press, 1927).

Walker, D. P. *The Decline of Hell* (London: Routledge and Keegan Paul: 1964).

———. *The Ancient Theology—Studies in Christian Platonism from the Fifteenth Century to the Eighteenth Century* (London: Routledge, 1972).

Webster, Tom. *Godly Clergy in Early Stuart England—The Caroline Puritan Movement, c. 1620–1643* (Cambridge: Cambridge University Press, 1997).

Willey, Basil. *The Seventeenth-Century Background* (London: Chatto and Windus, 1934).

Woodhouse, A. S. P., ed. *Puritanism and Liberty* (London: J. M. Dent and Sons, 1938).

Worden, Blair. "Providence and Politics in Cromwellian England," *Past and Present* 109 (1985), pp. 55–98.

———. "Toleration and the Cromwellian Protectorate," *Studies in Church History* 21 (1984), pp. 200–230.

INDEX

INDEX

Thomas Aquinas, 25, 26, 35, 144
Tillotson, John, 13
Toleration, 44; in Conway, 41; in Cudworth, 21; in Culverwell, 28–29; in More, 3; in Smith, 31–32; in Sterry, 37; in Whichcote, 13
Toleration Act (1650), 50
Toleration Act (1689), 52
True Intellectual System of the Universe, The (Cudworth), 20–21, 22, 24
True Levellers, 49
Truth, 7–8
Tuckney, Anthony, 12

Underhill, Evelyn, 52–53
Union with God, 26–27, 42, 53
Unity, 36

Van Helmont, Francis Mercurius, 38, 39, 41, 42, 43
Vane, Henry, 32
Voluntarism, 17, 24, 26

Wakefield, Walter, 53
Ward, Richard, 18, 19
Wesley, John 29–30
Whichcote, Benjamin, 2, 5, 12–15, 18, 19, 20, 21, 25, 27, 29, 31, 32; aphorisms, 135–36; and Cudworth, 19, 20; mind and body, 11; moral life, 8–9; and Smith, 29, 31; and Sterry, 32; texts, 95–136
Worden, Blair, 34
Worthington, John, 20, 29

Zeno, 137–38

Other Volumes in This Series

Other Volumes in This Series

Other Volumes in This Series

Other Volumes in This Series

The Classics of Western Spirituality is a ground-breaking collection of the original writings of more than 100 universally acknowledged teachers within the Catholic, Protestant, Eastern Orthodox, Jewish, Islamic, and Native American Indian traditions.

To order any title, or to request a complete catalog, contact Paulist Press at 800-218-1903 or visit us on the Web at www.paulistpress.com